A SOCIETY ORDAINED BY GOD

English Puritan Marriage Doctrine In the First Half of the Seventeenth Century

studies in christian ethics series

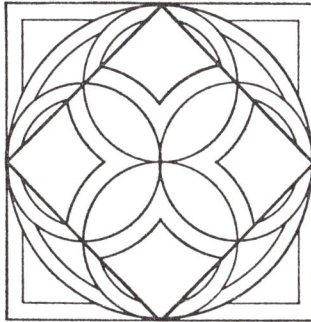

JAMES TURNER JOHNSON

Nashville   Abingdon Press   New York

A SOCIETY ORDAINED BY GOD

Copyright © 1970 by Abingdon Press

ISBN 0-687-38933-X

Library of Congress Catalog Card Number: 77-124759

SET UP, PRINTED, AND BOUND BY THE
PARTHENON PRESS, AT NASHVILLE,
TENNESSEE, UNITED STATES OF AMERICA

For Pamela

PREFACE

It is safe to say that the popular conception of Puritanism today is largely one of a cold, repressive theological and social system dominated by a blue-nosed God who would brook no levity among his saints. The economic virtues inculcated by such a system might be admirable, but surely the same discipline, the same soberness, the same deferral of gratification of one's own needs and those of one's family which tend to make a man prosperous in business are exactly those virtues which become vices when applied to personal life. And the general repudiation of Puritanism which has become popular today is fed by such recollections as that spouses might not kiss in public in colonial Massachusetts, on pain of a fine or the stocks or both.

This popular conception has enough basis in fact to make it durable, but in important ways it is a misconception. It is nothing short of ironic that studies can be written showing how Puritan thought contributed to the advance of political liberty while at the same time the personal morality of the Puritans is held to be narrowly legalistic and repressive. This book is not intended to be a refutation of popular misconceptions of Puritanism; in particular it does not take up and refute twentieth-century notions of what the Puritan sex ethic was. What it does do is explore how certain Puritan writers in the first half of the seventeenth century conceived of the relationship of marriage, that is, what they said marriage should be ideally and what grounds they allowed for ending it when it fell short of the ideal. Insofar as a composite picture of Puritan marriage doctrine emerges from this study, it does not tend to support that notion which finds everything bad in modern man-woman relations to emerge from Puritanism.

The Puritans were men of the sixteenth and seventeenth century—perhaps also of the eighteenth, if we stretch the name a bit. In some ways they were in total agreement with their contemporaries on how men and women should relate to one another. For example, women were universally regarded as naturally inferior to men. Puritan writers assert that the wife occupies the second place in marriage, but so do non-Puritan writers of the same period. To lay the subjection of women at Puritan feet is thus an error.

But more striking—and more at odds with modern conceptions—is the liberality and warmth of many Puritan writers in the early seventeenth century. They place a high premium on mutual love and a high level of intellectual and emotional compatibility in marriage, setting themselves off from their contemporaries, whom they saw as overly concerned with matrimony's biological aspects. In fact, some Puritans even move toward arguing that two persons who are not compatible in this profound way should be allowed to divorce if they wish. These men are innately practical, and typically they give a high rating to the orderly life, but a disciplined life is for them the best way of expressing the mutual love husband and wife should have for each other in a good marriage. Critics of this attitude should be reminded that spontaneity is not in itself a virtue, and discipline not necessarily a vice.

I have been saying, first, that some of the evils which are now popularly traced to Puritan social attitudes are not specifically Puritan but come out of the general social fabric of the time in which Puritanism flourished.

Second, I have suggested that my study reveals that in certain ways Puritan marriage theory is more "modern" than other approaches to marriage in the early seventeenth century.

I do not wish to imply that there is no grain of truth in the modern popular conception of the Puritan outlook on life. This would be to state more than my evidence warrants. But I do wish to say as forcefully as possible that it is time a more balanced understanding of Puritan ethics and institutions replaced the misconception that all Puritans were sexually and socially repressed bluestockings. To contribute to formulating such a more balanced view is one of the intents of this book.

Behind this reason for the study which follows is, however, another one: it is an important part of self-understanding to explore and seek to understand the sources of one's ideas and attitudes and of society's institutions and mores. Much has been done to trace the relations of capitalism and liberal democracy to Puritan thought; this book is an attempt in the direction of doing the same for personal ethics, in particular the matter of marriage.

Last, the third reason for this study is to indicate how two disparate theological systems can, because of their divergence of outlook, draw from the same raw social data two quite different ethical imperatives. Anglicans and Puritans alike witnessed the strains placed on marriage in the early seventeenth century, yet to a considerable extent they interpreted the issues differently and prescribed different remedies through their pictures of ideal marriage as God wills it. One of the intentions of this book is thus to indicate the fundamental difference theological presuppositions make in dealing with the raw facts of society's predicaments.

Most of the research for this study was carried out in the Firestone Library of Princeton University. The availability there on microfilm of virtually every source I have wished to consult from the sixteenth and seventeenth centuries has greatly facilitated my investigations. The McAlpin Collection of the library of Union Theological Seminary, New York, and the Speer Library of Princeton Theological Seminary supplied works not otherwise available to me. My gratitude goes to the staffs of these libraries for their help when it was needed.

Thanks go to the editors of *Studies in Christian Ethics,* particularly James Gustafson, John T. Noonan, Jr., and Paul Ramsey, for helpful criticism directed toward greater clarity of ideas and expression, as well as investigation of some materials not earlier incorporated into this study. Special gratitude is due to Paul Ramsey, who first suggested the topic of Puritan marriage doctrine to me and helped to guide me through a doctoral dissertation on the subject. The present volume represents the results of a continuation of the study. Professor Ramsey's major aid has been in the application of his powers of critical analysis and in tutoring me in the development of such powers. Insofar as the analysis of Puritan marriage doctrine contained herein is successful, it is a reflection of a successful tutor.

John Wilson of Princeton University has helped in most valuable ways to shape my perspective on the Puritans. From the earliest stages of this study, his criticism of my ideas, suggestions of bibliography, and knowledge of major Puritan figures have shaped the direction of my investigations.

It would not be right to fail to mention two men who freely gave of their time and their advice to aid me in understanding John Milton. Roland Frye of the University of Pennsylvania helped me at an early stage to shape my inquiry and avoid pseudo-questions. Don Wolfe of Brooklyn College provided me in conversation a perspective on Milton I would otherwise have missed. To these men, whose help was in the best traditions of scholarly investigation, I owe a unique gratitude.

Whatever aid and advice I have received, however, the faults of this study of Puritan marriage doctrine must remain my own.

JAMES TURNER JOHNSON

CONTENTS

INTRODUCTION

This book is a study of Puritan marriage ethics in the first half of the seventeenth century. It is an attempt to follow the course of certain ideas about what form the relations of husband and wife ideally should take and whether this relation can and should be ended in the case of a bad marriage. Thus it is an attempt to analyze a certain tradition of thought concerning the state of matrimony in its inception, its continuation, and its dissolution.

The method followed herein is that of the identification and analysis of ideas. This implies, in the particular case of Puritan marriage ethics, concentration on what might broadly be termed theological reflection. It does not mean that consideration of contemporary events and practices will be systematically avoided, but it does mean that such consideration is a secondary concern. For the purposes of this book, the study of events and practices occupies a supportive role only. The primary concern remains what the writers treated herein thought about marriage as a focal point of their understandings of Christian doctrine and of man as a being made for relations with other human beings. All the writers treated in the following pages hold the conviction that marriage represents God's gift to man to rescue him from his primal loneliness. This idea is embellished differently by different writers, but all agree that marriage is a society ordained by God as a result of God's decision recorded in Gen. 2:18: "God said, 'It is not good that the man should be alone; I will make him a helper fit for him'" (RSV).

The idea that is traced in this book, then, is that marriage is a society ordained by God for the relief of human loneliness. This tracing will entail investigation into the character of that loneliness, the nature of God's intent in granting marriage as its relief, and the possibilities for ending a match that demonstrably does not fulfill God's purpose for man.

A study of this sort has never been undertaken previously for the Puritans, though there are several works which must be noted to have bearing on this topic in spite of their different concerns. Chilton L. Powell's *English Domestic Relations, 1487-1653* approaches the subject of English family life in general through literary and legal sources as well as by consideration of the broad historical background out of which the literature and laws concerning marriage arose. Historically Powell finds two events to be of primary importance: the "king's affair," or the marriages and divorces of Henry VIII, and the controversy between Puritans and Anglicans on divorce in the period from Henry through Charles I. To amplify the implications of these Powell surveys the laws governing marriage and the attempted "reform of the laws" (*Reformatio Legum*) begun in the last days of Henry VIII. Shifting his focus to the domestic conduct books of the sixteenth and seventeenth centuries, he further attempts to discern attitudes toward marriage and divorce through developments in advice to married persons on how to live together in harmony. Powell's breadth is shown in that he even considers domestic drama briefly in trying to round out his understanding of domestic relations in the latter part of the period covered.[1]

Another broad approach is that of Louis B. Wright's *Middle-Class Culture in Elizabethan England.* Wright treats marriage only as part of a more inclusive description of middle-class life during the reign of Elizabeth and afterward. His title is misleading, for the period treated actually includes the first part of the seventeenth century, at least up to the end of the reign of James I. Elizabethan England, he argues, does not end until a generation and more after Elizabeth's death. Wright's

---

[1] Chilton L. Powell, *English Domestic Relations, 1487-1653* (New York: Columbia University Press, 1917).

concern with marriage and domestic life as one aspect of middle-class culture causes him to look only briefly at the laws governing matrimony, but for the same reason he devotes more space than Powell to consideration of the conduct books and development of intrafamilial roles in the growing middle classes.[2]

While Powell and Wright approach the subject of marriage from a secular point of view, other writers show more concern with marriage as a relation to be governed by Christian norms. A. R. Winnett's *Divorce and Remarriage in Anglicanism*,[3] T. A. Lacey's *Marriage in Church and State*,[4] and D. S. Bailey's *Sexual Relation in Christian Thought*[5] all exemplify the latter approach. Winnett's and Lacey's books provide masses of data for the student of Christian marriage doctrine; the portions of both books which deal with the sixteenth and seventeenth centuries are directly comparable to Powell's and Wright's treatments, though theological concerns now dominate the historical inquiry. Bailey is a different sort of writer, for his history is not so detailed, and he seeks for an issue in a historically aware "theology of sex"—something the other writers show no interest in developing.

All the above works treat periods more broadly defined than that of this book, and none of them offers a systematic discussion of the marriage doctrine of Puritanism. The last three of the above books, however, are valuable for their picture of Anglican marriage theory, which should be set in contradistinction to the Puritan marriage doctrine outlined in the following pages. For knowledge about Puritan views on marriage one might better turn to secular historians than to Winnett, Lacey, or Bailey, though the secular writers have little interest in purely theological matters.

The present study, then, fills a spot not otherwise occupied, between secular historical works which provide considerable information about the Puritans and histories of theological development which tell much about Anglican but little about Puritan thought. Further, this study stands apart from chronicles of events, whether secular or theological, as it seeks to follow an idea as it develops from one generation to the next.

[2] Louis B. Wright, *Middle-Class Culture in Elizabethan England* (Chapel Hill: University of North Carolina Press, 1935).
[3] New York: St. Martin's Press, 1958.
[4] London: S.P.C.K., 1947.
[5] New York: Harper & Brothers, 1959.

13

Charles H. and Katherine George's *The Protestant Mind of the English Reformation, 1570-1640* raises the question of whether a meaningful distinction can be made between Puritan and Anglican in the period of the English Reformation. Their contention is that to speak of an Anglican-Puritan controversy on questions of doctrine, of ecclesiology, of social and institutional structure is to oversimplify what the evidence reveals. It is better, they argue, to speak only of "English Protestantism," including thereby men of all stamps not specifically Roman Catholic. Differences exist, to be sure, between specific men on specific issues, but these are offset by agreements on other questions. To give just one example, the Georges link Perkins, Gouge, and Richard Rogers, all Puritans, together with such Anglicans as Hooker and Cosin in marriage doctrine.[6]

The Georges stand alone in their assertion of Puritan-Anglican nondifference. This is not the place to cite all those authors who take the opposite position or to give all the evidence, but since the present study proceeds partly by assuming and partly by demonstrating a substantial difference between the two wings of the English Church, one response to the nondifference theory might be noted. John F. H. New, writing in his book *Anglican and Puritan,* explicitly takes issue with the Georges' contention. He admits that there are difficulties in classification of Anglican and Puritan positions, but he maintains that a "workable, though not infallible" classification is possible. New faults the Georges on their reading of the historical evidence and on their own oversimplification of the data. The one serious defect of their book, he writes, is "an unwillingness on the part of the authors to admit theological distinctions between Anglican and Puritan."[7] The Georges have been too interested in setting English Protestants over against Catholics to see that there are also basic dissimilarities between the two main types of Protestants, Puritan and Anglican.[8]

The following study proceeds largely on the basis of assumptions much like New's and the preponderance of scholarship on the English

---

[6] Charles H. George and Katherine George, *The Protestant Mind of the English Reformation* (Princeton: Princeton University Press, 1961), pp. 265-75.

[7] John F. H. New, *Anglican and Puritan* (Stanford: Stanford University Press, 1964), pp. 107, 104.

[8] New's criticism of the Georges' book is found *ibid.*, pp. 104-11.

Reformation. Some evidence will be advanced, however, to show that Puritan marriage doctrine is significantly different from Anglican in the first half of the seventeenth century. In Chapter I it is explicitly argued that Puritan marriage doctrine should be understood as an application of covenant theology to the man-woman relationship. The resultant covenantal conception of marriage is characteristically different from the Anglican teaching, which borrows heavily from Roman Catholic theory and emphasizes the procreative purpose of marriage. Further, at various points throughout this book I argue that Ramist logic leads Puritans to quite different conclusions about matrimony from those reached by Anglican theorists, who proceed on the basis of a Scholastic-Aristotelian logic. In these two major cases and on many more smaller points this book stands opposed to the Georges' assertion that there is no meaningful difference between Anglican and Puritan.

Whether John Milton can properly be treated as a Puritan is another question on which a side has had to be taken in this investigation. I have chosen to argue that the influence of Puritan theology is great in Milton's divorce tracts and in fact that these tracts represent a kind of continuation and completion of the tradition on marriage begun around the turn of the century by such men as William Perkins and Robert Cleaver. In arguing thus I am supported by such students of Milton as William Haller and Arthur Barker.[9] Those familiar with Milton studies will recognize the indebtedness this book owes to the article of William and Maleville Haller, "The Puritan Art of Love,"[10] which argues that Milton's attitude on marriage and divorce is prefigured in certain Puritan writings on marriage doctrine of the two generations before him. The implications contained in the Hallers' article go far beyond this fairly narrowly defined thesis, however, and the present study is an attempt to explore some of them. My chief concern is with the marriage doctrine that develops within Puritanism as a result of theological grappling with a problem of human relations. Milton represents one of the stages of development of this doctrine. To be sure, his stage is a highly significant one; it is the completion of a certain under-

---

[9] See William Haller, *The Rise of Puritanism* (New York: Columbia University Press, 1938), and Arthur Barker, *Milton and the Puritan Dilemma* (Toronto: University of Toronto Press, 1942).

[10] *Huntington Library Quarterly,* V (1941-42), 235-72.

standing of the Puritan marriage doctrine. But my emphasis rests on Puritan theology, not on Milton, and this book is therefore not a chapter in Milton studies but an investigation of Puritan theological ethics in the specific case of marriage. All this implies that I find Milton to be importantly Puritan.

The alternative position is that Milton is not a Puritan but a child of the Renaissance, specifically that what he says on marriage comes not from Puritan marriage doctrine but from the classical humanism of the English Renaissance. This latter position is represented by Don M. Wolfe, general editor of the Yale Press edition of Milton's works and author of *Milton in the Puritan Revolution*. The following passage expresses Wolfe's judgment:

> The shadowy cloak of Calvinism, the glasses of theology, the grating accent of Puritan contumely—these Milton has thrown aside for a broad humanism fresh as the spirit of Plato's praise of music or Sidney's paeans for poetry. From his reading, from his meditations, his mind has distilled a new richness and a zestful loftiness more Greek than Puritan.[11]

Though the above passage comes during a discussion of *Areopagitica* and not of the divorce tracts, Wolfe could easily say the same thing about the viewpoint of the latter writings. For in treating the divorce tracts he reminds his readers that Milton ultimately accepted no authority except "his own insight" into marriage; he further explains Milton's attitude this way: "For himself he would face the future and find truth anew."[12] Wolfe emphasizes the references to Justinian, Cicero, and Aristotle in Milton's works as the sources for his understanding of the law of nature, so that when Milton identifies the law of nature with the law of God, it is not Puritan but Ciceronian theology that is thereby expressed. This is important for the doctrine of marriage since Milton there relies on the law of nature knowable by all men as one of the arguments for divorce of incompatibles.

Wolfe sees little good in the Puritanism of Milton's day, but the breadth of the Renaissance is for him an unequivocally happy phenome-

[11] Don M. Wolfe, *Milton in the Puritan Revolution* (New York: Humanities Press, 1963), p. 124.
[12] *Ibid.*, p. 327.

non. While Wolfe describes Puritanism in phrases pointing to its narrow-news, its closedness, its pettyness, he characterizes the Renaissance as that which inspired men to reach beyond their frontiers. It is not Perkins or Ames but Shakespeare, Raleigh, and Bacon whom Milton is like.[13] Milton may have been born a Puritan, but from his earliest exposure to the classics he began to move toward the ideals expressed there.[14] In this view Milton is best understood as embodying the best of the English Renaissance. His individualism, his reliance on reason, his use of the law of nature, and his breadth of spirit all stem directly from his eager learning at the feet of classical authors.

It would be unfair to Wolfe to suggest that he does not recognize in Milton some remnants of Christian theological influence. He can speak of Milton's "Christian individualism" even while describing it in Renaissance terms.[15] The law of nature is also not unchristian; "it presents a mixture of Stoicism, Aristotelianism, and Christianity."[16] But Wolfe does not connect the Christian with the Puritan, since he finds Puritanism so totally opposed to Renaissance motifs.

In spite of the argument for Milton's debt to the Renaissance, this study follows Haller's lead in emphasizing the Puritan elements in Milton's thought. This is not to assert that Milton owes no debt to Renaissance influence. Rather he seems to be a product of both Puritan and humanist learning, and it would distort much of his writing to make him either Puritan or Renaissance man alone. In the divorce tracts, however, the Puritan influence is quite obvious, and for this reason as well as for our purposes in exploring Puritan marriage doctrine it is possible to leave aside the Renaissance influence on Milton's humanism, though a treatment centered on Milton would have to consider this factor too. As Barker and Haller argue, Milton remained a Puritan even after the influx of classical ideas. He is not the type of Puritan that Wolfe describes in such derogatory language, but he is a Puritan in the tradition of another man of breadth and learning, William Perkins. Thus it is fitting that a historical treatment which begins with Perkins should end with Milton.

[13] Don M. Wolfe, general ed., *The Complete Prose Works of John Milton*, I (New Haven: Yale University Press, 1953), 2.

[14] *Ibid.*, pp. 3-4.

[15] Wolfe, *Milton in the Puritan Revolution*, p. 326.

[16] *Ibid.*, p. 330.

While events fade into the background with the passage of time, ideas live on in the ideas they beget. Human nature too persists throughout time. The immediate questions answered by Puritan marriage doctrine and the terms in which the answers were couched will never repeat themselves the same way. But the understanding of God's relation to man and that of man's relation to his fellows which are at work in the Puritan attempt to delineate a Christian approach to marriage are more timeless. A history that is antiquarian is irrelevant for the present, but an ethics which has no historical awareness is relevant only for the moment. Were this study more broadly based, I should be tempted to conclude, like Bailey, with my own historically aware "theology of marriage." But such a conclusion would be presumptuous on the basis of only this one case study. Nevertheless, I wish to make clear that the analysis which appears on the following pages is intended to be open-ended toward the present, so that hopefully the Puritans' thought on marriage is not irrelevant for consideration of a Christian ethic of marriage in our own time, different though this world is from that of the early seventeenth century.

I

The Covenant Idea and the Puritan Doctrine of Marriage

Puritan writings are laced throughout with covenant imagery and terminology. Considerable work has been done in elucidating the influence of the covenant idea in politics and economics, but its implications in matters of personal ethics still need fuller exploration. This chapter looks at the doctrine of the covenant in relation to the Puritan understanding of marriage and represents an attempt to show how the covenantal relationship between man and wife was conceived in English Puritanism. In order to illustrate the divergence of this marriage doctrine from the other important conception of matrimony in the sixteenth and seventeenth centuries, the last section of this chapter sketches briefly the Thomistic position.

As a beginning point the idea of the covenant discussed here must be identified. There are two extremes between which all Puritan covenant thought ranges: the individualistic "covenant of grace," borrowed from the New Testament through Calvin, and the sociopolitical doctrine of the federal theology, drawn from the Old Testament via analogies between Englishmen and the patriarchs.

The former states the terms of the God-man relationship for the individual elected to salvation by God. Since he is of the elect, he has the power to do what is pleasing to God, that is, to fulfill God's law, the terms of the covenant.

In the case of the federal theology it is the whole society of the elect who have been drawn into structured fellowship with God, not just individuals separately. This relationship is definitive not only of man-God interaction but also of strictly human social interaction. As Thomas Hooker describes it, "The Covenant which passeth between God and us, is like that which passeth between a King and his people; the King promiseth to rule and govern in mercy and righteousnesse; and they againe promise to obey in loyalty and in faithfulnesse." [1] What begins as a way of describing the individual's relation to God ends in the federal theology as a political pattern for structuring New England society, and by implication that of old England as well. Drawing not only from biblical patterns (mainly those of the Old Testament) but also from the developing legal theory of contracts,[2] the doctrine of the social covenant set out by federal theologians in both Englands provides a way of transforming what had been solely an individualistic ethic into one having social relevance as well.[3]

The Puritan marriage doctrine examined in this book is manifestly the result of applying covenant thinking to the problems of a Christian understanding of marital union. This result is a particular type of covenant doctrine, or rather the doctrine of a particular type of covenant—that between man and wife—yet one which is closely similar to

[1] Quoted in Perry Miller, *The New England Mind: The Seventeenth Century* (Boston: Beacon Press, 1961, p. 413.

[2] For discussion of this development in its theological context see David Little, *Religion, Order, and Law* (New York: Harper & Row, 1969).

[3] Too much, in my opinion, has been made of Puritan individualism. Giving the covenant theology proper weight would require a rethinking of those theses based on the individualist concept alone. R. H. Tawney is a case in point. Tawney admits that for the Puritans secular obligations come from religious commitment, but by stressing the personal relation of each man with God and the necessity for every one singly to abide by religious discipline, he obscures the social cohesiveness Puritanism requires. Discipline is everybody's affair, in fact; this is why the congregation can act to straighten out a wayway member. Tawney has ironically mistaken a highly structured relationship for no relationship and has forgotten the social impact of covenant thought in his concern to point up Puritan individualism. See R. H. Tawney, *Religion and the Rise of Capitalism* (13th ed.; Mentor Books; New York: New American Library, 1954), pp. 164 ff.

covenants between friends, among business partners, within nations, and in the church.

It is this notion of marriage as covenant which sets off the Puritan position most sharply from High Anglican marriage doctrine, which in the sixteenth and early seventeenth centuries remained essentially that set out by Thomas Aquinas under quite different social and theological conditions. One way of comparing these two doctrines of marriage would be to argue that the Puritans see marriage as covenantal, the High Churchmen as sacramental, implying a distinction between them on the locus and manner of God's action in Christian matrimony. This is a helpful way of contrasting the two positions thematically, but at this point I propose to follow a different approach. The Puritans define marriage in two ways, by looking to the Bible and by comparisons with other social forms. Instead of attempting thematically to typologize Puritan marriage doctrine over against High Anglican, I shall briefly show the biblical roots of the Puritan doctrine and then, in the body of this chapter, describe four analogies used by English Puritans to explain the nature of covenantal marriage.

Gen. 2:18 is a definitive passage for Puritan marriage doctrine: "And the Lord God said, It is not good that the man should be alone; I will make him an help meet for him" (KJV). The relief of man's loneliness is the primary reason for God's institution of marriage in paradise; God responds to Adam's need by giving him a "help meet." The words of one Puritan writer sum up this understanding of God's intent for marriage: husband and wife are to help each other to live "togither for a time as copartners in grace here, [that] they may reigne togither forever as co-heires in glory hereafter."[4] The man-wife relationship requires mutual help, not only in the everyday concerns of earthly life, but also as a preparation for the life of bliss awaiting the elect of God. The character of this mutual help is carefully defined in Puritan sermons and treatises on marriage, with duties for each spouse listed in terms derived from scripture. The duties of mutual meet help in marriage are the terms of the covenant entered into by the spouses upon their marital union.[5]

[4] Thomas Gataker, *Marriage Duties* (London, 1620), STC 11667, p. 48. This work and others dating to the sixteenth and seventeenth centuries will be identified herein by the numbers assigned to them in Pollard and Redgrave's *Short-Title Catalogue* (abbreviated STC).

[5] Fuller discussion of this point will be deferred until Chaps. II and III below.

21

In contrast, both Prayer Books of King Edward VI list the first end of marriage as procreation.[6] Following this lead the High Churchmen of this period looked to the injunction to "be fruitful, and multiply" of Gen. 1:28 as the principal proof text defining the institution of marriage. For this side of English Christianity the good of mutual society of husband and wife never takes precedence over the procreative purpose of marriage. Since this end of marriage is regulated in nature, there are no Anglican homilies on the duty of procreation to compare to Puritan sermons on the duties of mutual help. Similarly there is no explanation of marriage as covenantal in High Church circles. The High Church position, with marriage conceived on a chiefly biological model, has no place for a covenantal conception of marriage because of the simplicity of achievement of the primary end, procreation.

The implications of this divergence in the understanding of the biblical foundation of marriage are many, but one common and fairly obvious result is the reversal, among Puritans, of the Prayer Book's listing of the marriage ends. Instead of procreation, restraint and remedy of sin, and mutual society, the list becomes mutual society, restraint and remedy of sin, and procreation. This reversal is explicitly accomplished by the time of Thomas Gataker (ca. 1620),[7] but it is already hinted in the writings of William Perkins a generation before.[8] When John Milton writes his divorce tracts in the 1640s, he accepts the ordering of the ends given by Gataker twenty years before, but he traces this order to the Bible, not to any man.[9] Similarly, Richard Baxter, writing about thirty years after these tracts of Milton's, subordinates procreation to mutual help.[10] This

[6] For example, *The Second Prayer Book of King Edward VI* lists the ends of marriage as follows: "One was for the procreation of children, to be brought up in the fear and nurture of the Lord, and praise of God. Secondly, it [marriage] was ordained for a remedy against sin, and to avoid fornication. Thirdly, for the mutual society, help, and comfort, that the one ought to have of the other, both in prosperity and in adversity." (Parker Society, eds., *The Two Liturgies,* A.D. 1549 and A.D. 1552 [Cambridge: The University Press, 1844], p. 303.)

[7] Gataker, *A Good Wife Gods Gift* (London, 1623), STC 11659, p. 9. Later chapters of this book explore this reversal more fully.

[8] Perkins, *Christian Oeconomie,* in *Workes,* III (Cambridge, 1609), STC 19649, p. 671.

[9] Don M. Wolfe, general ed., *The Complete Prose Works of John Milton,* II, ed. Ernest Sirluck (New Haven: Yale University Press, 1959), 246 (from *The Doctrine and Discipline of Divorce*), 601 (from *Tetrachordon*), also *passim* throughout both tracts. Hereafter cited as: Milton, *Doctrine and Discipline* (or *Tetrachordon*).

[10] Richard Baxter, *The Practical Works of the Rev. Richard Baxter,* I (London: Henry G. Bohn, 1854), 937 (from "Of the Celebration of Matrimony," Baxter's reformed marriage service).

reversal of the ends of marriage listed in the official liturgy is thus a common feature of Puritan marriage doctrine, one which supports the covenantal character of the marital relationship.

The Puritan Doctrine of Marriage as Covenant: Four Analogies

Four analogies drawn from other types of human relationships— friendship, government, church, and business partnership—reinforce and amplify this biblically inspired covenantal model of marriage. All four are commonly employed by Puritan writers on marriage, but for brevity and explicitness I shall here treat them as they appear in representative writings.

A popularly intended book which nevertheless reveals its theological foundations yields the first example of Puritan use of analogy to explain the marriage covenant. Alexander Niccholes' *Discourse of Marriage and Wiving* draws from one of Augustine's images to inform readers that woman is to be man's "middle companion," since she was made from Adam's rib, a bone from the middle of his body.[11] But in a more serious vein Niccholes continues, "In thy Marriage, the very name whereof should portend to thee Merry-age, thou not onely unitest unto thy selfe a friend, and comfort for society, but also a companion for pleasure, & in some sort a servant for profite too."[12] Here plainly stated are all the factors Puritan writers commonly name as characteristic of ideal marriage. First of all, it is to be a union for life and aims at a happy old age for husband and wife. Second, the wife is the husband's friend, and third she is his companion. What is obscured here is that the wife's friendship and companionship imply the husband's also, for these relationships cannot by their nature be one-sided. Fourth, the wife is the husband's servant in some sense. This must be carefully explained. The wife is not to be grouped among the household servants, for she has authority over them. But she derives her authority from her husband, who has final say in the household. Niccholes goes further than other Puritan writers in calling the wife "servant." More typically Gataker in his *Marriage Duties* calls her the husband's "assistant . . . in his Travels [i.e., his travails], and in his Troubles."[13] This understanding of the wife's role vis-à-vis her

---

[11] (London, 1615), STC 18514, p. 1.

[12] *Ibid.*, p. 5.

[13] P. 20.

husband dominates Puritan thinking, and it is expressly pointed out in nearly every Puritan treatise on marriage that the wife, far from being ranked with the household servants, is second only to the husband in ruling them. But she *is* second, not equal.[14]

That Niccholes himself intends a severe qualification of the term servant when he calls the wife such only "in some sort" is apparent from the rest of his book. His emphasis is continually on the necessity for husband and wife to be evenly matched companions who help each other in a friendly way through life. "Conveniency and fitnesse in choyce, is more to be regarded, than either beauty, riches, or any other addition, of minde or fortune," he writes. "I meane not equality or fitnesse of nature, for the more equal conjunction & action, but fitnesse in affection.[15] Only slightly later he cites an "Italian proverb" to make his point clear:

> Hee that a fit wife to himselfe doth wed,
> In minde, birth, age, keepes long a quiet bed.[16]

And in the most practical manner he advises those who have had a riotous youth to "smell thee out a wife a little tainted," while he counsels merchants, farmers, and sailors to marry instead wives "of some phlegmaticke humor." [17]

It should be clear from this that Niccholes has in mind a particular kind of relation between husband and wife, one most closely analogous to the relation of friendship. That the husband has the ascendancy in this special kind of friendship is a bow to social conventions in seventeenth-century England, and the fact that the wife is called the husband's servant should therefore not be misunderstood. Gataker makes this point about marriage, and indeed all friendships in general, when he writes,

---

[14] She is second to the husband in authority in the family, for she is second to man in the order of nature. So any seventeenth-century man might have argued; it had nothing to do with Puritan theology. But the Puritans found this natural ordering at work also in the Bible. Alongside this hierarchical ranking by sex, however, they also found in the Bible a doctrine of equality in grace regardless of sex or station. For most Puritan marriage theorists, nevertheless, equality in grace does not imply equality in nature, for this would be to offend God's law for the world.

[15] Niccholes, *Discourse of Marriage and Wiving*, pp. 13-14.

[16] *Ibid.*, p. 15.

[17] *Ibid.*, p. 16.

"There can bee no ordinary intercourse and commerce or conversing betweene person & person, but there must be a precedencie on the one part, and a yeelding of it on the other." [18] The analogy of marriage to friendship and human relationships considered more generally is clear from this. Niccholes, though, restricts his comparison to the relation of friendship and thereby offers an uncluttered example of one way Puritan writers conceive of the husband-wife relationship.

The second commonly employed analogy is that of marriage to the relations that obtain as a result of government. Robert Cleaver's *Household Government* affords the best example of this kind of comparison. This treatise is a mammoth and significant work on marriage doctrine, with much space given to explaining the duties implicit in the marriage covenant. Here I shall not go beyond explication of Cleaver's first definition of marriage (he has two, one sociopolitical and the other theological in basis), in which he assumes the analogy with which we are interested: "A Household is as it were a little common wealth, by the good government whereof, Gods glorie may be advaunced, the common wealth which standeth of severall families, benefited, and al that live in that familie may receive much comfort and commoditie." [19]

In this definition it is not friendship between husband and wife which is held up as the goal of marriage. Their partnership is not so much that of friends as of fellow citizens. The companionship and meet help the members of the household give one another vary according to status as husband, wife, child, or servant, but in each case there is a comparable status in the state. It would be tempting to push these comparisons and turn them back on themselves to illuminate Cleaver's political theory

[18] Gataker, *Marriage Duties,* p. 8.

[19] Robert Cleaver, *A Godlie Forme of Household Government* (London, 1598), STC 5383, p. 13. Cleaver is a much more shadowy and less appreciated figure than his younger contemporary William Perkins. Cleaver spent much of his life avoiding punishment for his openly nonconformist views, and the fact that he often wrote and preached using assumed names does not make study of his theological position a simple matter. His name is frequently linked with that of John ("Decalogue") Dod in writings principally attributed to the latter. Cleaver, in fact, had a hand in the preparation of the commentary on the Decalogue which gave Dod his nickname. Cleaver's influence is hard to trace, but he was well known in Puritan circles during his lifetime. *A Godlie Forme of Household Government* is the only major work published under his name alone, but he also wrote several minor treatises on various subjects and, as noted, collaborated with Dod in the preparation of other longer works. A fuller discussion of Cleaver follows in Chap. II.

as well as his doctrine of marriage, but that would lead far beyond the scope of this book. That such as interpretation is possible, however, reveals that Cleaver is most serious about his "little common wealth" model of the family.

The roles of husband and wife in the household are most pertinent to the present discussion. Cleaver generally calls them the two "governours" of the household, but he also explains their roles as arising from their various relations. Regarding each other, they are husband and wife; to the servants they are master and mistress; to the children they are father and mother. Certain duties pertain to each role, but Cleaver sees no irresolvable conflict coming from the necessity to play several roles at once. Significantly for our picture of Puritan marriage theory the husband has final authority: "The governours of families, . . . upon whom the charges of governmēt lyeth, though unequally, are, first the Cheefe governour, which is the Husband, secondly a fellow helper, which is the Wife." [20] Together they rule the household in "wisdom." The end of their government is twofold, the advancement of "Christian holinesse" in members of the family and provision for their physical well-being.

Now what of the analogy to the state? The well-known examples of Bolingbroke and Laud serve as reminders that the political structure of England in this period allows for a "fellow helper" or first minister to aid the monarch in his government of the nation, though final responsibility remains with whoever holds the throne. Furthermore, the king rules his country with wisdom just as wisdom is the guide of the householder. And finally, the twofold aim of household government is reflected in the English monarch's position as head of both state and church, as "protector of the faith" as well as protector of his people's lives and fortunes. Hooker's analogy stated earlier, with slight expansion, holds for Cleaver as well: as God is to the individual, so is king to subject, and so is husband to wife.

Cleaver's marriage-state analogy reaches fullest development not in England but in New England, where the Puritan fathers, wishing to create a godly commonwealth, wrote implications of their theology into civil law. Edmund S. Morgan, in his book *The Puritan Family,* de-

[20] *Ibid.,* p. 19.

scribes the relation of family government to civil government as conceived in Massachusetts:

Civil government, once established, did not supersede the family as a means of enforcing the laws of God. The state made no demand that the heads of families should "yield up their Family-Government over their Wives, Children, and Servants, respectively, to rule them in common with other Masters of Families." Rather, it gave additional support to their authority.[21]

The analogy between marriage and the state is carried so far in New England that the family becomes an aspect of civil life, its government an integral part of civil government. Two examples cited by Morgan will illustrate the extent of this reasoning. In 1629 the Massachusetts Bay Company ordered John Endicott, a deputy governor, to divide a group of male servants under his direction into artificial "families," setting up in each one as head a servant "grounded in religion." The chief end was disciplinary, to keep order among these servants who had no connection with a regular household. Second, both Connecticut and Plymouth enacted laws requiring any unmarried man with no servants to attach himself to an established household and submit to discipline by the family head.[22] Such extremes are never reached in England, but the reasoning used for New England is latent in precolonial Puritan writers like Cleaver.

Cleaver's point that life in a family is like life in a national commonwealth is echoed by Robert Pricke, who takes as his nominal beginning point the fifth commandment, "Honour thy father and thy mother." Moving from this base in the scriptural tradition bearing on proper family relations, he notes wider duties that are required by this commandment. Honoring one's father also implies honoring "Kings, Princes, and Magistrates, Ministers of the worde of GOD, Householders, Schoolemaisters, and Teachers." [23] This reveals that Pricke, like Cleaver, understands the familial structure to be of the same nature as the civil. Directly to the point of this chapter is this further implication Pricke

---

[21] Edmund S. Morgan, *The Puritan Family* (rev. ed.; Harper & Row, New York: 1966), pp. 142-43. The quotation is from John Davenport.

[22] *Ibid.*, pp. 144-45.

[23] Robert Pricke, *The Doctrine of Superioritie, and of Subjection* (London, 1609), STC 20337, p. B4.

27

draws from the fifth commandment: as to the father from the children, so subjection and honor are due from the wife to the husband.[24] In general Pricke's reasoning moves in the opposite direction from Cleaver's; it is the national government that is defined from the familial, according to Pricke. That there is a direct analogy, nevertheless, between relationships in the state and those of husband and wife (and other members of the household) is assumed by both men.

Pricke takes us one step further when he compares the relation of husband and wife to that of God and the elect. The reason that the wife should honor her husband and subject herself to him is that he is like God, who "hath joyned to himselfe, and as it were married in a speciall covenant of mercie and compassion, al the faithfull and elect ones; so that he is head and husband of his people." [25] Notably the analogy is not between husband and Christ, wife and church, as it would be if Pricke had in mind Eph. 5:21-33; rather he compares husband to God, wife to the chosen people of God. Marriage is like the covenantal relationship between God and Israel, a comparison which stresses the commonwealth nature of marriage. God works his covenants directly, and by analogy the covenant between husband and wife is also direct. Pricke does not compare marriage to the mystical union of Christ and the church, a comparison central to the conception of marriage as a sacrament of the new law. For Pricke marriage is a covenant relationship, not sacramental in nature, in which the husband is like God and the wife like the elect whom God has chosen.[26]

From the example of Pricke it can be observed how the Puritans merge their analogies into one another. Most commonly one analogy (such as marriage with friendship or nation) is not used by itself in Puritan writings on marriage, and the examples employed thus far in this chapter have been chosen partly for their single-minded imagery. The analogy between marriage and the relations of Christians in the church needs now to be explored, and there is no one treatise like Pricke's or Cleaver's to examine in this case. Nevertheless comparison

---

[24] *Ibid.*, p. B6.

[25] *Ibid.*

[26] Cf. the position taken by Calvin, *Institutes of the Christian Religion*, Bk. IV, Chap. XIX, secs. 34-37.

of the Puritans' understanding of marriage with their doctrine of the church yields some of the most interesting parallels of all.

There is no need here to explain how various types of Puritans conceived of the church. This ranges all the way from those who would accept bishops and could get along remarkably well with High Anglicans, through the Presbyterians, on to the Congregationalists, ending with those radical sectarians, the Baptists. It is the broad middle range of Puritanism with which we are here concerned, the part of the spectrum including those who were in church polity Presbyterian and Congregationalist. So far as the individual congregation was concerned, these two groups were in close agreement as to polity, and it is with the church as congregation that the analogy to marriage is made.[27]

The people of God should live a disciplined life, most of all in the church to which they become united by their election. At the center of congregational organization, in this conception, was "a godlie discipline." At the head of the congregation, taking ultimate responsibility for the spiritual well-being of his flock, stood the minister, the spokesman for God to his people. Seconding him were laymen who helped in the day-to-day affairs of the congregation and who watched to make sure discipline was kept. Last in the scheme came the rest of the members of the congregation, who had responsibilities not only to themselves but to the others in the fellowship as well. It must be noted that these differences within the congregation were conceived to be of function only, not of grace. All men who are elect are equal before God, and no one in the church should presume to usurp God's place and say who is elect and who is not. Thus it is only function within the congregation (the minister to preach God's word and oversee the maintenance of discipline, the elders to maintain discipline) which gives some authority over others. In this scheme all members of the congregation, from minister to ordinary layman, are conceived to have responsibility for mediating Christianity to their families. Here too the responsibility of the man is functionally determined; Puritan writers often admit that the wife can surpass the husband in grace, but the authority for maintaining true religion in the household remains the man's. In all this the similarity to John Calvin's

[27] See Haller, *The Rise of Puritanism*, Chaps. III, IV, *passim*, for a discussion of this matter. Cf. Miller, *The New England Mind*, Chap. XV, "The Church Covenant," for a study of New England congregational Puritanism.

scheme for the organization of the Genevan Church is evident. But so is this congregational structure similar to all patriarchal forms of social organization, the nation and the family no less than the Genevan Church. What separates Puritan church polity from more general forms of patriarchal government is its discipline, taken directly from the pages of God's word—"not the filthye canon lawe"[28] but a structure of life for all the elect which would ensure their keeping of the terms of the covenant of grace in their personal and corporate lives.

Now let us investigate the relation of this understanding of the church to the Puritan doctrine of marriage. Were these duties of the householder not labeled as such in Puritan writing, they might easily pass as duties of the minister: First, he should get everyone to worship services together and on time. "Secondly, hee must set an order in his house for the service of God." "The third dutie . . . is private instruction . . . in matters of religion."[29] The rest of the discipline in the household is administered in a way closely comparable to the administration of church discipline. In both are found "fellow helpers" who take the burden from the head while still leaving him final responsibility. Likewise, the ordinary members of the Puritan congregation function similarly to the children and servants in the household.

One basic reason for easy comparison between marriage, the state, and the church is that all three were in this period conceived after a patriarchal model. Ultimately it is the biblically inspired idea of a covenant, whose terms are given in a discipline according to God's word, which sets off each of these, in its own way, from patriarchalism in general. Since each is a form of covenant relationship, moreover, it is the discipline proper to each which sets it off from the others—which makes the state the state, not the church or the family.

If discipline is the key within the church even as law is necessary in the commonwealth, so is a particular kind of discipline necessary to the proper ordering of the family. In the family, notwithstanding the clear primacy of the husband/father/master, this discipline carefully imposes duties on him as well as on other members of the household. Similarly, the idea that the king is bound by God's laws as are the people, a feature

[28] Quoted from Usher in Tawney, *Religion and the Rise of Capitalism*, p. 178.
[29] Cleaver, *Household Government*, pp. 34, 43, 49.

of Puritan covenant thought, works itself into social contract political theory as the seventeenth century progresses.[30] The Levellers and the Diggers, the Long Parliament, the thought of Perkins and Milton on liberty, and many other examples could be developed to demonstrate this point, but it is a familiar one.

The ultimate implication of covenant thought is that the Christian can call God to account if he fails to fulfill his promises, just as in social theory the people can ultimately call their monarch to account—and execute him if need be, as in the case of Charles I—for his failure to abide by the contract he has implicitly or explicitly made with them. One Puritan divine, fastening duties on both God and man when they are in covenant, declares, "We must not make Gods Covenant with man, so far to differ from Covenants between man and man, as to make it no Covenant at all." [31] In this covenant between man and God there are "as it were indentures drawne between God and man, conditions on both sides agreed upon," [32] and each party must be ready to account for his actions toward his covenant partner. Of course this is purely theoretical, since the Puritans hasten to remind themselves that God, who in his mercy initiated the covenant with man, always keeps his promises, while man habitually breaks his. But the covenant between God and man remains "a true contract of mutual obligation" nevertheless.[33]

The covenant theology also makes "true contracts of mutual obligation" of the relationships between ruler and people and between husband and wife. This implies that each relationship can be dissolved for nonperformance of covenant duties: a king can be deposed, an errant marriage partner divorced. But as in the case of calling God to task, these implications are approached gingerly by the Puritans. While their marriage doctrine seems to point toward requiring divorce when the duties of the marriage covenant are not performed, writers before Milton are extremely slow to move to this conclusion. Similarly, Charles I remains the only victim of the ultimate implication of the covenant theology in politics.

Moving the other way, the Puritans conclude that God, monarch, and husband have the right to demand performance of certain duties from

---

[30] See the Georges' *Protestant Mind of the English Reformation* for discussion of this interrelationship of ideas.
[31] Quoted in Miller, *The New England Mind*, p. 376.
[32] *Ibid.*
[33] *Ibid.*, p. 377.

the elect, the subject, and the wife and household, respectively. Dissolution of the covenant can result from the latter's not living up to his part. But again the Puritans are reticent to carry this principle through. Once God elects, he elects for eternity. The husband may go so far as to take his wife to the magistrate, if he cannot handle her, but in general he may not divorce her except for adultery or desertion.[34] In the political sphere expatriation receives little attention among English Puritan writers.

What is foremost in all these cases is that failure to keep to the prescribed discipline, which is implied in the covenant itself, can result in punishment. But ultimate punishments, breaking up the covenant relationship, are not what interest Puritan writers. Among commentators on marriage it is the terms of the covenant, the duties it implies, the appropriate discipline, which one finds emphasized in tract after sermon after treatise. Understanding how to live according to divine law and the ability to live according to this understanding are assumed in Puritan theology to be characteristic of God's elect, who live their lives in covenant with God. So in the covenant of marriage the partners are assumed to know what is required of them and to have the power to keep to the terms of their agreement. Thus William Gouge can write a treatise *Of Domesticall Duties,* which runs to some six hundred pages, never doubting that a Christian spouse can fulfill all six hundred pages' worth of requirements if he will only try.[35]

It is William Ames who, considered along with John Preston, most completely develops the covenant theology in Puritanism.[36] When Ames speaks of marriage, it is the analogy with partnerships in business which most often emerges. In making such a comparison he is, of course, representative of a much broader tendency in Puritanism. No one need accept the Weber-Tawney thesis uncritically to admit that Puritans were disproportionately prominent participants in the new economic structure, the

---

[34] Perkins, *Workes,* III, 692.

[35] (London, 1622), STC 12119.

[36] William Ames was a pupil of William Perkins at Cambridge. Eighteen years younger than his tutor, he was less willing to make peace with the compromise English Church of the Elizabethan Settlement, and in 1610 he left England for the Continent. There he became well known and influential among Calvinist theologians, writing the works which gained him a sizeable niche in Puritan history. Puritans on both sides of the Atlantic admired his *Medulla Theologiae (The Marrow of Sacred Divinity)* and *De Conscientia (Conscience, with the Power and Cases Thereof).*

corporation, which arose in the Elizabethan period. To the stanch Puritan the contract which effected a corporate partnership was defined not only by common law or royal patent; it had its real meaning in being a form of covenant. Conversely, in the case of marriage the covenant entered into by the spouses is commonly described as being created by mutual contract. Thus in both corporate partnership and marital partnership there is a covenant relationship between the partners which is entered into by their mutual contract.

Ames explains that it is the contract between spouses which initiates their marriage. For this, mutual consent is necessary, and it is defined by eight conditions, all of which must be fulfilled. Consent is to be (1) declared by words, (2) mutual, though possibly given at different times by the two spouses, (3) voluntary and free, (4) not binding on those without the use of reason, (5) not binding if caused by fear, (6) not binding if caused by error (about the person, as in the case of Jacob and Leah, or about the "quality" of one person or both, as in the case of Joseph and Mary), (7) binding if any error is only in a condition or quality not "essential to the nature of marriage," (8) seconded by the consent of the parents of both spouses.[37]

These conditions placed on the binding power of the consent of those marrying are unexceptional if regarded only in the light of High Church marriage doctrine as it treats consent. In the marriage theology of late medieval Catholicism, which is reflected in the High Anglican position, consent is binding only when certain conditions are fulfilled, for which Ames's list of eight is an abridgment. Both Thomas Aquinas and Gratian seem to be recalled in Ames's catalog of conditions, and the example of Jacob and Leah is drawn directly from Gratian.[38] But two factors show that Ames is utilizing the tradition in a way different from that chosen by the scholastics. First, the context of Ames's theology is given by the covenant of grace, so that his marriage ethic describes what is normative for those in such a covenant with God. Unlike the Catholic doctrine, in which the divine binding power enters marriage through the *ex opere*

[37] William Ames, *Conscience, with the Power and Cases Thereof* (London, 1639), STC 550, pp. 200-201.

[38] The definitive list of conditions binding consent in the Catholic traditions is given in the *Supplement* to the *Summa Theologica* of Thomas Aquinas, Questions 44 ff. For the example of Jacob and Leah see Gratian, *Decretals, Dictum,* Chap. 29, Q. 1.

operato effect of the sacrament at the moment of the marriage vows, in Ames's theory God works by enabling the partners, all through their courtship, to fulfill the conditions necessary for marriage—or by enabling them to refrain from marriage if they cannot meet the conditions. That is, for Ames, God works in the hearts of the elect long before the marriage ceremony, drawing together persons who can be married and separating those who cannot. The second differentiating factor is the similarity, in Ames's thought, between the conditions governing a business contract and those governing consent to marry. Two general conditions are required for a business contract to be binding; it must be made by "persons fit to a contract," and they must give "either formall, or virtuall consent," which must be "free," "promissive," and "expressed by some outward signe." [39] The eight requirements governing marital consent are but applications of these general terms to a specific kind of contract, that to enter into matrimony.

The similarity Ames assumes between marriage and business partnerships can be illustrated in a negative way by exploring the question of when the contract to enter each kind of relationship can be broken. It is here, according to Ames, that the only real difference exists between these two kinds of contractual relationships. "Matrimony cannot by any at his pleasure be dissolved," writes Ames, it having "this privilege above other contracts, not only from Christs institution, but also from the Law of Nature. . . . The reason is, because Matrimony is not only a Civill but a Divine conjunction." [40] While marriage, considered as a "Civill . . . conjunction" only, is like other contracts, its character as also a "Divine conjunction" means that the analogy is not perfect—but if it were, it would be an identity, not an analogy. There are four possible conditions under which a business contract may be broken: (1) "when the thing promised becomes unprofitable, unlawful, or impossible"; (2) "if the state of the things & persons is so changed that in the judgement of wisemen, the promiser is thought, that hee would not have comprehended such an event"; (3) "if the other party would remit it"; (4) "if hee which promised on the other side, will not fulfill his promise." [41] Marriage, on Ames's understanding, may be dissolved only in cases of

---

[39] Ames, *Conscience*, p. 227.
[40] *Ibid.*, p. 208.
[41] *Ibid.*, p. 232.

contagious disease of one spouse, desertion, absence for long periods, danger from the other spouse, and adultery.[42] Missing here is the possibility of ending marriage by mutual consent or by decree of the magistrate, both of which are open to the partners in a business contract. But if marriage were only a civil conjunction, these possibilities would pertain to it too.

William Perkins, whose discussion of marriage includes a strong emphasis on its contractual character, distinguishes between the civil and the moral or religious in a way that foreshadows Ames. Writing of the Mosaic divorce law, Perkins argues, "This law was not morall, but civill, or politicke, for the good ordering of the Commonwealth." Explicating this point, he continues:

The force and effect of this law was this, It made the Bill of divorcement for any cause given, to be tolerable before men; and marriage after such a divorce, lawfull and warrantable in the Courts of men, Deut. 24.4. But yet in the court of conscience before God, the divorcement it selfe, and second marriages made thereupon, were both unlawfull.[43]

To recapitulate, the concept of marriage here being described supposes an analogy between the contract of marriage and contracts of corporate partnership. So far as the making of marriage is the only concern, this analogy is drawn rather specifically, and the contract to marry is treated as a subtype of the more general form of contract, that to enter partnership. But when the question is of ending the contracted partnership, Puritan marriage theory insists that the analogy between marriage and business contracts is not an identity, for the contract to marry has both a civil and a religious aspect, while business contracts are civil only. But both Ames and Perkins, as well as the entire tradition they exemplify, would agree that if marriage were only a civil partnership, it would be dissoluble in the same way as contracts of incorporation or any other contractual agreements in the world of business. It is the divine aspect of marriage that makes it indissoluble by mutual consent, not the civil aspect, and thus the analogy remains closest between business partnerships and marriage conceived as civilly contracted partnership.

[42] *Ibid.*, p. 209.
[43] Perkins, *An Exposition of Christs Sermon in the Mount,* in *Workes,* III, 68.

The analogy here defined could be further developed by investigating various statements of duties imposed in the marriage contract and comparing them to promises made by parties to civil contracts. But there is no space here for such a minute investigation. To show that such comparison might prove fruitful is not, however, too time consuming. When William Whatley argues in *A Bride-Bush* that failure to fulfill marriage duties can "stretch" the marriage bond even to the breaking point,[44] Ames's fourth condition for breaking a business contract is recalled: "If hee which promised on the other side, will not fulfill his promise." And when John Milton comes to argue for divorce by mutual consent for incompatibility, all four of Ames's conditions spring to mind. Milton's argument is far too complex for attention at this point, but it is worth noting that a prime feature in that argument is that Milton pushes the analogy made by Ames to the point of identity. That is, Milton denies a special "divine" or "religious" or "moral" aspect to the marriage contract, saying that it is no different from contracts of business or government.

For so the covnant which Zedechiah made with the infidell King of Babel is call'd the covnant of God, Ezech. 17.19. which would be strange to be counted more than a human covnant. So every covnant between man and man, bound by oath, may be call'd the covnant of God, because God therein is attested. So of marriage he is the author and witness; yet hence will not follow any divine astriction more then what is subordinate to the glory of God and the main good of either party.[45]

In the same locus Milton identifies this "main good" as mutual meet help between the spouses. By denying that marriage has two aspects, civil and religious, this most radical of Puritan writers on marriage opens the way to ending the marriage contract when "the main good of either party" is not being served—precisely Ames's reason for voiding a business contract.

These four analogies—with friendship, government, the church, and partnerships in business—serve in the development of Puritan marriage doctrine to support and amplify the concept of marriage the Puritans

[44] William Whatley, *A Bride-Bush* (London, 1617) STC 25296, pp. 5-7. See also Chap. III below for discussion of his position.
[45] Milton, *Doctrine and Discipline*, p. 276.

find in the Bible. All four relationships are, to the Puritan mind, cove-nantal in character, and each adds something to the concept of covenantal marriage for mutual meet help which Puritan theorists develop in con-tradistinction to official Church of England doctrine, rooted in High Anglican theology and ultimately similar to the Thomist position. To show what the Puritans were reacting against is the motive for the brief sketch of Thomist marriage doctrine which completes this chapter.

Catholic Marriage Doctrine and Puritan Reaction: Points at Issue

Prior to the Reformation, Christian marriage doctrine in the West was simply that promulgated within the Catholic faith. In attempting to set forth certain aspects of the Catholic theory as a way to better under-standing the Puritan conception of matrimony, two kinds of issues emerge: those in which the Puritans take over the tradition, in general accepting the position and arguments of canonists and theologians in the main line of the developing tradition on marriage, and those in which the Puritans repudiate the traditional formulations they have in-herited. The most systematic Puritan commentators on marriage not only know medieval matrimonial theology intimately but throughout presuppose it as the basis for their own work. This is true whether the use made of the tradition is positive and supportive or negative and destructive. That Puritan theorists make positive use of Catholic marriage doctrine should, however, not be taken as a way of eliding Puritan into Catholic on issues stemming from sexuality and the marriage relationship. The opposite conclusion ought rather to be drawn: that agreement on certain points makes Puritan divergence from Catholic marriage doctrine all the more striking and significant. This is true both of sober, scholarly, well-balanced writers like William Perkins, who enters into serious debate with Catholic marriage doctrine in order to refute it, and of polemical writers like John Milton, who always puts Catholic doctrine in the worst possible light so as to disagree radically with it.

No attempt will be made here to encompass the full range of the Catholic tradition on marriage. There are two points at which Puritan writers are most uncomfortable with this tradition: the issue of the nature of marriage, whether it is sacramental or covenantal, and the issue of the ends of marriage, whether procreation of offspring or companionship between the spouses is the primary end. The discussion of the following pages concentrates on these points.

I wish to clarify what Catholic canonists and theologians were saying about marriage in order to show how the Puritans use this tradition in a different way, in some cases making different assumptions and in others drawing different conclusions from similar assumptions. The presence of a minority tradition within Catholic writings on marriage, represented by such figures as Martin Le Maistre and John Major,[46] a position which in large part is in agreement with Puritan marriage doctrine, does not seriously complicate this task. The position of the majority is easy to isolate, and it is this position I have in mind when I speak of the Catholic tradition on marriage. That there is a dissenting minority with teachings coincident with those of the Puritans is instructive on two counts: first, it shows that even though they are Protestants, the Puritans are not totally aloof from the development of doctrine in the Catholic Church (it may in fact be said that they thought of themselves as rediscovering the Catholic tradition); second, it argues that the Puritans are on the mark in discerning the weaknesses and difficulties in the majority position in Catholic marriage ethics. Finally, the peculiar ambiguities of the English Reformation suggest this argument: in the English context, one test of whether, in doubtful cases, a given writer is a Puritan can be marriage doctrine. Application of this test will be eased if the following pages successfully lift up and explore relevant aspects of the Catholic doctrine on marriage.

A full historical treatment of Catholic marriage doctrine would reach far back into the early history of Christianity; a reasonably complete treatment would begin at least with Augustine. But since the intent here is to provide a context for the development of Puritan marriage doctrine, it is justifiable to limit discussion to the Catholic position as it was developed in the Middle Ages, and specifically to use the teaching of Thomas Aquinas as a representative example. It is, after all, the medieval form of the doctrine which the Puritans know and to which they react, and by their time (as in our own) Thomas Aquinas had come to be the chief theological spokesman for the Catholic Church.[47]

[46] See John T. Noonan Jr., *Contraception* (Cambridge, Mass.: Belknap Press, 1965), pp. 306-40.
[47] The quotations from Thomas Aquinas given herein are from the discussion of

38

In a catechism published in English in 1604, Cardinal Robert Bellarmine, a contemporary of Cleaver and Perkins, expressed a central tenet of the Catholic tradition: that marriage is good, but virginity is better. He writes:

The Apostle S. Paul hath cleered this doubt, having written, that who joyneth himself in Mariage doth wel, but who kepeth virginitie doth better. And the reason is, because Mariage is a thing humane, virginitie is Angelical. Mariage is according to nature, Virginitie is above nature. And not only virginitie but widowhood is also better than mariage. Therefore wheras our Saviour said in a parable, that the good sede yelded in one fild thirtie fold fruite, in an other threescore, in an other a hundred fold: the holie Doctors have declared, that the thirtie fold fruite is of matrimonie, the thre-score fold of widowhood, the hundred fold of virginitie.[48]

The distinction made in this passage among states pertaining to matrimony is a common one. Underlying such distinctions wherever they appear, however, is a common assumption: that a special danger for the souls of men is somehow connected with the married state. More correctly, the danger is inherent in sexual intercourse, which lust drives all men toward, and the state of matrimony aims at removing this danger and controlling human lust. Thus Thomas asks "whether the marriage act is altogether sinful" and answers, no, it is not *altogether* sinful, for "since the inclination to beget an offspring whereby the specific nature is preserved is from nature, it is impossible to maintain that the act of begetting children is altogether unlawful." [49] This is one phrasing Thomas gives to the scholastic doctrine of procreative intent in intercourse, an idea which he takes from Peter Lombard, who had found it in Augustine.[50] This doctrine teaches that the lust which accompanies

---

matrimony in the *Supplement* to the *Summa Theologica,* which is an arrangement of relevant sections of Thomas' commentary on the *Sentences* of Peter Lombard. Thomas also treats marriage briefly in his *Summa Contra Gentiles,* Book III, Chaps. 122-26. The references below are to *The Summa Theologica of St. Thomas Aquinas* (New York: Benziger Brothers, 1948), vol. III, *Supplement* (hereafter referred to as *Supp.*).

[48] Robert Bellarmine, *An Ample Declaration of Christian Doctrine,* trans. Richard Haddock (Douai, 1604), pp. 257-58. For one Puritan polemic against divorce as treated in this document see Appendix A below.

[49] *Supp.,* Q. 41, A. 3.

[50] Noonan, *Contraception,* pp. 193-94.

coitus somehow transmits original sin, and that the only excuse for the sin of concupiscence in intercourse is the direction of that act toward its natural end, which is identified with the procreation of offspring. Nature also gives a second reason for the existence of marriage, according to Thomas: the "mutual services which married persons render one another in household matters." [51]

From Augustine, Thomas has inherited the idea that there are three goods in marriage: *fides,* faith; *proles,* offspring; and *sacramentum,* sacrament.[52] This list, Thomas argues, sufficiently enumerates the goods of marriage. The first two correspond directly to the natural reasons for marriage stated above, yet the content of these goods needs further explication. *Proles* as an end of marriage is not just the *having* of offspring but the *intention* to have them, as Thomas reasons from the tradition. This follows from what was said above: the intent to procreate excuses the marriage act. But *proles* also includes the education of any children who may be born into a family.[53] The entire causal chain, beginning with the parents' willing to have children and ending with the last child's emergence from the family to seek his fortune in the world, is what *proles* denotes; it is the entire process of transmitting human life.

Fides has an even more extensive set of meanings, of which the one already given (mutual service in household matters) is but a single example. Clearly *fides* is a natural end of marriage: it does not denote the theological virtue "faith" (as in "faith, hope, charity, these three"); rather it pertains to justice, a natural virtue, since marriage is a state entered into by mutual promising and maintained by justly keeping those promises. Among the promises the spouses make and must keep are those to pay the marriage debt to each other and to have intercourse with no third parties.[54] That payment of the marriage debt is directed toward the restraint and remedy of sinful concupiscence as a good to be given faithfully to one's partner and that sexual intercourse (even as payment of the debt) must be excused by intent to procreate together show that this aspect of *fides* is, in fact, defined by the good of *proles.*

[51] *Supp.,* Q. 41, A. 1.
[52] Noonan, *Contraception,* pp. 127-28.
[53] *Supp.,* Q. 49, A. 2.
[54] *Ibid.*

Thomas obviously wishes to maintain the separateness and parity of the two natural goods of marriage, but the logic of his position seems to drive toward a subordination of *fides* to *proles*. This is an especially sore point among the Puritans, who, as I attempt to demonstrate in the following chapters, tend to do precisely the opposite, subordinating the good of procreation to that of companionship. The Puritan championing of the cause of mutual companionability in marriage is not wholly comprehensible unless it is seen against the background of a powerful theological tradition which asserts the primacy of procreation among the reasons for the existence of marriage and among the goods toward which married couples should aim.

The tradition with which Thomas is working is the result of Christian opposition to two denials of the good of offspring in marriage. Both the Manichees, in Augustine's time, and the Cathars, in the Middle Ages, held that to procreate was to enslave souls in matter. These groups therefore opposed even the intent to have offspring, but they did not consistently oppose intercourse for other purposes, or even modes of intercourse other than vaginal. In opposition to the Manichaean and Catharistic challenges the Catholic doctrine on marriage came to assert the primacy of procreation among the ends of marriage and the necessity of procreative intent to justify all sexual intercourse.[55]

The Puritans, then, do not misread the intention of Catholic doctrine, though Milton perhaps overstates the case when he accuses the English courts of canon law, because of their adherence to medieval canons governing marriage, of making "the minde of man wait upon the slavish errands of the body." [56] In Thomas, besides the evidence already cited, his very language suggests that *fides* is secondary to *proles* among the ends of marriage. In one place he defines *fides* as simply that "whereby a man has intercourse with his wife and no other woman." Again, though *fides* is "the entire communion of works that exists between man and wife as united in marriage," it is so only as long as these works aim at the rearing of offspring. Finally, no Puritan could ever pronounce such a statement as this one of Thomas: "The offspring like a principal end includes another, as it were, secondary end," namely *fides*.[57] Thomas wishes to maintain parity between the natural ends of marriage, but he

[55] Noonan, *Contraception,* Chaps. IV, VI.
[56] Milton, *Tetrachordon,* p. 599.
[57] *Supp.,* Q. 49, A. 2.

is prevented from doing so by the logic of his position. Given his definitions of *proles* and *fides* and the presence in the inherited doctrine of the requirement of procreative intent, *fides* comes out second best. In their different context, influenced by Renaissance humanism and not a Catharistic threat, the Puritans create a marriage doctrine in which the ranking of *fides* and *proles* (or, as they would put it, companionship and procreation) is just inverted from the Catholic order.

Two other ends of marriage need to be considered at this point. First, what of the restraint and remedy of sin, listed second after procreation in the English Prayer Book and always one of the ends in Puritan listings? In the marriage doctrine of Thomas Aquinas this end is clearly subordinated to the other natural ends, *proles* and *fides:* to the former insofar as any intercourse needs the excuse of procreative intent and to the latter insofar as the intercourse which restrains and remedies sin is in payment of the marriage debt. Raising restraint and remedy of sin to the level of an independent end of marriage alongside procreation and companionship seems to be a departure from both Augustine and Thomas, and it is in fact a departure from their language, for though this function is always admitted in Catholic doctrine, it is not there given independent status among the marriage ends. But too much can be made of this difference between Puritan and Catholic. For the latter the end of restraint and remedy is integral to marriage and is internally related to *proles* and *fides*. For the Puritans, as it is argued in the two following chapters, the real issue is the primacy of companionship over procreation; and the end of restraint and remedy of sin, though stated, is largely left to one side, out of the debate over priority among the ends. Moreover, whichever of procreation and companionship is primary gives definition to the idea of restraint and remedy of sin, and so there is an internal relation of this end to the others among English Christians also. Thus to a Thomist, having intercourse to limit concupiscence must be, at least in intent and objective nature of the act, procreative, while to Thomas Gataker or John Milton or other Puritan marriage theorists the act of intercourse is simply the most companionable of all acts of mutuality between husband and wife.

The last end to be considered belongs to the Catholic marriage doctrine but not to the Puritan: the end of *sacramentum,* sacrament. This is not a natural but a supernatural end; it is an end only of marriage between Christians. Its relation to *fides* and *proles,* according to Thomas, is as follows:

[F]aith and offspring may be considered in their principles, so that off-spring denote the intention of having children, and faith the duty of remaining faithful. . . . Taking faith and offspring in this sense, it is clear that offspring is the most essential thing in marriage, secondly faith, and thirdly sacrament; even as to man it is more essential to be in nature than in grace, although it is more excellent to be in grace.[58]

Besides reiterating what has been described above, the priority of *proles* over *fides,* this passage makes two other points: *proles* is the most essential of all three ends of marriage, outranking even *sacramentum* in this respect, and the good of *sacramentum* is of a different sort from the other two.[59] The first point simply reinforces the Catholic position in the argument with the Puritans over the ends of marriage. The second point introduces us to the second major issue between Puritan marriage theorists and the Catholic doctrine: that of the nature of marriage, whether it is sacramental (as conceived by the Catholics) or covenantal (as with the Puritans). In making this distinction I am aware of a problem of language: that in Catholic doctrine also marriage may be said to be a covenant, since the Latin word for "contract" can also be rendered in English as "covenant." But just as for the Puritans marriage is emphatically nonsacramental, for the Catholics marriage is definitely not covenantal, if this term is defined as in the first part of this chapter, with the covenant of grace as upper limit and analogies with other human covenantal relations as a lower limit. In fact the issue between Puritan and Catholic on the nature of marriage transcends this linguistic problem and is largely a question of where to locate the activity of God and the spouses in courtship, in the moment of the marriage vows, and in sustaining the matrimonial union. But before answering this question, it is necessary to explore briefly what Thomas means when he argues that marriage is a sacrament.

[58] *Ibid.,* A. 3.

[59] Together these two points mean that marriage between unbelievers is valid. Even they can fulfill the natural ends, which are more essential, though less excellent, than the supernatural end.

Sacramentum as the third good of marriage derives, of course, from Augustine. Noonan writes:

Augustine uses the term *sacramentum,* here translated "symbolic stability," for the third value of marriage. Later usage was inevitably to identify the term with "sacrament" in the more specific sense of a sacrament instituted by Christ. The latter meaning is not entirely alien to Augustine's thought. He proposes this value as a result of reflection on the indissolubility of Christian marriage. The bond made for the purpose of procreation cannot be set aside if procreation is impossible.[60]

In Thomas the more specific sense of sacrament is the one applied to marriage. But the connection made by Augustine between *sacramentum* and indissolubility remains. Neither of these points is accepted by the Puritans.

A sacrament, in the narrow sense, is a visible sign of an invisible grace. While it does not cause grace to come, performance of the symbolic act with the right intent will always be accompanied by grace. Sacraments are efficacious *ex opere operato* and not by virtue of the holiness of the person or persons performing them. Is matrimony a sacrament, then; that is, does it confer grace? Thomas replies to two objections that it does not confer grace:

Reply Obj. 1. Just as the baptismal water by virtue of its contact with Christ's body is able to touch the body and cleanse the heart, so is matrimony able to do so through Christ having represented it by His Passion, and not principally through any blessing of the priest.

Reply Obj. 2. Just as the water of Baptism together with the form of words results immediately not in the infusion of grace, but in the imprinting of the character, so the outward acts and the words expressive of consent directly effect a certain tie which is the sacrament of matrimony; and this tie by virtue of its Divine institution works dispositively to the infusion of grace.[61]

A Christian couple who marry, then, so long as they observe the proper form and have correct intent, are assured of God's blessing on their

---

[60] Noonan, *Contraception,* pp. 127-28.
[61] *Supp.,* Q. 42, A. 3.

life together. So far as intent is concerned, they must aim at fulfillment of the three ends of marriage: *fides, proles, sacramentum;* so far as form is concerned, "consent expressed in words of the present between persons lawfully qualified to contract makes a marriage, because these two conditions are essential to the sacrament, while all else belongs to the solemnization of the sacrament, as being done in order that the marriage may be more fittingly performed." [62] The marriage is performed by the man and woman themselves, not by the priest, and if they observe the conditions, God's grace is given to their union. But what does this grace do? It sustains the marriage. In the same way that natural virtues are infused by grace in cooperation with human striving to attain these virtues, the grace of matrimony cooperates with the spouses in their attempts to gain the virtues proper to married life. These latter virtues pertain to the various institutions of matrimony: "Nature inclines to marriage with a certain good in view, which good varies according to the different states of man, wherefore it was necessary for matrimony to be variously instituted in the various states of man in reference to that good." [63]

Matrimony ordered to the procreation of children was instituted in paradise before sin (interestingly the Puritans generally view this original institution as ordered toward providing a companion, a "help meet," for Adam); matrimony directed toward remedying the "wound of sin" was instituted "after sin at the time of the natural law" and is in certain respects part of Mosaic law; as representing the mystical union of Christ with his church marriage is instituted in the new law; and "as regards other advantages resulting from matrimony, such as the friendship and mutual services which husband and wife render one another, its institution belongs to the civil law." [64] The sacramental grace present in Christian marriage works through husband and wife to help them realize marriage in all its institutions in their own union.

One of the perfections of marriage is indissolubility. Though in the definition of matrimony given by Peter Lombard and seconded by Thomas Aquinas the indissolubility of the union is explicitly associated with its sacramental character,[65] nature itself creates the tendency toward

[62] *Ibid.,* Q. 45, A. 5.
[63] *Ibid.,* Q. 42, A. 2.
[64] *Ibid.*
[65] *Ibid.,* Q. 49, A. 3.

indissolubility. That is, when a man and a woman come together intending to have offspring, they commit themselves to a lifelong union by the nature of the object of their commitment.[66] The raising up of children is a lifetime task, not only in intent but in fact, given the extended period of childbearing possible for human beings and the length of time it takes for a child to grow and be educated (the latter, as Thomas argues throughout his discussion of marriage, is always an essential part of *proles*). Though this tendency toward marital indissolubility is present by nature, the presence of sin tends to prevent natural marriages from reaching this perfection. But grace, working against sin, supports nature in giving husband and wife strength to hold to this object of their marriage: "Wherever God gives the faculty to do a thing, He gives also the helps whereby man is enabled to make becoming use of that faculty.[67]

In regard to the institution of marriage in the new law, the everlasting character of marriage mirrors the everlasting union of Christ and church. As man now is, therefore, matrimonial indissolubility comes from grace alone, and that by special divine institution, Christian marriage as *sacramentum*. Once two persons are married, similar considerations apply in understanding the action of grace. These considerations, in turn, affect Catholic and Puritan conceptions of marital indissolubility. Both doctrines agree that it is consent which makes marriage—the consent of the two parties who become husband and wife. Thomas writes of this consent that though it

is not everlasting materially, i.e. in regard to the substance of the act, since that act ceases and a contrary act may succeed it, nevertheless formally speaking it is everlasting, because it is consent to an everlasting bond, else it would not make a marriage, for consent to take a woman for a time makes no marriage. Hence it is everlasting formally, inasmuch as an act takes its species from its object; and thus it is that marriage derives its inseparability from the consent.[68]

[66] *Ibid.,* Q. 67, A. 1. "By the intention of nature marriage is directed to the rearing of offspring, not merely for a time, but throughout its whole life. . . . Therefore, since the offspring is the common good of husband and wife, the dictate of the natural law requires the latter to live together for ever inseparably: and so the indissolubility of marriage is of natural law."

[67] *Ibid.,* Q. 42, A. 3.

[68] *Ibid.,* Q. 49, A. 3.

In the same locus he argues that the character imprinted by the sacramental nature of marriage is power to perform bodily actions, not spiritual ones. For the Puritans, on the other hand, the consent which makes marriage must be everlasting materially; that is, the partners must throughout their life together continually renew their consent. For Thomas the grace of God enters marriage primarily at the moment of the marriage vows, for this is the nature of the sacrament, but for the Puritans grace works at all points in the historical continuum of married life, helping the partners to renew their mutual consent so long as they both shall live. As I elsewhere indicate, the perseverance of mutual consent is assumed by the Puritans wherever mutual duties are performed. Lacking performance of mutual duty in a particular union, the question arises for them whether God's blessing is on this union, indeed, whether it is truly a marriage in the sight of God.

What is at stake in this sacramental conception of marriage, so far as the development of Puritan marriage doctrine is concerned, is the understanding of where and how God acts and how his acts are related to those of the marriage partners. In the doctrine of Thomas, grace in marriage operationally *accompanies* and logically *follows* the acts of the partners. This language, which is not that of Thomas, must be explained. I mean that when the partners consent to marry, it is their action first, God's action to support them second. Leaving aside the entire matter of the grace which has preceded matrimony, that of baptism, of confirmation, of penance, and of the Mass, matrimonial grace arises when two people decide to marry (it accompanies their decision) and logically can be discussed only after treating the decision of the partners. For the Puritans, however, grace necessarily *precedes* the decision of two Christian persons to marry and is in a certain way the cause of that decision. What I assert here about the decision to marry obtains, *mutatis mutandis,* throughout the matrimonial state. In this conception, just as God gave Eve to Adam, so he guides men and women together who will be right for each other. This conception of God's activity was introduced earlier in this chapter during a discussion of William Ames. In the next chapter the same topic arises in connection with William Perkins' understanding of proximate and remote causation (the partners' and God's, respectively) in marriage, and in Chapter III it is reintroduced as a consideration of the role of special providence, as opposed to general providence, in bringing together certain men and women, following the thought of Thomas Gataker. Finally, John Milton's peculiar twist on this understanding of God's action is explored in the remaining chapters. This difference in the way God's action in marriage is conceived is basic to understanding Puritan repudiation of the sacramentalist notion of marriage.

Relation of the above to the *ex opere operato* efficacy of the sacrament of matrimony should be indicated. Since for Puritans grace precedes and in some way causes the human acts that make marriage, the idea that God works in the sacrament *ex opere operato* is redundant. Given their conception of the working of grace, the question which the Catholic doctrine answers never arises.

Once marriage is contracted, those Puritans who argue for matrimonial indissolubility do so on the ground of its divine nature alone (Ames and Perkins, already treated in this chapter, are examples) and so depart from Thomas Aquinas' teaching that indissolubility comes from nature, namely the intent to live together and procreate. The Puritans argue that Christian marriage is indissoluble only because God is working through the mutual love of the spouses to support their union. Those Puritans who argue for divorce for incompatibility accept this point but assert that in marriages where there is no mutual love, God is not working because he never intended this couple to be together in marriage. Milton makes this argument quite explicit.

In closing this discussion of two main issues in Catholic marriage doctrine I must reiterate that they are the two around which, in my judgment, Puritan dissatisfaction with the tradition clusters. There are points of lesser importance which might have been introduced here (for example, the question of the object of consent in matrimony, whether consent is to procreation or to companionship, and the implications of both positions), but they are related to the two main issues discussed here and can best be treated in particular contexts elsewhere. Likewise I have not explicated portions of the tradition which the Puritans accept by taking for granted, though some of these too are indicated elsewhere. I have attempted in these pages to sketch briefly only those parts of Catholic marriage doctrine which relate to Puritan distinctiveness. This aim has dictated omission of much that would belong in a full discussion of the Catholic position.

II
Early Statements of the Puritan Marriage Doctrine

From the time of Henry VIII onward isolated cases can be found of movement toward an understanding of marriage based on the covenant between husband and wife. Most significant among these is the *Reformatio Legum Ecclesiasticarum,* which stands as the earliest attempt to modify English law so as to allow for full divorce with remarriage rights on certain grounds, notably desertion and adultery.[1] But while the beginnings of the Puritan marriage doctrine can be traced back as far as "the king's affair," there are no systematic works on marriage written by Puritans until around 1600. This chapter begins the historical analysis of the Puritan marriage doctrine, then, with an examination of works by three Puritan divines of the turn of the century: Robert Cleaver, William Perkins, and William Ames. This examination aims not only at clarifying the total perspective on marriage of each of these men but also at pointing to those particular ideas which are most significant for the later development of the Puritan marriage doctrine.

[1] Powell, *English Domestic Relations,* p. 63. See also his Chap. III, pp. 61 ff., for a discussion of the changing attitude toward marriage after Henry VIII.

Louis B. Wright examines "The Popular Controversy over Women" which simmered and boiled both during Elizabeth's reign and on into the 1600s.[2] Wright argues that some of the concern precipitating this controversy arose from there being a female monarch on the English throne. By her prominent position Elizabeth became the (of course unnamed) butt of the satires of the "new woman" as well as the ideal to be defended by friendly writers. But the continuation of this controversy into the days of James's reign shows that the queen was only a partial cause. The fact is that there were abroad in England at this time women who were self-assertive and concerned with gaining access to prerogatives which had previously belonged to men only. Whether such women sought to educate themselves to the level of the men they knew or whether they became sexually aggressive—two manifestations of the "new woman" noted by Wright—they aroused both ire and sympathy and precipitated the writing of books and pamphlets both derogatory and comlimentary.

In general, according to Wright, the middle class favored tendencies of women to better themselves, but with important reservations. A woman could go too far in aping the man or seeking to supplant him. Those who supported education for women did not necessarily approve of the "froward" fashions of the day. The way in which a woman of the court asserted herself was, in middle-class eyes, quite a different matter from the way a good wife might assert her rights in the family unit. Much of the support the "new woman" received from middle-class writers, Wright argues, was simply support for a set of virtues developed within the middle-class family. Here wives were expected to play a responsible role as junior partner in a joint enterprise, and therefore women had to prepare themselves to exercise this responsibility. The "new woman" of the middle classes was thus not the same as the "new woman" of the court, who was recognizable by her provocative clothes and mannish manners. This latter would find no kind words about her in a middle-class defense of women's rights.

Puritan writers play a large part in the production of controversial literature concerning women, Wright notes. The Puritan contribution is of two sorts: argumentative pamphlets written for some immediate

[2] *Middle-Class Culture in Elizabethan England,* Chap. XIII.

purpose and highly controversial in nature and theoretical works which stand aloof from the in-fighting of the pamphlet world so as to explain better what is proper for a woman to do and to be. The works discussed in this chapter fall into the second category. For an illustration of some relatively high-level pamphleteering, see the discussion of Edmund Bunny's and John Rainolds' tracts in Appendix A.

Robert Cleaver

An example of a Puritan theoretical writing on the general subject of the controversy over women's rights is Robert Cleaver's *A Godlie Forme of Household Government: For the Ordering of Private Families According to the Direction of Gods Word*.[3] This treatise is bourgeois: it takes up the subject of women's rights within the framework of typical middle-class marriage; it is Puritan, as can be seen from the reference to "Gods word" as the final source for authority in the family; it is mildly revolutionary, in that it allows for a high interpretation of woman's rights in the family and outside it when representing the family's interests. Besides being timely it expresses both theological and social concerns and ways of dealing with them which are typical of Puritan writings in Cleaver's day and into the next generation as well.

Cleaver is most interested in the practical aspects of life in the household, and particularly he is concerned that the husband and the wife order their mutual relationship properly. The plan of his work is a contrast to the typical Puritan marriage sermon of a generation later, and it is even more strikingly different from the typical Anglican homily on marriage. Nearly the first hundred pages are devoted to defining a household and explaining the roles of the two "governours" of it under various headings. Only on the basis thus prepared does Cleaver become theoretical, and approximately the next hundred pages deal with the definition of marriage, the proper way of entering into it, and whether and how it can be dissolved. Even here the practical concern intrudes, as theory is seen by Cleaver to imply certain duties for the husband and wife. The final two hundred pages of the book return explicitly to practical matters and deal with the various duties members of a house-

---

[3] See Chap. I, n. 19 above.

hold have toward one another. Whereas the initial treatment of this theme concerns only husband and wife, the concluding longer treatment takes up their duties once more and those of children and servants as well. All duties of one member of the household toward another imply reciprocal duties until finally the household is explained as a marvelous matrix of requisite acts performable in certain directions and for certain reasons, all for the good of the entire household together and the individuals making it up separately. No contradiction is seen between such constant talk of duties and individual freedom, for freedom's place is in how the duties are performed. And finally, all through his book Cleaver refers again and again to biblical injunctions and patterns of family life as almost his sole authority.

What sets off this tome from one an Anglican of the period might write is its overwhelming practical concern. An Anglican typically would outline the doctrine of marriage and discuss practical aspects of marriage only as a result of the implications of the doctrine. Part of this is a result of the Ramist "plain" logic (start with what is most obvious and build upon it) over against the Aristotelian (begin with definitions, then deduce to cases). But perhaps more of the reason is cultural: the Puritan writings, especially Cleaver's, express a middle-class concern with the ordering of day-to-day activity, whatever the theory behind it.

But there is a difference from Puritans of the next generation too. Cleaver's work would be in outline, as well as in much of its content, like the marriage sermons of a Gouge or a Whatley, both writing a generation later, were it not for his initial discourse on the household and its two "governours" and his attempt by this discourse to place family government within a larger framework.[4] Cleaver's book is an attempt to set the godly family within the nation as a whole, which is for him capable of being godly too. Gouge and other later writers have a more narrow concern, that of keeping their own houses in order. This should not be taken to imply that these latter do not share Cleaver's belief that the family and the nation are best ordered in the same way, out of God's word to man in the Bible. Nor does it mean that Cleaver is more interested in authoring a work on social order in general than in prescribing rules for Christian families. One might read too much into

---

[4] *Household Government,* p. 15. See also Chap. I, pp. 25-26 above.

what may be only an accidental difference in outlines, yet one should be careful to note the possibility that this difference arises out of the changed conditions that faced the Puritans after Laud became Archbishop of Canterbury.

Cleaver's preoccupation with the more practical or at least more ready-to-hand aspects of his subject makes his treatment of the theological aspects of it the more interesting. His position on what the family ideally should be is one that does not seem to rise directly from the Scriptures, though there is some link with the Bible as well as with the culture of late Elizabethan England. As it is set forth here, there is a tension within Cleaver's marriage doctrine as to what the purpose of the family is and what the means of obtaining its ends ought to be.

"A Household is as it were a little common wealth, by the good government wherof, Gods glorie may be advaunced, the common wealth which standeth of severall families, benefited, and al that live in that familie may receive much comfort and commoditie." [5] A Christian household is different from any other in that a Christian householder exercises "a christian care" [6] over it. What this immediately means in this: if he only seeks to provide the material necessities of life for the subordinate members of the household, "then Papists, Atheists, yea, Turkes, and Infidels, do yeelde this dutie as well as [he]." [7] The Christian head of family is to do what unbelievers do but is to add Christian instruction as well. "The government of a familie tendeth unto two things especially. First, christian holinesse, and secondlie the things of this life." [8] The responsibility for seeing to this lies with the husband, but he is closely seconded by his wife: "The governours of families . . . upon whom the charge of governmēt lyeth, though unequally, are, first the Cheefe governour, which is the Husband, secondly a fellow helper, which is the Wife." [9]

Cleaver never departs from maintaining a high position for the wife, though he carefully holds to the doctrine of the husband's final superiority of station. To the children and servants, the wife is to be regarded

[5] *Ibid.*, p. 5.
[6] *Ibid.*, p. A4.
[7] *Ibid.*, p. A3.
[8] *Ibid.*, p. 17.
[9] *Ibid.*, p. 19.

as having the authority of the husband when he is absent and as his near equal when he is present. She is to be obeyed and revered just as he is. Yet toward the husband the wife must show submission, thereby both returning the love which he gives her as his proper duty and also setting an example for the children and servants to follow.[10] The closeness of the wife's position to the husband's is indicated by Cleaver's relative silence when he comes to discuss her duties. He spends pages on the husband's role; then he quickly sets the wife to seconding her husband when he is present and taking his place when he is not. The image called up is at least that of her being like a junior partner in a business enterprise; at most it is that of an executive officer on a warship.[11] It is never forgotten that husband and wife are cofounders of the household, even though the original initiative was properly the husband's.

If a household is a "little common wealth" with "two governours," what is a marriage, the nucleus of the household?

Wedlocke or Matrimonie, is a lawful knot, and unto God an acceptable yoking and joyning together of one man, and one woman, with the good consent of them both: to the end that they may dwell together in friendship and honestie, one helping and comforting the other, eschewing whoredome, and all uncleannesse, bringing up their children in the feare of God: or it is a coupling together of two persons into one flesh, not to be broken, according unto the ordinance of God: so to continue during the life of either of them.[12]

There are here two definitions set side by side, and Cleaver seems not to realize that they do not say exactly the same. Or perhaps he does, for he continues this inaugural discussion of marriage with various warnings that by "one flesh" he does not mean only the result of the spouses' having sexual intercourse together: it implies "an uniforme agreement of minde" as well as "outward dwelling together" and "common participation of bodie and goods."[13] It may be the case that he is actively trying to join the differing implications of the two parts of

[10] *Ibid.,* pp. 60-61.
[11] For Cleaver on convenantal marriage see above, Chap. I, 25-26.
[12] *Household Government,* p. 98.
[13] *Ibid.*

his definition of marriage so as to make a new definition; perhaps the conjunction should be "and," not "or."

The ambiguity in Cleaver's theory of marriage may, I suggest, be traced also to his failure to carry through the implications of the Ramist system of logic within the framework of which he seems to move.[14] Some Ramist elements are quite obvious. Analysis by successive dichotomization, a dependable sign of the presence of Ramist method, is present throughout *Household Government*. One example will illustrate this aspect of Cleaver's use of Ramism. The idea of "good government" introduced in the first definition of marriage is explicated first by considering right and wrong ways of governing. Next Cleaver dichotomizes the right way by bringing to view the two sorts of persons in every household, the governors and the governed. The governors are two, the father and the mother, also called master and mistress, since each has a dual role. Similarly the governed are of two sorts: children and servants. After setting forth the basic structure of the household in this fashion, Cleaver further defines the parts by describing the duties that pertain to each role. This too is done by dichotomization. The two governors of the household have two sorts of duties, those concerning spiritual matters and those relating to things of this world.[15] The husband has two kinds of duty to the wife, and so has she toward him. Similarly Cleaver works through all the duties of members of the household in their relations with one another. But this method of dichotomization is not the only clue to Cleaver's Ramism. Two more are present: movement from the general to the particular in listing duties, when Aristotelian method would suggest the opposite procedure, and utilization of cause-effect language throughout to describe this movement.

Cleaver neglects, however, in his definitions of marriage to make as full use of cause-effect categories as Ramism would suggest. A Ramist definition is formally correct only when it lists in order the efficient, material, formal, and final causes of the thing defined. While Cleaver's two definitions of marriage can be broken down by Ramist analysis, they are not formal Ramist definitions. Had Cleaver been more carefully Ramistic in defining marriage, he might have avoided the ambiguity

[14] See Appendix B for a brief discussion of topics in Ramist logic which are relevant for study of Puritan marriage doctrine.
[15] *Household Government*, p. 17.

that mars his marriage theory. One is never sure on just what basis he makes his judgments about the household. One way of ensuring clarity about this would have been to state what is the efficient cause of the household, and this is precisely what is lacking in Cleaver's definitions. It takes little imagination to find a probable reason for this omission: marriage, the root of the household, is "a society ordained by God" in the Prayer Book of the day. God is therefore the efficient cause, as, Cleaver assumes, all men know. But the proximate efficient causes, social pressures and the wills of the spouses, need to be considered too, and here Cleaver begins to be ambiguous. He is never clear about the efficient causation of marriage, and so he is never univocal about the nature of marriage. If this analysis is correct, then it is Cleaver's incomplete appropriation of Ramist logic that underlies the lack of clarity in his doctrine of marriage.

Whether the tension in Cleaver's thought is intentional or accidental, it is there. Present in the definition of marriage, it shows itself more clearly when the subject is the causes of marriage. Cleaver lists them according to the Prayer Book order: "The first is, the procreation, begetting, & bringing up of children: Gen. 1.27.28. & 9.1." [16] "The second occasion why Marriage was ordeined, was, that the wife might bee a lawfull remedie to avoid whoredome, fornication, and all filthie uncleane lusts. I Cor. 7.2.3. &c. . . . The third and last cause was, for mans commoditie, to the end to avoid the inconvenience of solitarinesse, that the one may helpe & comfort the other." [17] But only a few pages away, where the subject is not "causes" of marriage but "common duties" of the married, a different order is followed: "The first common dutie is praier." [18] "A second dutie of pietie is, that they admonish one another." [19] "Againe, there is another mutuall dutie pertaining to themselves: to witte, that neare conjunction, even in regard of their bodies, for an holy procreation of children." [20] Other common duties follow, but these state what is *first* to be done. How can procreation be the first of the "causes" of marriage (i.e., *final* causes or ends) when it

[16] *Ibid.*, p. 157.
[17] *Ibid.*, p. 158.
[18] *Ibid.*, p. 181.
[19] *Ibid.*, p. 182.
[20] *Ibid.*, p. 183.

is only third among the duties? How can mutual "helpe & comfort" be the last of the ends of marriage, ranked *after* procreation, when "that they admonish one another" is the second common duty, ranked *before* procreation? Cleaver here is quite inconsistent. From the standpoint of logic, either Ramism, which would emphasize the efficient causation implied in the duties, or Aristotelianism, which would emphasize the final causation of the marriage ends, would be preferable to the uneasy mixture of the two attempted by Cleaver.

Another interpretation of the tension in Cleaver's marriage doctrine arises from consideration of his sources. Two distinct sets of data inform his conception of marriage. One is the analogy of the household with the nation, of the "little common wealth" with that "which standeth of severall families." Here the principal model is the national structure of England with its monarch as head and a complex system of duties arising from its intricate social structure. When he speaks of the husband's duty to make sure the family has access to the word,[21] to provide for worship in his household,[22] to catechize his family privately,[23] he could be admonishing the monarch to set up the nation in this fashion. Indeed the analogy, once introduced, becomes circular: as the concept of the monarch governing the nation reinforces that of the husband governing his household, likewise the reverse happens, so that the monarch is more and more seen to be like the petty householder. Their duties are much the same, but on a different scale.

Within the family conceived in such an analogy the wife's role as helper is the definitive one. She is a deputy of the husband; she is indeed one of the two "governours" of the family. Cleaver would be long dead when William and Mary ruled England, and their sort of rule may not have been what he had in mind anyway. But who would be the "wife" in the larger commonwealth, under only the monarch, the "husband," is not so important as noting that in the family the wife's role is high indeed and has mainly to do with her being alongside and yet subordinate to her husband in the government of the family. Thus the emphasis is on her role as helper (even "help meet"), not her role as defined by man's procreative instincts.

[21] *Ibid.*, p. 20.
[22] *Ibid.*, p. 43.
[23] *Ibid.*, p. 45.

The case is quite otherwise when one looks at the second set of data informing Cleaver's view of marriage. When he attempts to discuss marriage from a purely theological viewpoint, he becomes concerned with the procreative aspects of the union of husband and wife: "The first [cause] is, the procreation, begetting, & bringing up of children." "The second . . . [is], that the wife might be a lawfull remedie to avoid whoredome." Yet it would be wrong to stress this. Cleaver's concern never rests with the first two causes of marriage; it remains predominantly with spelling out the implications of the third. In this work of some four hundred pages he devotes only paragraphs here and there to marriage as a union for procreation. The reason seems to be that he frankly assumes this is what makes marriage unique among commonwealths and, furthermore, he reads it in the Bible.

Even though there is an important tension in Cleaver's thought between the two views of the purpose of marriage, he is not interested in reconciling the two. In his mind they are already reconciled. With his discussion of the mutual duties of husband and wife Cleaver begins a slow enlargement of the notion of marriage as primarily for companionship, an enlargement which takes place at the expense of the view of marriage as primarily a procreative society. Cleaver is one of the fathers of the covenantal doctrine of marriage.

Cleaver's concern with mutual society in marriage can be illustrated by investigating what he says about divorce. Adultery is the only basis for divorce. But the reason is not first of all that it breaks the one-flesh unity that has been created by the spouses' copulation together. It is that adultery "breaks the covenant of God" which has been created by the two partners with God as witness.[24] The important thing is the breaking of the contract which God witnesses. And the terms of the contract are love, trust, and the performance of mutual duties in the family. Thus here the social understanding of marriage is in control, though it works in a framework given by the understanding of marriage as primarily a fleshly unity sanctified by God. For Cleaver what God blesses is the

---

[24] John Dod and Robert Cleaver, *A Plaine and Familiar Exposition of the Ten Commandments of Almightie God* (London, 1612), STC 6956, p. 292. Though Dod gained the nickname "Decalogue Dod" for producing this work, Cleaver also contributed to it. The opinions it expresses on marriage are consonant with those of Cleaver's *Household Government,* and therefore I cite it in this chapter to fill out Cleaver's doctrine of marriage.

contract, not the act of intercourse. The latter is only one of the terms, though a most important one, of the contract. This makes marriage a peculiar form of contract, and Cleaver is ready to admit this:

All other agreements and contracts made by mutuall consent may be broken and dissolved by the like consent of both parties: but in the contract of marriage, Almightie God commeth in as a witnesse; yea, he receiveth the promise of both parties, as joyning them in that estate.[25]

The place to void a bad marriage is before it is contracted, and there are certain safeguards which make this possible. Cleaver goes beyond the rules of consanguinity and affinity to counsel that prospective spouses take into account religion and more subjective factors as well.[26] When all care is taken to ensure a free choice of spouses, there is no need to allow for divorce too. But "freedome and libertie" in espousals are not the last safeguard to marriage; the consent of parents on both sides is necessary. Especially the father's power of witholding consent is important, for God's power to deny a contract is exercised through the earthly father.[27]

When the contract is made properly, God blesses the marriage, and there is no undoing it except for adultery. "A Contract, is a voluntarie promise of marriage, mutually made betweene one man and one woman, both being meete and free to marry one another, and therefore allowed to do so by their Parents." [28] This contract, otherwise known as espousal or betrothal, must be made in words of the present tense, and it should spell out certain duties for both parties. This is already virtually marriage, for only fornication (cf. adultery) can break the contract once made.[29] After a decent length of time the marriage ceremony is itself held, and here God gives his final approval, witnessing in his own stead (and not in the persons of the earthly fathers) to the terms of the contract. After this ceremony, conducted in church before the minister according to the proper forms, the contracted pair are sanctified in their

[25] *Household Government,* p. 195.
[26] *Ibid.,* pp. 101, 104 ff.
[27] *Ibid.,* p. 135.
[28] *Ibid.,* p. 116.
[29] *Ibid.,* p. 126.

union. They are now free to procreate and produce a holy seed, and their union is inseparable.

More conservative writers in this period argue that even adultery is no cause for full divorce, only for separation *a mensa et thoro*.[30] Cleaver's position is that adultery does not *have* to mean breakup of marriage. His concern appears largely pastoral. While adultery breaks the covenant of God, no one, understood strictly, is free from adulterous thoughts and acts. No one ought to pride himself on being above adultery, for even King David fell into that sin.[31] Adultery (in the sense of coitus with another person than one's spouse) alone *can* dissolve the marriage contract, but for the Christian couple, who ought always to be ready to forgive each other if there is true repentance, real dissolution occurs only lacking forgiveness. Divorce for adultery is thus possible, but it is not automatic.

Cleaver makes so much of the contracting before the marriage ceremony that it is clear that he finds the important element in marriage here, in the contract. It is in this contract that the prospective husband and wife declare that they are going to do their duty by each other: the husband that he will love his wife and the wife that she will be submisive to her husband. Again, God is present in somewhat the same sense as in the ceremony of matrimony, because the minister is present at the contracting as well as the parents, and the announcement of the contract is made in the church. Further, since only intercourse with someone outside the contract can break it, the bonds holding the two contracting parties together are as strong as those holding together persons who have been through the marriage ceremony.

It would be better to say that there is not first the contract and then the marriage, but that the actual performance of marriage takes place over a period of time beginning with the contracting and ending with the full ceremony of matrimony. There is support for this view in Cleaver's work:

Every marriage, that hath been well and orderly used, either of the heathen (which were only enlightened with the law of nature) or of the people of God, who also were directed by his word, was perfected by two solemne

---

[30] For example, Edmund Bunny. See Appendix A.
[31] Dod and Cleaver, *Ten Commandments*, p. 289.

actions: by an apparent & open contract and by publicke marriage, the true
& unfained cōfirmation therof.[32]

The reason for dividing the performance of marriage into two parts,
contracting and marriage ceremony, is to set off man from the beasts,
as Cleaver points out in various places.[33]

What is obvious from this is that Cleaver wishes to emphasize the
concept of marriage as covenant for mutual help and not mainly for the
purpose of procreation. Beasts procreate promiscuously; man should not.
Even reason tells him this, and God's Word makes it more plain. Any
two persons of opposite sex can do what is necessary to procreate, and
while this still may be said to be the "first cause" of marriage, the
exercise of marriage is carried out so as to ensure companionable spouses.
This is why God may be said to bless the contract above all in marriage,
and it is why Cleaver can call only "publicke marriage, the true & unfained cōfirmation" of the contract.

Cleaver's doctrine of marriage occupies a place at the very beginning
of the tradition discussed in this book. His position is, as later chapters
will show, far removed from that of Milton in the tracts on divorce.
Cleaver's idea of companionship in marriage is severely restricted by his
legal language and his entire concept of marriage duties. There is in
Household Government no sense of the free loving in wedlock which
Milton later extols. The ring of finality which the marriage contract
has for Cleaver is too harsh for Milton to accept. But already in William
Perkins' doctrine of marriage there is expressed a more liberal attitude.
Furthermore, the ideas that work themselves out in the Puritan marriage
doctrine are already germinally present in Cleaver's treatise. Most significantly he emphasizes the necessity for covenantal, "helpful" society in
marriage over a partnership justified mainly for procreation and the
restraint of sin, even though his understanding of marital companionship
is restricted by duty language and the analogy with the state. The tone
of *Household Government* is conservative, however, in spite of the significant opening toward a covenantal view of marriage. Theologically
what Cleaver says is highly orthodox, and he seems unaware that there

[32] *Household Government*, p. 111.
[33] *Ibid.*, pp. 135 ff.

is any tension between this theological base and his more practically grounded arguments.

It must be stressed that his position is that marriage once contracted and confirmed is indissoluble except for adultery. Incompatibility, even desertion, cannot break the marriage bond.

William Ames

William Ames stakes out in his *Conscience, with the Power and Cases Thereof* a position less ambiguous than Cleaver's. He defines marriage as "ordained by God for the bettering men's position, Gen. 2:18" and "secondly, Because that since the fall, it hath that end, and use that it directly makes for the avoiding of sinnes and temptations: I Cor. 7.2.5.9."[34] Ames too emphasizes the contract, arguing for the marriage ceremony "not so much in respect of them that are to bee married as in respect of the community, to which they are subject." The marriage may be performed by a civil magistrate, but having it done in church by a minister makes the ratification of the contract "more weighty." When Ames turns to the duties of husband and wife to each other, he puts the emphasis on those duties that make for companionable life together, not on the duty to produce offspring. The first mutual duty is "a speciall love," the "conjugall"; the second, "conjugall honor"; the third, "living together"; and finally, in fourth place, "mutuall communication of bodies according to the right end and limits of Wedlock."[35] Other mutual duties follow, defining in more detail the couple's life together, but these mentioned show how Ames rates the duties of companionship and procreation. The duty of procreation is a poor second to the three kinds of duties of companionship. The tension noted in Cleaver—and also, as we shall see, present in Perkins—is not present in Ames; marriage is for companionship primarily, with procreation a result of the company.

This does not make Ames any the less strict on divorce. He writes:

Matrimony cannot by any at his pleasure bee dissolved, and for that cause, simply and absolutely considered is rightly termed indissoluble, Matth. 19.9

[34] Ames, *Conscience,* p. 197.
[35] *Ibid.,* pp. 205-6.

Rom. 7.1. . . . Matrimony hath this privilege above other contracts, not only from Christs institution, but also from the Law of Nature. . . . The reason is because Matrimony is not onely a Civill, but a Divine conjunction, whose Institutour and Ordainer is God himselfe.[36]

Nevertheless, God may himself approve dissolution in certain cases. Ames lists five causes for divorce: contagious disease of one party, desertion, absence from the household for a long time, danger of one party from the other, and adultery. But in all these cases except the last Ames allows only separation or divorce *a mensa et thoro.* Only in the case of adultery does he state that the "bond" as well as the "use" of marriage is nullified. Divorce for adultery alone is "totall" divorce.[37] Even so, the consent of the innocent party can "continue" and "renew" the marriage bond in the case of adultery without there having to be a new marriage. This seems to imply that Ames would argue that some authority higher than the married parties would have to declare the divorce, though he does not specifically say this. A position of this sort is taken by William Perkins, however.[38] If Ames is correctly understood as taking this stand, then he argues that while the bond of marriage is broken by the act of adultery, a court must grant the divorce decree certifying that the bond has been broken.

William Perkins

William Perkins, like Robert Cleaver, wrote a treatise of household government. His *Christian Oeconomie; or, A Short Survey of the Right Manner of Erecting and Ordering a Familie, According to the Scriptures* is, furthermore, highly similar to Cleaver's treatise in both intent and content. In the case of Perkins, however, there is the possibility of setting the treatment of household government within a systematic theological system, thereby gleaning whatever additional understanding comes from examining the more general theological statements on the basis of which judgments about marriage are made.[39]

---

[36] *Ibid.,* p. 208.

[37] *Ibid.,* p. 209.

[38] See p. 76.

[39] William Perkins (1558-1602) is one of the foremost figures of Puritan theology. Educated at Christ's College, Cambridge, he was fellow there for ten years (1584-94) and became popular as a teacher and lecturer. Most of his writings date from this period. Perkins wrote and preached on a variety of subjects and was widely influential. A contem-

In addition to the obvious similarity that comes from their having been written for the same purpose—to teach Christians how to order their families—Perkins' and Cleaver's treatises on household government share an underlying ambiguity on what needs to be said about Christian marriage. In Cleaver's case we identified this as the tension arising out of statements about marriage based on two different sets of data, arguing that on the one hand the analogy of the family with the state makes for a definition of the family that stresses its social purpose, and that on the other hand the biblical injunction to Adam and Eve to be fruitful and multiply tends toward a concept of the family that stresses its procreative purpose. In Perkins' writings on marriage, and no less in the treatise on the family than elsewhere, there is a similar tension, but it is more subtly expressed than in the case of Cleaver. In this case the two sets of data which produce divergent ideas of the end of the family and of marriage both come from theological consideration of biblical statements about marriage and the family.

Here we shall examine Perkins' writings on marriage and the family to show how the two ways of conceiving marriage arise and how they manifest themselves. It must be said at the outset that Perkins' contemporaries, as well as Perkins himself, saw no inconsistency in what he was saying, just as in the more obvious case of Cleaver the tension was overlooked.

Perkins approaches his discussion of marriage in *Christian Oeconomie* through the more general notion of the family, which he, like Cleaver, understands as "the Seminarie of all other Societies."[40] The following abridges his movement from the general to the more specific society:

A familie, is a naturall and simple Societie of certaine persons, having mutuall relation one to another, under the private government of one.

A Familie, for the good estate of it selfe, is bound to the performance of two duties: one to God, the other to it selfe.

A Familie is distinguished into sundrie combinations or couples of persons.

porary account describes his style as incorporating both profundity of ideas and plainness of language. He wrote in both Latin and English, and works appearing in one were normally soon rendered into the other. Perkins' contribution to Puritan thought is mainly in two regards: first, in his systematization of Puritan principles in such comprehensive works as *A Golden Chaine* and *Christian Oeconomie* and second in his advocacy of Ramist logic while he was a fellow in Cambridge.

[40] *Workes,* III, 10.

The principall, is the combination of maried folkes: and these are so termed in respect of Mariage.

Mariage is the lawfull conjunction of the two maried persons; that is, of one man, and one woman into one flesh. So was the first institution of Mariage, Gen. 2.21. . . . Wherefore this is an eternal law of mariage, that two, and not three or foure, shall be one flesh.[41]

In this Perkins says nothing unusual. His progression from the case of the family to that of marriage is carried through in a way reminiscent of Cleaver's, but much more quickly and without raising the problem of a distinction between marriage as instituted in paradise and marriage as the seminal society in the state. The underlying tension between marriage as a companionable union and as a procreative union reveals itself as Perkins spells out further his understanding of marriage.

Mariage of it selfe is a thing indifferent, and the kingdome of God stands no more in it, then in meats and drinkes; and yet it is a state in it selfe, farre more excellent, then the condition of single life. For first, it was ordained by God in Paradise, above and before all other states of life, in Adams innocencie before the fall. Againe, it was instituted upon a most serious consultation among the three persons in the holy Trinitie. . . . Jehovah Elohim said, It is not good that the man should be himselfe alone, I will make him an helpe meete for him. Thirdly, the manner of this conjunction was excellent, for God joyned our first parents Adam and Eve together immediately. Fourthly, God gave a large blessing unto the estate of mariage, saying, Increase and multiplie, and fill the earth. Lastly, mariage was made & appointed by God himselfe, to be the fountaine and seminarie of al other sorts and kinds of life, in the Common-wealth and in the Church. . . .

The ende of mariage is fourefold.

The first is, procreation of children, for the propagation and continuance of man upon the earth, Gen. 1.28. . . .

The second is the procreation of an holy seed, whereby the Church of God may be kept holy and chaste, and there may alwaies be a holy companie of men, that may worship and serve God in the Church from age to age, Malach. 2.15. . . .

The third is, that after the fall of mankind, it might be a soveraigne meanes to avoide fornication, and consequently to subdue and slake the

---

[41] *Ibid.,* pp. 670-71. This is a formally correct Ramist definition. See Appendix B.

burning lusts of the flesh, I Cor. 7.2. . . . And for this cause, some Schoolmen doe erre, who hold that the secret comming together of man and wife, cannot be without sinne, unless it be done for procreation of children. . . .

The fourth ende is, that the parties married may thereby performe the duties of their callings, in better and more comfortable manner, Prov. 31.11.[42]

So long as Perkins or any other theologian of this period is speaking of the ends (for Cleaver the "causes") of marriage, the listing is always the same. Perkins leaves the well-beaten road marked out by the Prayer Book's listing of the ends of matrimony only to divide the first one into two.[43]

There are two places in the above, however, where Perkins marks out a more independent position, one which allows more weight to be placed on the companionable or social understanding of marriage. One is the comment on his third end of marriage that intercourse does not have to be for procreative purposes. The other is a curious sandwiching of the procreative purpose of marriage between two statements of its social purpose in the first paragraph quoted above, where the subject is the origin of marriage in paradise.

The first point here is that man and wife may have sexual intercourse without having procreation as their purpose.[44] In the context of this

---

[42] *Ibid.*, p. 671.

[43] To facilitate further discussion it will be helpful here to compare Perkins' listing of the ends of marriage to that given in the English Prayer Book of his day. See the marriage service of *The Second Prayer Book of King Edward VI* (1552), found in Parker Society, *The Two Liturgies,* p. 303.

Perkins' list of the ends of marriage:
1. Procreation "for continuance of man upon the earth"
2. Procreation "of an holy seed"
3. To avoid fornication and to "subdue" and "slake" lust
4. Mutual comfort

The Prayer Book's list of the ends of marriage:
1. "The procreation of children, to be brought up in the fear and nurture of the Lord, and praise of God"
2. The restraint and remedy of sin
3. "Mutual society, help, and comfort"

Perkins' first two ends together correspond to the Prayer Book's first end; the remaining two in each list directly correspond. As compared with Catholic tradition, the end of *sacramentum* is dropped in both listings given here, and both retain the ends of *proles* and *fides,* with the latter defined as "mutual comfort." Both English sources, furthermore, make explicit the end of restraint and remedy of sin, a goal of marriage which in Thomas Aquinas is treated as implicit in *fides* and *proles.*

[44] That is to say, Perkins denies the scholastic doctrine on procreative intent in intercourse. The roots of this doctrine are to be found in Augustine's teaching on marriage and sexuality, but this teaching is restated for the Middle Ages in the influential

criticism of "some Schoolmen" Perkins' statement at first seems to mean only that the second end of marriage, the restraint and remedy of sin, must be allowed to stand separately. If this is all it means, then nevertheless this statement represents a qualification of the notion of the primacy of procreation among the ends of matrimony. If this is all that Perkins means to say, then he is opposing not an attempt to reduce the ends of marriage to the procreative, for no schoolman ever suggested that, but rather a tendency to make the ends of marriage two, the procreative and the companionable, with the restraint and remedy of sin subsumed into the former. That is, if marriage as the vehicle for restraining and remedying sin is to be so only if the intent and purpose of the spouses is to procreate, then the emphasis is so heavy on the first end that the second must be fulfilled only in the process of fulfilling the first. Perkins is not in this statement we are discussing raising the question of birth control. He is rather attempting to keep the end of restraint and remedy of sin autonomous as over against the end of procreation. The "secret coming together of man and wife" can be for purposes only of subduing and slaking "the burning lusts of the flesh" and does not have to be aimed at producing children.

The assertion of the autonomy of the end of restraint and remedy of sin vis-à-vis the procreative end produces a new balance within the statement of ends. The character of this second of the Prayer Book's ends of marriage (Perkins' third) is that it always tends to become a part of either the procreative or the companionable end. This is especially so in the context of the Puritan-Anglican debate on marriage.

Sentences of Peter Lombard. The position is reaffirmed and implications of the doctrine are treated more fully in Thomas Aquinas' *Commentary on the Sentences, Summa Contra Gentiles,* and *Summa Theologica.*

Noonan summarizes Lombard's version of this doctrine as follows: "Original sin is transmitted by an act of generation, an act which is preceded by concupiscence. Adam's descendents are in turn infected with concupiscence (*Sentences* 2.25.7; 2.30.8, 10; 2.31.4, 7; 2.32.2). As the result of this transmission of original sin and its consequences, there is 'the law of lethal concupiscence in our members, without which carnal intercourse cannot occur.' Therefore, 'coitus is reprehensible and evil, unless it be excused by the goods of marriage' (*Sentences* 4.26.2). Here the basic Augustinian assumptions are succinctly combined. . . . Because concupiscence accompanies intercourse, intercourse needs to be excused. The excuse is provided by the goods of marriage. These goods are the familiar Augustinian triad, *fides, proles, sacramentum* (4.31.1). Of the three, however, only the seeking of the good of offspring is sufficient to excuse intercourse (4.31.5)." (Noonan, *Contraception,* p. 194. For full discussion of this issue see pp. 194-99, 246-57, 307-16, 321-30, 354-58, 371-72.) Another aspect of this issue is discussed slightly later in the present chapter.

There is no independent notion of marriage as a vehicle for controlling and curing sin. The debate over the purpose of marriage, over what it essentially is, centers rather around whether the main end is procreation, with the proof text God's injunction to "be fruitful, and multiply," or whether it is companionship, with the proof text: "It is not good that the man should be alone; I will make him an help meet for him."

What this implies is that if sexual intercourse can be conceived even momentarily as existing for some purpose other than procreation, it tends to become a way of reaching the end of marriage as companionship. That this is not a serious warping of Perkins' thought can be shown by looking to another section of *Christian Oeconomie,* that which treats "Of the Duties of Married Persons." Perkins here lists these duties as "principally two: Cohabitation, and Communion. Cohabitation is their quiet and comfortable dwelling together in one place, for better performing of mutual duties." [45] This first duty is not one which stresses the procreative end of marriage. It has to do with married persons living in the same household; it is the duty they have to each other to join in mutual society together. If the ordering is significant (as it almost certainly is, given Perkins' Ramism),[46] placing cohabitation before communion amounts to placing the social end of marriage before the procreative.

Perkins divides the duty of communion into two parts, one requiring mutual communication of "both their persons, and their goods each to other, for their helpe, necessitie and comfort," and another which requires satisfaction of the marriage debt. The satisfaction of this debt, or "due benevolence," as Perkins terms it, is achieved in three ways: first, by intercourse ("the right and lawful use of their bodies, or of the marriage bed"); second, by "cherishing one another," that is, by "the performing of any duties, that tend to the preserving of the lives one of another"; and third, "by an holy kind of rejoycing and solacing themselves each with other" (here Perkins mentions kissing specifically). Sexual intercourse here is called an "essential dutie" and termed morally "indifferent," though capable, through "holy usage," of being "sanctified by the word and prayer." [47]

---

[45] *Christian Oeconomic* in *Workes,* III, 686.

[46] See Appendix B and n. 51 below.

[47] *Christian Oeconomie,* in *Workes,* III, 686-90.

What is notable about this listing is the fact that procreation is not mentioned as the reason behind the first "benevolence." Rather "the right and lawful use . . . of the marriage bed" is to be understood as a kind of communication between spouses. It must be admitted that Perkins presents "communion" as governed by concepts of duty and debt, so that what takes place between the couple in the marriage bed seems to be for him primarily a mutual performance of duty. Furthermore, he severely qualifies the injunction to rejoice in one's partner: "Prov. 5.18. Rejoyce with the wife of thy youth. . . . This rejoicing and delight is more permitted to the man, then to the woman, and to them both, more in their yong yeares, then in their old age." [48] But this is not to depart from the idea that marriage is for companionship; it is only to state what is meant by companionship. Perkins' position forms the basis on which Milton later builds, but the latter has been influenced deeply by the Renaissance, and his understanding of companionship is more romantic than dutiful.

Perkins' categorization of sexual intercourse as morally indifferent recalls his repudiation of the need for procreative intent in intercourse and places him within an argument of long standing among Catholic theologians and canonists. The issue is this argument is this: Is intercourse itself sinful, as Augustine appears to hold, and only excused by its ordination toward procreation? The affirmative answer is given by the main line of opinion from the Middle Ages until our own time. But a minority deny this opinion throughout its history, arguing that coitus is not sinful per se and so need not be excused by procreative intent. Perkins undeniably supports the latter position. Two corollary points commonly follow, in the Catholic debate, from this denial of the need for procreative intent: that intercourse may be discussed apart from procreation as a separate moral issue and that intercourse should be linked somehow with marital love. Perkins' marriage doctrine exhibits both points: the second by treating the duty of the marriage bed as deriving from the need to show companionship, that is, to manifest love; the first by defining the sin of adultery in a way which bypasses the Thomist description of that sin as primarily against the offspring which might result from it.[49]

[48] *Ibid.*, p. 690.
[49] *Supp.*, Q. 49, A. 5; cf. *Summa Contra Gentiles,* Bk. 3, Chap. 122.

A full discussion of Perkins' conception of adultery follows later in this chapter. One point bearing on this question arises from the text that is presently being considered, however: that "the right and lawfull use . . . of the marriage bed" is that use which avoids adultery. This means for Perkins and most of his contemporaries not only staying away from other beds and persons other than one's spouse; it includes as well "strange pleasures about generation," such as copulation with beasts, with the devil, with others of the same sex, with those within degrees of consanguinity or affinity, and with one's menstruating wife, as well as "nocturnall pollutions" and "effeminate wantonness." [50] The terms "right and lawfull" thus do not refer to whether the purpose of intercourse is procreative or to slake the thirst of lust—or to provide companionship.

In addition to the qualification of the second (or third, as Perkins has it) end of marriage, Perkins in his exposition of the institution of matrimony sandwiches the purpose of procreation between two statements of the companionable purpose of the union of the first man and woman. While Perkins does not make of the "help meet" passage what some other Puritan writers do, the fact that he lists it before the injunction to "increase and multiplie" may be significant. In Genesis the latter comes in the first chapter, the former in the second. Since the context, in Perkins' discussion, is that of reasons for marriage being "farre more excellent, then the condition of single life," it appears that the primary purpose of marriage is represented here as being for companionship, with the directive to procreate an added blessing on the marriage made "immediately" by God between the man and the woman created especially for him.

Put in brief form, the reasons given by Perkins for the excellency of marriage are (1) its origin before the Fall, (2) its satisfaction of the needs of loneliness, (3) its being made directly by God, (4) its being blessed as the vehicle for populating the earth, and (5) its being the basis for all other unions, particularly those in church and state. It appears, then, from the context that procreation is an addition to the companionable end of marriage. Furthermore, if there is a significant logical progression from the first reason to the last, this would explain why marriage

[50] Perkins, *A Golden Chaine*, in *Workes*, I, 59.

as the basis for other societies is mentioned last, after the injunction to procreate: there can be no other sorts of unions of men until after Adam and Eve have produced offspring. Marriage is the primary relation of humankind, and all others are derived from it. But secondary relations therefore derive from the procreative purpose of man and woman. To speak of these secondary relationships of companionship last, then, is not to undermine the relationship of companionship in the primary union of man with woman. Is the order of the listing significant? If that of the last two items is, then likely the rest is as well. Moreover, if Perkins is using Ramist method, as he seems to be, the logic requires him to move from what is original to what is derived from it.[51] The important thing in the institution of marriage is God's action to satisfy the needs of man his creature. Man's being accepted as "procreator" in filling the earth thus comes only after the first man has been united with the first woman in satisfaction of loneliness. Finally, it is significant for what was said earlier about the second end of marriage (the restraint and remedy of sin), namely that it never has the stature of the other two ends, that this end arises only after the Fall, while both companionship and procreation are ends of marriage before the Fall.

Once all this has been said, however, it must be said equally forcefully that Perkins does not carry through his statements on the companionable end of marriage to the point at which this end becomes what it does for some Puritans of the next generation and notably for Milton in his divorce tracts. Marriage as companionable society never, in Perkins' writings, achieves the status of clear priority over marriage as procreative society. What, then, has been the point of the discussion of the last several pages? It was intended to demonstrate two points. First, Perkins does have a strong idea of marriage as for the purpose of companionship between meet helps. Secondly, this idea always remains in carefully

[51] In Ramus' system "method" has a particular meaning. It signifies that way of ordering ideas or facts ("arguments," in Ramist terminology) from the more general to the more particular, in direct opposition to syllogistic ordering, which proceeds from the specific to the general. Proper application of Ramist method requires that each new item be clear because of what has preceded it in the ordered array of arguments. Each new item is regarded as implied in those which go before it. In the case of Puritan marriage doctrine, the movement from a definition based on Gen. 2:18 to a statement of the ends of marriage, and from that to a statement of the duties of the parties to marriage, illustrates the use of Ramist method. For further discussion see Appendix B.

achieved balance with the understanding of marriage as for procreative purposes. For Perkins it would simply be erroneous to say that marriage is primarily for companionship. But it would be equally wrong to say the opposite: that marriage is chiefly for adding to even the holy race. Marriage in his writings is represented as being for both purposes conjointly. The contradictions that may arise from saying both things at the same time are not dealt with at all, and there is no reason to suppose that Perkins recognized them. Especially is this so since Cleaver, writing at about the same time, incorporates more glaring contradictions into his marriage doctrine and seems blissfully unaware of them. The most notable characteristic of what Perkins has to say is its balance. But because he implicitly presents the case for companionable union so well, his position forms the basis for later departures in Puritan tracts which emphasize this end of marriage as unequivocally primary, relegating the procreative end to a distinctly subordinate position.

So far we have been considering the thought of William Perkins on the institution of marriage in its origin and continuation. The subject of the dissolution of marriage remains to be treated.

Death, adultery, and desertion end marriage. When one partner dies, the other is free to marry again if he wishes; likewise, after divorce for adultery the innocent party is free to remarry. The only other ground for divorce Perkins considers seriously is desertion.[52] Yet he maintains that a Christian cannot use this means of ending wedlock; indeed, the one who departs is no longer a Christian.

The malitious and wilfull departing of the unbeleever, doth dissolve the marriage; but that is no cause of giving a bil of divorce: onely adulterie causeth that. Here the beleever is a mere patient, and the divorce is made by the unbeleever, who unjustly forsaketh, and so puts away the other.[53]

The one left behind is free to seek out a new mate and marry again. Perkins' solution to the problem of divorce for desertion is that there can be such only in the case of one partner's not being a Christian. In this

[52] Powell is more liberal in his interpretation of Perkins. He states that Perkins allows divorce in the case of "malicious dealing" of the spouses with each other. I find Perkins somewhat ambiguous on this matter. Cf. Powell, *English Domestic Relations*, pp. 79-80.

[53] Perkins, *An Exposition of Christ's Sermon in the Mount*, in *Workes*, III, 69.

way he finds scriptural warrant for his position in I Cor. 7:15.[54] Yet there is a curious twist to his thinking: in the judgment of Perkins, if one of the partners in the marriage leaves the other, he signifies thereby that he is no Christian. This is not a hard statement for one who holds that there are elect and reprobate persons in the world, even among the baptized, and only God knows which is which. It is noteworthy that the departer need not commit adultery to end the marriage; he may do so, but that is another sin on top of the desertion.

Why does Perkins insist, against what seems to be the intention of Paul, that anyone who deserts his marriage partner is an unbeliever? I suggest the following answer: Perkins is trying to modify the traditional teaching that desertion is cause only for separation *a mensa et thoro* so as to allow full divorce for this cause. He finds support for his position in the so-called "Pauline privilege," defined in the cited passage from I Corinthians. Since there is full divorce whenever an unbeliever separates from a believer, as both the New Testament and the tradition agree, Perkins assimilates the case of desertion to this one, arguing that a deserter is by definition an unbeliever. If this be granted, then the forsaken partner, assuming he or she is a Christian, is free to marry again.

For Perkins' argument to succeed, two elements must be allowed to be essential in defining who is a Christian. Baptism alone is not sufficient; it must be supported by a demonstrably godly life. Since it is not godly to desert one's spouse, the deserter is not Christian. On the other hand, the desertion does nothing to impugn the faith of the one left behind; he or she continues to live righteously if the household is maintained, the children are fed and educated, and so on. But the old marriage is ended, and the forsaken partner is free to find a new mate, one who hopefully will prove to be a godly person, since only the presence of Christ makes a true marriage.[55]

[54] I Cor. 7:12-15b reads as follows: "To the rest speak I, not the Lord: If any brother hath a wife that believeth not, and she be pleased to dwell with him, let him not put her away. And the woman which hath an husband that believeth not, and if he be pleased to dwell with her, let her not leave him. For the unbelieving husband is sanctified by the wife, and the unbelieving wife is sanctified by the husband: else were your children unclean; but now are they holy. But if the unbelieving depart, let him depart. A brother or a sister is not under bondage is such cases."

[55] A traditional treatment of the Pauline privilege is that of Thomas Aquinas in *Supp.*, Q. 59: "Of Disparity of Worship as an Impediment to Marriage." Thomas argues

Perkins' language is curious, for he says that the Christian gives the divorce in the case of adultery, while the departing unbeliever does so in the case of desertion. It would seem that the two cases are analogous and that the same language should be used for both. In each case there is a sin which breaks the marriage bond, and in each case the Christian is set free to marry again. It is not at all apparent why Perkins insists that in the case of adultery the Christian "puts away" the sinning partner, while in the other case it is the sinning deserter who "puts away" the Christian partner. The matter seems to be one of inconsistency of language only, for in each case, adultery or desertion, the courts declare the divorce. "Here we must know, that divorcement, or mariage after, must not be done privately by man and wife upon their owne heads, but by order of law, before the Magistrate, according to the custome of that Church or common-wealth whome it concernes." [56]

Still, this is primarily a stipulation for the sake of order, and the bond

---

that disparity of worship *is* an impediment to marriage (A. 1). Marriage between unbelievers is valid according to nature but not according to grace, while believers are validly married in both senses (A. 2). Disparity of worship in marriage may arise when one of the partners is converted to Christianity and the other is not. In such case the believer *may* remain with his partner, though he is not *required* to do so. That is, the marriage tie, valid according to nature, is not broken when one partner becomes a Christian (A. 3). Assuming that the husband is the one converted, he may remain with his wife in chastity, since danger to the offspring might result from the wife's unbelief (*ibid.*), or he may put her away, even though she is willing to cohabit with him "without insult to the creator." In the absence of this condition he may of course put her away (A. 4). Subsequently he is free to marry again, so long as he marries a believer, for their marriage, perfect according to both nature and grace, "dissolves the marriage previously contracted in unbelief," since "the marriage of unbelievers is not altogether firm and ratified." The wife, on the other hand, may not remarry (a punishment for her refusal to be converted) unless she is converted after her husband's remarriage. In this case she too may marry a Christian (A. 5).

Though Perkins departs from this tradition in assimilating cases of desertion to those covered by the Pauline privilege, his break with the tradition is not complete. Allowing for some difference in language and order of treatment, he seems to put the same conditions on remarriage as does Thomas. Specifically, the one forsaken is free to remarry as long as it be to a Christian while the deserter may not take a new spouse on pain of adultery or bigamy. While Thomas would allow the unbelieving partner who has been put away to marry again if only she convert, Perkins cannot allow the deserter to do so. If such a one sees the error of his ways, he can but go back to his spouse. If the spouse has remarried in the meantime, he must live the rest of his life without a marriage partner and chaste. The reasoning is precisely the same as in the case of adultery. See Perkins, *Sermon in the Mount*, in *Workes*, III, 69-70.

[56] Perkins, *Sermon in the Mount*, in *Workes*, III, 71.

of marriage is actually broken when the sin of adultery or desertion occurs. Perkins would not, however, grant the innocent party in either case the liberty to decide by himself to remarry unless there is a "lawfull" divorce. Freedom operates in the framework of the law. What Perkins says about divorce for adultery applies equally to divorce for desertion: "The partie offending breaks the bond of mariage, and so sinneth grievously against that commandment [against adultery]: but the partie innocent marying againe after lawfull divorce, onely taketh the benefit of that libertie, whereto God hath set him free, through the unlawfull breaking of the bond, by the partie offending." [57]

There are other possible grounds for divorce which Perkins disallows. He admits in these cases that living together may only be just tolerable, but nevertheless it is God's will for the spouses that they remain married, with all their mutual debts still due. "A contagious disease may cause a separation for some time, but no divorce; & if that disease bee incurable, and disable the partie from the dutie of mariage, then such parties must thinke themselves, as it were, called of God to live in single life." [58] The example Perkins gives of an incurable disease is leprosy. If one party is a leper, the only way for the other party to be freed from the bond of matrimony is for the diseased person to leave or to commit adultery. Again, "enmitie may cause a separation for a time, till reconciliation be make, but the bōd of mariage must not therefore be brokē." [59] If there is no reconciliation, then once more the parties must live as called to be single.

There are other examples of this sort, and in all cases except those of desertion and adultery Perkins declares that there can be no divorce. Though life together may be only just tolerable for a man and wife, they must tolerate it so long as the marriage bond remains, for it is God's will for them.

Perkins' reasoning is like Cleaver's on this point. Before the actual marriage takes place there must be a contract between the couple, "a mutuall promise of future marriage, before fit & competent Judges and

---

[57] *Ibid.*, p. 70.

[58] *Ibid.*, p. 69. This argument, even to the example given, seems to derive from Gratian, *Decretals,* Title 8, Bk. IV.

[59] *Ibid.*

Witnesses." [60] This promise is made in words of the present tense and is almost as binding as marriage itself. Between the making of the contract and the "solemne Manifestation of the Contract, by that which properly we call Marriage," [61] there should be a period of some weeks in which the prospective marriage partners get used to what will be required of them in their married life. In theory if the two discover they cannot live together because of some incompatibility, they may break the contract. This saves the marriage bond itself from being broken when an arch incompatibility is discovered. But in fact Perkins makes breaking the contract such a weighty matter that it is almost as hard to do this as to get a divorce. Leprosy is again used as an example, but here it is sufficient cause for ending the engagement, while a curable disease is not.[62] The similarity with Cleaver's position is evident.

The role of Ramist logic in producing the above formulation is considerable. Though Perkins utilizes language and examples from long-standing Christian tradition on marriage, he organizes this material along with his own ideas in a new pattern suggested by the dialectic of Ramus. This is most apparent in Perkins' treatment of causation. The efficient cause of the marriage contract can be said to be either God or the two parties consenting. The two parties are the proximate efficient cause, but God is the remote cause. The words "proximate" and "remote" are Ramist terms defined in such a way as to allow both to operate independently though together (when they are called "conficient," after Cicero).[63] Logically this is the way Perkins (and the other Puritan Ramists) chose to deal with the doctrine of human responsibility in spite of divine foreordination. In marriage God is the cause of the parties' consent, yet it is in fact *they* who consent to the contract. God exercises his efficient causality through implantation of his love in the elect. God's will in the institution of marriage is that man should not

[60] Perkins, *Christian Oeconomie*, in *Workes*, III, 672.

[61] *Ibid.*

[62] *Ibid.*, pp. 683 ff.

[63] Here "remote" does not signify any diminution of power but in fact the contrary; it is the term applied to the first cause in a causal chain, just as "proximate" is the term for the last. There are other causes between these, but Ramus and his followers choose to discuss these in pairs of remote and proximate—another example of the method of dichotomy.

be alone but should have a meet help; in all marriages he efficiently works his will through that love of the spouses for each other which manifests itself in care of each for the other. An important implication of this reasoning is that marriages which lack mutual love and helpfulness do not have God as remote efficient cause and are therefore not complete marriages. On the other hand, this reasoning implies that so long as the proximate efficient cause remains, the marriage remains. Perkins makes a dichotomy between the two types of efficient cause of the agreement to marry, but for him it is a logical dichotomy, one which is not felt as such by the parties contracting. It is their love which unites two persons in matrimony, but Perkins sees that it is also God's love and explains this by Ramist method. The result is that the love of a man and a woman who contract to marry cannot be separated from the will of God in instituting marriage to relieve human loneliness. This is what Perkins means by God's "presence" in the marriage covenant or his "witnessing" to it. Ramist reasoning here thus tends to support the covenantal view of marriage.[64]

Desertion and adultery are alike in ending marriage because in each case one party separates himself from God as well as from his partner. Perkins explicitly says that the adulterer incurs damnation by his act, and the deserter becomes no Christian by his. But one may separate himself from God without putting away his partner in wedlock. Idolatry is no ground for divorce. "Idolatrie is a more hainous sinne then Adulterie, . . . and yet it comes short of Adulterie, in this quality of breaking wedlocke: for wedlocke may be kept of those which are Idolaters."[65] The marriages of heathen are valid marriages and are broken only by the same two actions as Christian marriage, adultery and desertion.

Perkins' position on divorce is as carefully balanced as his position on marriage itself. He avoids agreeing with those who would make marriage indissoluble for any reason or who would grant only separation

<hr>

[64] My interpretation of Perkins on this point draws from several of his writings, all contained in his *Workes*. Most important is *Christian Oeconomie*, III, 672-84; cf. *A Golden Chaine*, I, 70-71; *An Exposition upon the Five First Chapters of the Epistle to the Galatians*, II, 356-57; *An Exposition of Christs Sermon in the Mount*, III, 34-35. See also David Little's discussion of "conscience" in Perkins' thought, contained in *Religion, Order, and Law*, 114-18.

[65] Perkins, *Sermon in the Mount*, in *Workes*, III, 53. This argument also seems to derive from Gratian's *Decretals*, in this case his excerpting of Augustine in chap. 28, Q. 1.5.

a mensa et thoro for adultery or desertion. And on the other hand he refuses to give in to those who would have divorce allowed with full remarriage rights for various reasons other than the two Perkins find in scripture. The objections he answers in putting forth his position on divorce come from both the more rigid and the freer sides, and he is careful to keep his balance between them while refuting both.

A characteristic of such a carefully balanced position is that it quickly ceases to be such when taken over by succeeding generations. Just as Perkins' doctrine of marriage forms the basis for later assertions of the companionable purpose of marriage, so his thoughts on divorce are appropriated by those who would argue for easier divorce than he allows. It is necessary now to explore what in Perkins' system allows such a phenomenon to occur.

Even though Perkins restricts divorce for adultery to cases in which actual sexual intercourse has taken place outside wedlock, his understanding of the problem of adultery is much broader than this position would suggest. First of all, it is admitted that adultery may be caused by both partners, though only one commits it. "[W]hen one partie is a manifest cause of the Adulterie of the other, and so becomes an accessorie to the others offence [this hinders remarriage after divorce]: for it seems unequall, that he who hath put his hand to the committing of a sinne, should reap any benefit or priviledge by the same." [66] The divorce is still granted for the cause of adultery; it is only the remarriage rights that are withheld, and this because there is no truly innocent party. There is no reason why such reasoning might not be applied to the case of desertion: if one party drives the other away, he seems to share the guilt the other incurs by leaving. But this matter is complicated by Perkins' insistence that it is the deserter who puts away the other, while it is the adulterer who is put away for his sin.

Divorce for adultery, in the case that there is no real "innocence" in either party, becomes in Perkins' theory divorce *a mensa et thoro,* since remarriage is not allowed. The subject here is enmity, for which cause Perkins will allow separation so long as it continues. In Milton's hands Perkins' conclusion becomes inverted: no one is ever singly at

[66] *Ibid.,* p. 71.

fault when a marriage breaks; therefore separation for enmity should be divorce, with both parties allowed to remarry if they wish.[67] Perkins' interest is in ensuring that sin does not receive a reward; Milton's is to assure that the parties are not bound by something not God's will. Perkins assumes that God blesses the marriage when it is contracted; Milton prefers to wait until after it proves itself. The key to Perkins' position is discipline: marriage, even a bad marriage, is a moral school. The key to Milton's position is Christian liberty informed by charity: it must be assumed that if a marriage is a bad one, it is not God's will that it continue, and the partners should be free to follow providence into a new marriage if it so leads them. For both men the prime purpose of matrimony is mutual companionship; they differ in defining companionship. For Perkins marriage is a companionable society in which husband and wife live disciplined, dutiful lives of mutual helpfulness and service to God. For Milton, conversely, companionability in marriage is free moving, directed only by charity.

Perkins is not totally without charity in his formulation, however, as is shown in his discussion of the Fathers on divorce and remarriage in another work. He quotes Augustine approvingly: "And it is so doubtfull in the Scriptures themselves, whether he (who doubtlesse may put away his wife for adulterie) be an adulterer if he marry againe, that surely I am of the opinion that any man may herein be pardonably mistaken." [68] What seems to be admitted here is that remarriage after divorce for adultery is not a mortal sin for the party who does not commit the act. If he remarries but actually is partly responsible for the other's sin, he can be forgiven.

It should be remembered that Perkins gives extremely broad and detailed definitions of adultery until he speaks of the particular case of adultery as grounds for divorce. One listing of all the things that are adultery has been given already;[69] elsewhere Perkins adds to this list as follows: looking lustfully on a member of the other sex, reading unchaste books, talking lightly and wantonly, wearing "vaine and light attire," acting in a loose manner, mixed dancing, keeping bad company,

---

[67] See Chap. V for a discussion of Milton's marriage doctrine.

[68] Perkins, *The Demonstration of the Probleme*, in *Workes*, II, 655. Here Perkins refers to Augustine's *De Fide et Operibus*, Chap. XIX.

[69] See above, p. 72.

and pampering the body.[70] Now if all these are taken seriously as adultery, that is, if adultery is really not just the physical act of intercourse out of wedlock, then Perkins' position comes close to the radical one of granting divorce for enmity or incompatibility. Perkins does not go so far, yet there is reason to think he should have, following his own presuppositions:

Adulterie properly, is the breach of wedlocke by such parties, some one whereof, at the least, is either maried, or espoused: I call it the breach of wedlocke, to note the propertie of this sinne, which is not in any other sinne, unlesse it be of this kinde, though the sinne be far more grievous. . . . Now, though the Lord under this one includes all the sinnes of the same kinde, . . . yet the Pharisies took this literall signification for the whole meaning, and taught that the sinne here forbidden, was bodily adulterie onely, and so made adulterie of the heart to be no adulterie; which exposition Christ here confutes.[71]

But when it comes to allowing divorce for adultery with remarriage rights for the innocent party, Perkins himself goes the way of the Pharisees. The sin which breaks marriage is for him "bodily adulterie onely," and not "adulterie of the heart." When Milton later inveighs against habitual unfaithfulness as worse, as more destructive of marriage, than one "accidental" act of intercourse,[72] he is doing no more than following through on the lines laid out by Perkins in his commentary on the Sermon on the Mount.

The Mosaic permission Perkins denies to have any force for Christians.[73]

This law was not morall, but civill, or politicke, for the good ordering of the Commonwealth. Now among their particular lawes, some were lawes of toleration and permission, which were such as did not approve of the evill which they concerned, but did onely tolerate and permit that evill which could not be avoided, for the preventing of a greater evill. . . . Such

---

[70] Perkins, *Sermon in the Mount*, in *Workes*, III, 54.

[71] *Ibid.*, p. 53.

[72] Milton, *Doctrine and Discipline*, pp. 331-32.

[73] This again sets Perkins off from Milton, who sees this permission as a law of God for all time. *Ibid.*, pp. 261-68.

was the law concerning usurie, . . . and the like was the law touching polygamie. . . . So likewise this law of Moses for divorce, was a law of permission, not approving the giving of a bill of divorce for every light cause, but tolerating of it, for the prevention of greater mischiefe, even of murther. . . . The force and effect of this law was this, It made the Bill of divorcement for any cause given, to be tolerable before men; and mariage after such a divorce, lawfull and warrantable in the Courts of men, Deut. 24.4. But yet in the court of conscience before God, the divorcement it selfe, and second mariages made thereupon, were both unlawfull; for God hateth this separation, Mal. 2.15. And whether partie soever marieth another upon this divorce, commits adulterie, Matth. 19.9.[74]

The error of the Pharisees was dual: first, they interpreted adultery to mean only "bodily adulterie"; second, they interpreted the Mosaic permission too loosely, allowing divorce on small cause. Perkins takes the opposite stance on both: he sees the message of Christ as first requiring emphasis on "adulterie of the heart" and second as abolishing the Mosaic permission. There is an inconsistency in Perkins' stance which we have already noted: the internalization of the meaning of adultery implies that the marriage bond is broken in many cases other than the one of simple "bodily adulterie."

It is possible to approach this same point through another channel, Perkins' conception of the law. Here a complementary inconsistency shows itself.

Before the Fall man's integrity consists in two parts: wisdom, or knowledge of God and his will, and justice, or conformity of the will of man to God's will.[75] The Fall introduces corruption in the first integrity; that is, sin is first of all the corruption of wisdom.[76] But it spreads to infect all man's being; beginning in the mind, it moves into the will and into the body as well, introducing in all three their respective imperfections.[77] It is notable that Perkins does not here list concupiscence as a major result of the Fall; he is not concerned with sexual sin except as a result of more general sinfulness.

Sin does not completely destroy the knowledge of God's will; it only

[74] Perkins, *Sermon in the Mount,* in *Workes,* III, 68.
[75] Perkins, *Golden Chaine,* in *Workes,* I, 17.
[76] *Ibid.,* p. 18.
[77] *Ibid.,* pp. 20-21 for a listing of these imperfections.

corrupts it. This will is manifested in the "Morall law" which is naturally imprinted in every man's mind. The grace of Christ is both to fulfill this law and to forgive man for not living up to it.

What the Morall law is, I will describe in three points: First, It is that part of Gods word, concerning righteousnesse and godlinesse, which was written in Adams minde by the gift of creation; and the remnants of it be in every man by the light of nature: in respect whereof it bindes all men. Secondly, it commandeth perfect obedience, both inward, in thought; & outward, in speech and action. Thirdly, it bindeth to the curse and punishment, every one that faileth in the least dutie thereof.[78]

Perkins continues by listing differences between the law and the gospel and then turns to the meaning of Christ's statement that he came not to destroy the law but to fulfill it. "In the elect he fulfilleth the law in two waies: First, by creating faith in their hearts, whereby they lay hold on Christ, who for them fulfilled it: Secondly, by giving them his owne spirit, which maketh them endeavour to fulfill the Law; which in Christ is accepted for perfect obedience in this life, and in the life to come is perfect indeede."[79] In non-Christians the law is fulfilled by their reprobation.

While Perkins accuses the Church of Rome of "confounding" the law and the gospel by saying that Christ reveals a new law, it would seem that he confounds the two by a different means. The big difference between the elect and the damned in this life is not that the former can perfectly fulfill the law while the latter cannot. Christ's spirit only makes the elect "endeavour to fulfill the law," and this striving is "accepted for perfect obedience in this life." Further, it is not the elect who for themselves fulfill the law; it is Christ who has fulfilled the law for them. To take this position seriously would lead to an antinomian position for Christians. Perkins never entertains such a possibility. The reason for this is that he never considers that one of the elect could be caught in such a position that obedience to the law is intolerable. While Milton worries about the Christian who is driven to sin by being bound in an incompatible marriage, such a possibility does not occur to Perkins. The reason is that for him Christian liberty is always subordinate to the law

---

[78] Perkins, *Sermon in the Mount,* in *Workes,* III, 33.
[79] *Ibid.,* p. 34.

given in creation and confirmed in Christ. And this means that the grace of Christ does not empower a Christian to break the law governing marriage, which antedates all other laws governing relationships of men. The gospel thus represents an entering into the full meaning of the law for the elect. To the reprobate it is the sign that they cannot in any way gain righteousness by doing what the law exacts. In the case of marriage the implication for the elect is that once married they will be empowered to live together in spite of hardships. The trials of such a union will serve only to perfect them for the life to come. They will not break God's ordinance by seeking divorce. But the reprobate, whom Perkins usually calls simply "unbeleevers," in the case of a bad marriage have no grace to help them in their "endeavour to fulfill the law." They will seek divorce, or worse, they will commit adultery or forsake their partners.

The problem in Perkins' position on the law is that he tries to make two divergent statements at once. He is caught in the Puritan dilemma of determinism versus freedom in a special way. First, he insists that Christians are bound by the law by virtue of their being men and bearing the stamp of creation. Second, he asserts that fulfillment of the law is done by Christ and not by the recipients of his grace. The way Perkins attempts to solve this dilemma is to conceive of Christians as never wanting to do other than the law requires. But even Perkins does not carry this through to its logical end, for he admits that perfection in action is reached only in the life to come. There is a streak of perfectionism in Perkins' thought in spite of his insistence on the totality of sin: one of the uses of the gospel is to "derive faith into the soule: by which faith, they which beleeve, doe, as with an hand, apprehend Christs righteousness." [80] It is their apprehension of the righteousness of Christ, who in his being fulfills the law, which makes them able to fulfill the law of marriage, if only to the point of not being moved to break the bond when the alternative is a life of trials and unhappiness within it.

It requires only a small shift in emphasis to make Perkins' position into a more liberal one. To emphasize the uncertainty of election and the omnipresence of sin even in the elect is one step; to emphasize the work-

[80] *Ibid.*

ing of providence is another. In Milton's divorce tracts both these move-
ments occur, and the result is a totally different doctrine of divorce
based on the same evidence from scripture.

Perkins, Cleaver, Ames and lesser writers of the period around 1600
faced different problems from those which later presented themselves.
One of these was the emergence of the "new woman" in her upper-
and middle-class variations. The other major problem was the question
of divorce, which arose both culturally and theologically. In response
to the first the Puritan writers generally sided with woman's rights,
though they carefully maintained man's superiority of station. In the
specific case of marriage this is seen in Cleaver's insistence that the
government of the household is centered in two heads, the husband and
the wife; though the wife is subordinate in rank to the husband, she
rules with him over the household. It is seen in another way in Perkins'
statement that both wife and husband have equal rights in suing for
divorce if wronged by adultery,[81] the reason being that "in regard to
the bond of mariage, they are equally bound one to another." The conservatism of the Puritan writers on this matter is revealed in that while
they support woman's acceptance of responsibility, they do not accept
any of her attempts to rule over men, especially those involving her using
her feminine attractions to gain ascendancy.

Theologically the question of divorce centers in this period around
whether remarriage should be allowed. Social pressure for relaxation
of the divorce law is reflected in Edmund Bunny's disparaging allusion
to divorce and remarriage as "so common a practice with many."[82]
The position taken at the first of the seventeenth century by men such
as Cleaver and Perkins is that maintained by Puritan orthodoxy all
through that century, but certain elements of that position could, when
interpreted in a different manner, be used as planks of a more liberal
divorce platform. The forces within Puritanism which made for the
more liberal interpretation were those which created separatism, but
Presbyterian Puritans could espouse the liberal view on divorce as well.
The point is that the position staked out by Perkins especially and also by

[81] *Ibid.*, p. 68.
[82] Bunny, *Of Divorce for Adultery and Marrying Again* (London, 1610), STC 5382,
p. 1.

Cleaver and lesser writers is an unstable one, an inconsistent one, one with internal tensions always threatening to unsettle the carefully achieved balance. In Milton's divorce tracts the balance is radically unsettled, but on the basis of orthodox opinion. The next chapter will show how even before Milton the liberal implications of Perkins' position came to light.

III

Dutiful Companionship: The Crystallization of Puritan Marriage Doctrine

The men to be discussed in this chapter are of a different order from Perkins and Cleaver as regards their importance in defining Puritan doctrine. While the "fathers" of the turn of the century influenced the thinking of their own as well as the following generations, these later writers build on the foundations of their predecessors while shaping the thought mainly of their contemporaries. Yet they are important for our study for two reasons. First, it is impossible to get closer to Milton's period than they in tracing the development of the Puritan understanding of marriage. If any relevant material was published during the 1630s, with the exception of occasional reprints of older, noncontroversial works, it was done clandestinely and has been lost. From William Whatley's *A Care-Cloth* of 1624 to Daniel Rogers' *Matrimoniall Honour* of 1642 and the first edition of Milton's *Doctrine and Discipline* a year later, a hush replaces the fairly spirited interchange of ideas on marriage that marked the first quarter of the seventeenth century. Thus to examine the thought of these men who wrote toward the end of that first quarter brings us as close as possible to the doctrine of marriage which Milton inherited.

Second, the direction of the thought of these men is significant for our thesis. Two trends suggest that here is a bridge from Perkins to Milton. One is a definite movement away from the ambiguity of Perkins and Cleaver to an acceptance of the companionable purpose of matrimony as primary. The other is an increased emphasis on duty with a linking of duty to love. Failure to do one's duty in marriage severely strains the marriage bond, and since God-given love is what enables marriage partners to do their mutual duties, the implication is that nonperformance of duty is due to a lack of God's blessing on the particular marriage. It is a short step (which, however, none of these men make) to the position advocated by Milton, that if God-given love is not in a marriage, the marriage is not and has never been. Later in this chapter there will be further discussion of these two trends and their significance.

Published opinion differs as to what exactly was happening in the theological understanding of marriage in the period we are about to discuss. As regards the doctrine of marriage, the importance of the men examined in this chapter was first noted by William Haller, who emphasizes the contribution of these little-known figures over that of the earlier and better-known works of Perkins and Cleaver.[1] Haller traces the the Puritan doctrine of marriage back to Bullinger's *Der Christlich Eestand,* published several times in different editions in English as *The Christen State of Matrimony,* sometimes with a preface by Thomas Becon. Haller further argues that the Puritans were forced to develop their approach to marriage into a real alternative to the Anglican position after they had failed to win control of the Church of England. Taking their lead from Bullinger, they attempted to offer a real choice in understanding the matter; they sought to develop out of their peculiar theological assumptions answers to the practical questions of life in society, answers which had to be different from those the Anglicans gave if the Puritans were to have any influence or indeed any identity in the English Church. While Haller nowhere makes such a statement, it would seem from his emphasis on comparatively little-known figures that he sees the critical confrontation of Puritan and Anglican on marriage as occurring around the end of the first quarter of the century.

Contrary to this interpretation of the evidence is that of A. R. Win-

[1] Haller, "The Puritan Art of Love."

nett.[2] Writing on the "indissolubilist" and "non-indissolubilist" views of marriage (respectively, that marriage once contracted cannot be dissolved for any reason and contrarily that there are reasons for dissolution of some marriages), he finds it impossible to set Puritans on one side and Anglicans on the other. Winnett connects a liberal posture on divorce with esteem of the continental reformers, but he does not draw a line from the continentals to either Puritan or Anglican on the question of liberalizing divorce. Now it must be agreed that the Puritan doctrine of marriage embraced more than relatively liberal views on divorce and remarriage, yet it follows from Haller's argument that the position of Milton on divorce comes out of Puritan theology. Furthermore, the argument of this essay has so far advanced this view. There is a real contradiction here in understanding the evidence.

Winnett's conclusion is a difficult one to reach on the basis of the evidence he cites. It is noteworthy that all the men he names as non-indissolubilists are connected in some way with Cambridge University, while the indissolubilists are all but one attached to Oxford. Since Cambridge was at this time the spawning ground of Puritan divinity and Oxford the intellectual bastion of Anglo-Catholicism, it would appear that Winnett's conclusion is unjustified, that Puritans and Anglicans did not agree on the permanence of the marital bond. To point out, as Winnett does, that such well-known Anglicans as William Laud and John Donne exemplify indecision on the matter of divorce hardly shows that the question received ambiguous treatment by all English churchmen of whatever stamp.[3]

Another way of looking at marriage is from the statement of its purpose. Is the prime purpose of matrimony companionship or progeny? Is there any significant difference of Puritan and Anglican on this point? D. S. Bailey cites Jeremy Taylor as maintaining that "marriage is the queen of friendships, and husband and wife the best of all friends,"[4] and he even more approvingly writes:

No Anglican divine of the sixteenth or seventeenth centuries, except perhaps Becon, shows so deep an understanding as does Taylor of marriage as a personal relation of sexual love. . . . Through their writings on matrimony

---

[2] *Divorce and Remarriage in Anglicanism.*
[3] *Ibid.*, pp. 60-101.
[4] Quoted in Bailey, *Sexual Relation in Christian Thought*, p. 197.

there breathes a new spirit, and their counsel to husbands and wives has the added authority which comes of knowing not only what marriage ought to be, but also what it is.[5]

Now, it is indisputable that Becon and Taylor emphasize the human aspects of marriage, but the preceding chapter reveals that Perkins does the same thing. Moreover, Haller's contention is that this very way of conceiving marriage goes back theologically to Bullinger, whom Becon seconds. It is just not the case, if Bailey is speaking of all varieties of English churchmen, that Taylor is so unique in the seventeenth century in emphasizing the friendly side of marriage. On the other hand, if Bailey is restricting himself to non-Puritans, then his singling out of Taylor suggests that High Churchmen in general did not support the covenantal doctrine of marriage. To point to Taylor's praise of friendship in marriage does not dispose of the fact that Puritans before Taylor as well as contemporary with him were developing this understanding of marriage in opposition to that based on propagation, which still held sway among High Churchmen.[6]

[5] *Ibid.*, p. 196. Again, is this truly a "new spirit"? In language similar to Taylor's, Thomas Aquinas calls marriage "the greatest friendship" and argues that "the greater that friendship is, the more solid and long-lasting will [marriage] be" (*Summa Contra Gentiles*, Bk. III, Chap. 123.6). If Thomas can write thus, what is the difference between his teaching on marriage and that of Taylor and the Puritans?

I leave Bailey to answer for Taylor, but as for the Puritans there is one decisive difference. Thomas describes marriage as friendship only in the previously established context of a definition of marriage as originally for procreation: "Woman is taken into man's society for the needs of generation" (*ibid.*, Chap. 123.3). But, Thomas argues, a man may not put away a woman when she is no longer suited for this need. Friendship makes an indissoluble marriage a pleasant association. Moreover, mutual love derives from indissolubility: "For thus, when they know that they are indivisibly united, the love of one spouse for the other will be more faithful" (*ibid.*, Chap. 123.8). Completely opposite to this conception of friendship in matrimony—that it is a secondary, supportive, and in some sense derived good—is the Puritan conception of friendship as the basis of matrimony, the undergirding soul of the marriage relationship and the good from which all other goods take their meaning. The argument advanced in this chapter and throughout this book, that Puritan marriage doctrine reverses the traditional listing of the marriage ends to put companionship first and procreation last, supports what here can only be stated. Another formulation of the same point is this: Thomas discusses friendship between husband and wife in the context of a marital relationship aimed at procreation; the Puritans discuss procreation in the context of a marital relationship founded on companionship and aimed at producing the greatest mutual love between the spouses. The two positions are quite opposite, and it would therefore be erroneous to make any argument for similarity rest on the coincidence in language noted above.

[6] It might be interesting for some future biographer of Taylor to investigate a possible

92

The conclusion must be that the Puritan doctrine of marriage at this time was discrete and well developed. The authors examined in this chapter, building on the writings of Perkins and Cleaver as well as looking back to the reformers, moved to emphasize companionship in marriage over the end of procreation, a companionship with terms defined by mutual duty, which is in turn inspired by love both natural and God-given. They move us as close as possible to the radical position of John Milton.

A Discrete and Well-developed Approach to Marriage

The practical tone of Puritan concern about marriage is demonstrated by these titles from the years 1615-25: *A Discourse of Marriage and Wiving; A Bride-Bush, or, a Wedding Sermon, Compendiously Describing the Duties of Married Persons; A Care-Cloth, or, a Treatise of the Cumbers and Troubles of Marriage; Marriage Duties; Of Domesticall Duties.*[7] Of these only the last, William Gouge's *Domesticall Duties,* attempts to be thoroughgoing; the rest are occasional works dealing with limited aspects of the subject of marriage. Gouge, moreover, admittedly bases his book on Bullinger's but expands his conclusions over some six hundred printed pages.

Essentially the concept of marriage that develops in Puritanism at the beginning of the seventeenth century has these characteristics: (1) marriage is an ordinance of God but no sacrament; (2) it is the normal state of man, with dispensation to remain single a special gift of grace to particular persons;[8] (3) it is a social estate, the microcosm of all human society, and at the same time a trial ground for salvation; (4) the lord of the family is the husband/father/master, but because of the existence of mutual duties the wife's position often approaches equality with her husband in certain respects; (5) depending on context, the purpose of marriage is now procreation, now companionship, with a significant emphasis on the latter emerging on the basis of God's wish to remedy Adam's loneliness in Eden.

---

relationship between Taylor and the Puritans on marriage. Since Taylor's boyhood and his early education were at Cambridge, it may be the case that his understanding of marriage represents a development of Puritan teaching, not an independent position.

[7] All these works are identified as discussed.

[8] On this one point cf. Calvin, *Institutes*, Bk. II, Chap. VIII, sec. 41; Bk. IV, Chap. XII, sec. 23; Bk. IV, Chap. XIX, secs. 34-37.

These characteristics are abstractions from the works consulted and may not hold in their entirety for all writers treated here or for all Puritans. Nevertheless their ubiquity in various forms in a large variety of Puritan works argues for their validity in general. These are the themes which begin to be developed by Perkins and Cleaver at the turn of the century, which are further explored by the writers discussed in this chapter, and which finally reach expression in a most radical way in John Milton's divorce tracts.

A most humane and at the same time soundly theological approach is that of Thomas Gataker, whose four published works on marriage show him to have been deeply concerned with the subject.[9] His thought exemplifies the two tendencies earlier identified: to emphasize the companionship within marriage over the call for progeny and to see companionship as best expressed in love-based performance of mutual duties.

In *Marriage Duties* Gataker argues that marriage is important primarily because "this societie is the first that ever was in the world" and "secondly, because this is the fountaine from which the rest flow."[10] Elsewhere he unequivocally asserts the significance of the companionable end of marriage:

A bad Wife is no Wife in Gods account. . . . For what is a Wife, but a Woman given to Man to be an Helpe and a Comfort to him? . . . And how is she a Comforter, that yeeldeth no comfort? How an Helper, that affordeth no helpe? . . . So is she a Wife in Name, but not in Deed, that affordeth not her Husband that Helpe and Comfort that a Wife ought, and that at first she was intended for.[11]

[9] Thomas Gataker was educated at Cambridge and taught there, in St. John's College and Sidney Sussex College, respectively. He was widely known and popular as a teacher and preacher, also enjoying a certain reputation as a Ramist logician. His stature is indicated by his appointment to the Westminster Assembly of Divines. For a while Gataker occupied a lectureship in Lincoln's Inn, a position which gave him access in political circles. Being a liberal among Puritans did not make Gataker less than orthodox in his writings, which were occasional, and in his sermons and lectures. He exhibits, nevertheless, a spirit of freedom in his writings which is totally uncharacteristic of another Puritan divine whose life parallels Gataker's in many ways: William Gouge. This spirit, which recalls the theology of Perkins, earned Gataker the dubious distinction of being once called (in print) an antinomian, an accusation he never seems to have taken seriously.

[10] Gataker, *Marriage Duties*, p. 3.

[11] Gataker, *A Wife in Deed* (London, 1623), STC 11659, p. 6.

Gataker consistently underscores the companionable purpose of marriage, with the result that for him issue is a secondary, derived end. God's gift to Adam was first and foremost a good wife. This "was one of the first reall and royall gifts that God with his owne hand bestowed upon Adam. And it must needs be no small matter that God giveth with his owne hand." [12] Gataker draws out the implications of this beginning of marriage by arguing that God in his providence sought foremost to end man's loneliness by providing a suitable companion for him. The primary purpose of marriage, then, is the remedy of man's loneliness.

Gataker is most explicit about two things: first, marriage, to be a good and proper marriage, must be the result of God's special providence; second, that the main blessing of marriage is a good, that is, a companionable, wife.

Is a good wife such a speciall gift of God? Then is Mariage questionles a blessing, and no small one, of it selfe: one of the greatest outward blessings that in this world man enjoyeth. In the first place commeth the Wife, as the first and principall blessing, and the Children in the next. . . . If Children bee a Blessing, then the root whence they spring ought much more to be so esteemed. . . . Children are the gift of God; but the Wife is a more speciall gift of God: shee commeth in the first place, they in the second.[13]

It is hard to imagine a more explicit statement of the reversal of the ends of marriage from the Prayer Book's ordering.[14] Because the wife if a gift of special providence, the union she has with her proper husband is a great blessing of itself. Children, being gifts of general providence, are a secondary blessing, calling attention not only to themselves but more importantly to the union which caused them to come to be. Gataker is the only writer I have discovered who makes this argument explicitly from the different kinds of providence. While in all Puritan writers the providential character of all life is a constant presupposition, Gataker's straightforward use of the Calvinist categories of the two kinds of providence is unique. The gift of a good wife is of the most special variety

[12] Gataker, *A Good Wife Gods Gift*, p. 9.
[13] *Ibid.*, p. 12.
[14] See Chap. II, n. 43 above.

of providence: "Gods providence is more especiall in a Wife than in Wealth." [15] A good marriage is the highest of gifts for this life because it provides a companion for life. The gift of a good mate compares in this life to the gift of salvation for the next, and both gifts are to be sought in the same way: through prayer, humility, and exercise of religion.[16]

Gataker's conclusion from this argument is to see the husband as also a special gift for the wife, thus asserting the mutually companionable purpose of marriage.

Lastly, if a good Wife bee such a speciall gift of God, then a good Husband is no lesse. For the Husband is needful for the Wife, as the Wife is for the Husband. . . . In a word, let both man and wife so esteeme either of other, as joyned by Gods counsell, as given by Gods hand; and so receive either other as from God, bee thankfull either for other unto God, seeke the good either of other in God; and then will God undoubtedly with his blessing, accompanie his gift to his owne glorie, and their mutuall good.[17]

All Gataker's published marriage sermons have a similar drift, and together they form a reasonably complete statement of a total doctrine of marriage. In *A Wife in Deed* the goods that come with a good wife are listed so as to put great stress on the need for companionship. The Prayer Book order of the goods of marriage needs once more to be recalled in order to understand the significance of Gataker's way of stating the goods: first, "societie"; "secondly, for assistance"; "thirdly, for Comfort and Solace"; "fourthly, for Issue"; "fiftly, for Remedie against Incontinencie." [18] The emphasis is so strong upon what is put last in the Prayer Book that this category has become three separate categories in Gataker's listing. What is for Gataker the fifth good is further demeaned by his notation that it is good for marriage only after the Fall. This means that of all the goods that were proper to marriage in paradise, the good of issue was last.

The most systematic treatment of marriage Gataker offers is in his

[15] Gataker, *A Good Wife Gods Gift*, p. 9.
[16] *Ibid.*, p. 15. Cf. Thomas Gataker, *A Marriage Praier* (London, 1624), STC 11669, *passim*.
[17] Gataker, *A Good Wife Gods Gift*, p. 24.
[18] Gataker, *A Wife in Deed*, pp. 27, 29, 31, 33, 36.

Marriage Duties. Here he takes his lead from Paul in Col. 3:18, 19: "Wives, submit yourselves unto your own husbands. . . . Husbands love your wives." [19] According to Gataker, Paul here mentions the wife's duty first both to show that she is in second place next to her husband and also to show that there duty begins. "For love goeth downeward; dutie cometh upward. . . . The wives dutie is the base or ground that the husbands dutie is built upon." [20] There must be a differentiation of husband and wife according to status, Gataker contends, because of the necessity for preserving order in the world: "There can bee no ordinary intercourse and commerce or conversing betweene person and person, but that there must be a precedencie on the one part, and a yeelding of it on the other." [21] The wife takes the lower part because "she was made to be an Helper or an assistant to her husband." [22] This assistance is to be given in two respects. First, the wife provides a good home for her husband and manages the household well so that he may be free of cares for labor in his calling. Second, she gives support to him when he is beset with troubles.[23] Gataker's favorite term for the wife in this connection is "yoke-fellow," a description which suggests that she is somewhat more than simply an inferior help to her spouse. Nevertheless the wife has the second place in the family and should not pretend to the first. What she offers to her husband is her duty to him, nothing more nor less.

On the other hand, the husband's action toward his wife Gataker describes as resulting from his "love." Duty comes upward, love goes downward. But this movement from language of duty to language of love is more verbal than substantial. It is as one of the mutual duties that the husband is called on to "love and affect" his wife and to "draw home his affection from loving any other." [24] The husband's love thus comes as a duty, and at the same time the wife's duty results in acts of love toward her husband. The two are intermingled because of the mutuality proper within the marriage relationship. There is nothing in

[19] See Gataker, *Marriage Duties*, p. 1.
[20] *Ibid.*, p. 5.
[21] *Ibid.*, p. 8.
[22] *Ibid.*, p. 20.
[23] *Ibid.*, p. 23.
[24] *Ibid.*, pp. 35-36.

Gataker's discussion of marriage duties that prevents his using the same language for what both husband and wife do with respect to each other except for the assumption that woman is naturally inferior to man. Given this assumption, grounded in scripture as well as cherished in popular opinion, it is all the more remarkable that woman's position is so high.

A significant feature of this treatise is that marriage is seen as a school for salvation. It is this notion that underlies the hope expressed at the end of *A Good Wife Gods Gift*,[25] but in *Marriage Duties* Gataker is more explicit. "In a word to conclude," he writes, "if Christian men are to observe one another, that they may whet on either other to godlinesse and good workes: then much more should Christian man and wife so doe: that having lived togither for a time as copartners in grace here, they may reigne togither for ever as co-heires in glory hereafter." [26] Such a statement implies a considerable modification of the view that wives are inherently inferior to their husbands. For now they are represented as "copartners in grace" and potential "co-heires in glory." The two levels in the family nucleus have with this representation become one, for in regard to grace here and glory hereafter man and woman are absolutely equal. A further implication is that in marriage neither one attains grace or glory without the other. No matter how much Gataker emphasizes the distinction of superior and inferior in marriage according to nature, the admission of equality before God undercuts this understanding of the family hierarchy. The covenant of marriage thus becomes almost a covenant of equals with regard to the state of grace.

Gataker's text for *Marriage Duties* is Col. 3:18-19: "Wives, submit yourselves unto your own husbands, as it is fit in the Lord. Husbands, love your wives, and be not bitter against them." Inspiration for his "word to conclude" might better be sought, however, in I Pet. 3:1-2, 7. That women are inferior to men in nature though they are equal with them in grace is an idea at least as old as the New Testament. The significance of Gataker's use of this idea comes from the context in which it is set forth. The immediate context, *Marriage Duties*, is a sermon in which love, given equally to Christian spouses through grace, is described

---

[25] See the quotation on p. 96 above.
[26] Gataker, *Marriage Duties*, p. 48.

as the motive force behind the performance of companionable duties in marriage. Equality and difference, nature and grace are blended into a particular unity in this formulation: Christian husbands and wives equally receive grace to do the unequal duties required of them by their positions according to nature. This formulation goes beyond that in I Pet. 3:7, where husbands are admonished to honor "the wife, as unto the weaker vessel, and as being heirs together of the grace of life; that your prayers be not hindered." In the larger context of a movement to assert the primacy of the end of companionship in marriage, Gataker's modification of a traditional idea stands as a guidepost, even though it appears as such only in retrospect.

Meditations on the state of grace of those whom God has truly joined together in this life are not seen by Gataker (or his immediate contemporaries) as having any implication for the rights of women in this life. An analogous case is that of salvation or damnation: they pertain to an eternal decision by God but have no bearing on whether one is wealthy or impoverished in this life. Receiving God's grace here and now does not destroy the natural order, which is itself a gift of God. God's immutable will expressed in creation is to give each creature a certain place in the world, and to attempt to move out of this place is characteristically scored in Puritan theology as rebellion against God. Even though it is admitted that a wife may surpass her husband in both gifts of grace and worldly wisdom, still because of the order of nature she remains subject to her husband in familial society. As one Puritan divine eulogizes a woman who had been an ideal wife, "The best time for commending her is yet to come.[27] In heaven God himself will commend and reward her; surely she can wait for that.

Even though Gataker does not follow through the implications of his own words, it is such reasoning as his on the necessity of mutual helpfulness in marriage for life in grace here and glory hereafter which underlies the emphasis on equality in Milton's doctrine of marriage.

Gataker's understanding of the character of marriage as revealed in its ordination is typical of Puritan writers of this period. In his conception the prime end of matrimony is companionship, the chief ways of proving a companion being love and performance of duty. Implicit in this con-

---

[27] Hannibal Gamon, *A Godly Womans Praise* (London, 1627), STC 11548, p. 23.

cept of marriage is also the idea that marriage is the normal state for man, that man needs companionship and therefore needs marriage. The relation between man's nature and the reason for marriage must be explored more fully.

In the preceding chapter it was argued that the second of the Prayer Book's goods of marriage, the restraint and remedy of sin, is not really a discrete good at all but always becomes a subordinate part of one of the other two goods. If procreation is put first, then it subsumes the restraint of sin; if companionship comes first, then restraint of sin becomes subsumed by that. In the writers discussed in this chapter there is such an unequivocal statement of the primacy of the companionable purpose of marriage that it ought to be the case, if our previous argument is valid, that they derive the purpose of marriage to restrain and remedy sin from that to provide companionship. This is in fact precisely the case.

Alexander Niccholes serves as an example. According to his *Discourse of Marriage and Wiving,* the character of marriage is implicit in its ordination by God. God's will that men should marry is shown by his gift of Eve to Adam. The reason for the gift indicates God's purpose: Eve was given to Adam as "a helper meet for him," a help, not a hindrance, "a companion for his comfort." God himself thus originally made marriage, and he was acting in the best interests of his creature man. It is only after setting up the reason for marriage as companionship (because "company is comfortable though never so small"!) that Niccholes admits in second place that God also had another reason: "The earth is large and must be peopled." [28]

Shortly after asserting the primacy of the companionable purpose of marriage in this manner, Niccholes adds that marriage is even more necessary since the Fall than it was before because the intrusion of sin makes man all the more in need of help. Marriage reduces man's "wilde and unbrideled affections . . . to humanity, to mercy and civility" and is therefore "at least equal" with virginity.[29] The nature of man requires marriage both before and after the intrusion of sin. But sin makes marriage even more necessary. What God gave originally as a remedy for man's loneliness becomes after the Fall a vehicle for controlling the

[28] Niccholes, *Discourse of Marriage and Wiving,* p. 1.
[29] *Ibid.,* p. 6.

sinful passions of man and preparing him for salvation. The need for companionship rules out the celibate life at this point in Niccholes' treatise, though elsewhere he can ask rhetorically, "[W]here is the man this day living whose Virginity may be compared with Abraham's Mariage, in whom all the nations of the earth were blessed?"[30] Though Niccholes makes such admission of the importance of offspring in marriage, the fact remains that he originally defines marriage using the language of God's gift to relieve loneliness. Furthermore, it is the companionship of marriage that after the Fall reduces man's "unbrideled affections" to "mercy and civility."

The key to understanding the Puritans on this point is to recognize that they assume that having issue normally comes from doing those things that manifest companionship. Their attitude toward procreation is uniformly matter of fact. But it is not for procreation that marriage was first instituted; the purpose of marriage is the relief of man's loneliness, the manifestation of God's concern through the presence of a companion in life. For these reasons denunciation of "virginity" should be understood always as denunciation of the attempt to live unnaturally, that is, alone. The result of trying to live alone is, according to Niccholes, the triumph of lust, which he characterizes venomously: "that boyling damned putrefaction of the bloud, that raging, ruling, headstrong sinne of this age, that is too likely to break out, though it went cloathed in sacke-cloath."[31] It is no accident that his imagery evokes thoughts of a monk, the archetypical Christian "virgin." This, to Niccholes, is the most sinful kind of life because it denies the purposes of God in making the gift of marriage to man.

Using similar arguments, William Whatley[32] praises marriage over celibacy and advances the companionable purpose of marriage. Taking

---

[30] *Ibid.* Other writers contemporary with Niccholes disagree with his assessment of Abraham's marriage on the grounds that his polygamy was sinful. Cf. Gouge: the patriarchs' polygamy "was their sinne, and a very great blemish in them" (*Of Domesticall Duties*, p. 115).

[31] *Ibid.*, pp. 22-23.

[32] William Whatley (or Whately) (1583-1639) attended Christ's College, Cambridge, advancing there to the B.A. For study toward the B.D., however, he went to Oxford. It was at a parish in Oxfordshire that he preached the two sermons treated in this study, the first of which earned him the censure of the High Commission. An irenic figure, this seems to have been the only controversy of his life. In spite of his Oxford B.D., Whatley was a Ramist, a fact observable from his sermons.

I Cor. 7:28 as his text in *A Care-Cloth* ("If thou marry, thou hast not sinned; and if a virgin marry, she hath not sinned. Nevertheless such shall have trouble in the flesh"), he like Niccholes upholds the notion that marriage is a necessary civilizer of sinful men.

Wee must have no world, or but a beastly and confused world, if marriage were not; therefore it must needs be lawfull. And let it be taken away from any sort of man, and that man will grow, by little and little, full of filthinesse and uncleannesse, and all viciousnesse, by being forced to forbeare beyond strength . . . and in affecting an inattainable purite, they fall into a most extreme impuritie.[33]

Implicit in Whatley's words is a denunciation of monasticism and the unmarried priesthood, but he should not be read as only engaging in a polemic against "popery." Rather there is here a deeper issue as well, that of the nature of man and his needs in this life. While the Puritan worldview may appear pessimistic to some, especially today, these people saw themselves as pragmatic realists. In no respect are they more realistic about man than in regard to his sexual appetites. This, and not just a dislike of Rome, is behind Whatley's statement excerpted above. Whatley makes the same point as Niccholes: man is too frail to combat the difficulties of life alone; he needs a helper. This is the reason for marriage.[34]

While companionship is the purpose of marriage and the chief end God had in mind in the institution of it, sexual desire is admitted as a strong incentive to marriage. Moreover, as already noted, to place companionship prior to progeny among the marriage ends does not imply that issue is unimportant for Puritan theorists on marriage. Quite the opposite is the case. Sexual desire is not to be smothered or denied, for that is both impossible (the desire is too strong) and wrong (it is rebellion against God's will in nature). The proper means of using sexual desire is to channel it into relations with a loving spouse. The natural result of this is offspring, yet the primary factor remains the love that exists between the spouses. The first consideration in marriage should always be companionability, not desire, and the reason is most practical: desire is best satisfied where there is true companionship.

[33] Whatley, *A Care-Cloth* (London, 1624), STC 25299, p. 27.
[34] *Ibid.*, p. 78.

Even in the face of admission of strong sexual desire, the first consideration in marriage should be mutual fitness or companionability. Love is never separable from companionship, though care must be taken not to confuse it with lust. Marriage does not indulge lust; it rather allows the channeling of sexual desire through love into what the Puritans euphemistically termed "benevolence."

To say that marriage is the foundation of all social life would be possible for all sorts of Englishmen in the early seventeenth century. For High Churchman and Puritan alike this statement would have two implications: that the family is a microcosm of society as a whole and that the existence of society can be traced to Adam and Eve's production of offspring. Both these implications have corollaries. To see the family as society's microcosm is to admit the possibility of making analogies from the form of one to that of the other. Sometimes the movement is up from family to society, but the example of Cleaver shows that it may also be downward from society to family. Second, to say that society would not exist were it not for the procreative activity of Adam and Eve is to say as well that the family exists for the production of members of society. In Puritan writings this latter normally becomes two statements, one about secular society and one about the church. It is a natural duty to provide members of the state; it is a further duty of Christian families to provide church members. This is the meaning of William Perkins' breaking of the procreative end of marriage into two parts.[35]

Marriage is a society in itself, a microcosm of society as a whole and at the same time that which furnishes members of the larger society. While all Englishmen could agree on this, the order of the two implications varied from Anglo-Catholic to Puritan. To see the procreative end of marriage as of higher importance than the companionable end requires putting first that interpretation of marriage as the foundation of society which emphasizes the production of members of society. Placing the companionable purpose of marriage higher in turn means that the family as society's microcosm should be placed first. In Perkins' writings the two are in tension, with neither coming out a sure superior.

[35] Perkins, *Christian Oeconomie,* in *Workes,* III, 671.

But only a few years later the lines are more clearly drawn, with Puritans taking one position and Anglo-Catholics another.

Conceiving the family as the microcosm of society as a whole means that the state of matrimony is the focal point for all social duties, and thus also the center of the most special strains. For the Christian the household is that locus in which all work together especially to help one another to glorify God. For the Puritan the peculiar sins that arise within the close confines of marriage are detrimental to the relationship with God as well as that between the spouses. But on the other hand Christians are aided in their life together by the grace which God gives his elect. The phrase that arises over and over is that marriage is "the covenant of God." That this phrase implies something special beyond ordinary agreements is not granted by Milton,[36] but it is clear that the Puritans before him use the figure of covenantal marriage to mean that God is present as witness to the covenant of husband and wife to be meet helps. God's grace holds marriages together. In the writers consulted, the way of describing God's presence in the marriage ranges from that of William Bradshaw, who uses the story of the marriage at Cana to say that Christ is present in all Christian weddings, to the higher analogy of Christ's presence with his church.[37] This latter, however, is quite unusual among Puritan writers.

Love and Duty

Another way of expanding the implications of the Puritan idea of the state of matrimony as a societal microcosm, however, is to investigate the category of duty and the love assumed to lie behind every cheerful performance of duty. For the Puritan each member of the family has specific duties appropriate to his station that define his place in that microcosmic society. It is largely in terms of duty that the writers discussed in this chapter conceive of companionship in marriage, and yet, as in the case of Gataker, it is sometimes hard to distinguish between language of duty and language of love. For this reason the companionable concept of marriage, though developed with a strong emphasis

---

[36] Milton, *Doctrine and Discipline*, pp. 245-47.

[37] William Bradshaw, *A Marriage Feast*, in Thomas Gataker and William Bradshaw, *Two Marriage Sermons* (London, 1620), STC 11680, p. 8. Gouge uses the latter analogy in *Domesticall Duties*, pp. 30 ff.

on performance of mutual duty, is easily accepted by Milton and modified by his romantic idea of companionship.

Gataker is not the only writer of this period to link duty and love so closely that which one is prior sometimes becomes ambiguous. While a "duty to love" sounds strange, especially to modern ears, this way of speaking is typical of the Puritans. In his compendious *Domesticall Duties* William Gouge sums up the husband's and the wife's duties as respectively love and fear, describing them thus: "Love as sugar to sweeten the duties of authoritie, which appertaine to an husband. Feare as salt to season all the duties of subjection which appertaine to a wife."[38] In one breath love is the sum of the husband's duties, but in the next it is the "sugar" sweetening the performance of all his duties. Gataker's characterization differs mainly in language: "In a word the wives maine dutie . . . is subjection, the mans principally love."[39] Like Gataker, Gouge does not hold to the dichotomy he sets up between husband's and wife's duties, reserving love only for the husband's action toward his wife. When he turns to speak of "common-mutuall duties" which are "absolutely necessary for the being and abiding of marriage," he makes no differentiation between husband and wife. Both are to exercise "a loving affection one to another" and "a provident care of one for another."[40] Here love is a duty of each in kind, as is care. As was the case with Perkins and Cleaver, here the wife is placed so high relative to the husband that even though she is theoretically inferior to him and subject to him, she shares in his duties. William Whatley never even sets up a dichotomy between husband's and wife's duties but moves immediately into a discussion of the duties they owe "each to other in a reciprocall debt." This last is all the more remarkable since Whatley

[38] Gouge, *Domesticall Duties*, p. 128. William Gouge, whose position is examined at several points in the rest of this chapter, was born two years after William Ames in 1578 and died twenty years after him in 1653. During his long lifetime, much of it spent at Cambridge, Gouge wrote profusely and compendiously, exercising wide powers of influence among Puritans. Many similarities in their lives invite comparison of Gouge and Gataker. As a teacher Gouge too was especially popular. He like Gataker was appointed to the Westminster Assembly. Like Perkins and Ames as well as Gataker, Gouge enjoyed a reputation as a logician and defender of Peter Ramus. But Gouge was a staunch Presbyterian and a theological conservative, and in marriage doctrine he was a strict disciplinarian, evincing none of the humane concern that marks Gataker's writings on marriage.

[39] *Marriage Duties*, p. 6.

[40] Gouge, *Domesticall Duties*, p. 213.

has taken as his text for this sermon Eph. 5:23: "The husband is the head of the wife." The main duties he cites are mutual chastity and cohabitation.[41] These correspond to Gouge's two kinds of "common-mutuall duties"—"matrimoniall unity" and "matrimoniall chastity."[42]

These examples show that the above-treated writers all were operating within a unique frame of reference. Their conceptions of duty in marriage are essentially the same, and so we may take them together as typifying the Puritan approach to family life. But what they say about the family also applies, *mutatis mutandis,* to life in the church and in society in general. The emphasis on duty implies a highly disciplined life lived within confines set by providence. Put another way, the agreement to marry is a covenant with certain duties implied. Living a disciplined life, performing these mutual duties, is what covenantal marriage requires. While a modern might balk at any linkage of discipline with love, to these Puritans such a connection is most natural. While most of the emphasis in these writings on marriage is on the duties of man and wife, considerable weight is also placed on spontaneous love as the source of the will to do one's duty by his spouse. The marriage covenant is initiated by love; it is fulfilled by performance of duty. The resulting link between duty and love makes it ultimately impossible to divide them and set one apart for the husband and one for the wife. This is so even in non-Christian marriages. There is a certain kind of love which is man's insofar as he is natural, and even heathen can love each other (and perform their mutual duties accordingly) in marriage with this natural love, which is itself a gift of God. Nevertheless, the Puritans never forget the effect of the Fall, as we noted above in discussing sexual desire. The effect of grace in a Christian marriage is both to purify and keep pure the natural sort of love and also to add a higher type of concern for the other. Haller's words are appropriate: "The Puritan, when he gave all for God or for love, did not as a rule lose the world, but he enjoyed the illusion, at least, of gaining something more besides."[43] But the illusion, if it is only such, takes on great importance in Puritan marriage theology. Whatley writes, "As for love, it is the life, the soule of marriage. . . . [I]t must be first spirituall,

---

[41] Whatley, *A Bride-Bush,* pp. 1-3.
[42] Gouge, *Domesticall Duties,* p. 213.
[43] Haller, "The Puritan Art of Love," p. 242.

then matrimoniall." [44] Matrimonial love is what is man's by nature, while spiritual love is based on Christ's command to love one's neighbor and comes as a result of grace to the elect. Spiritual love, inspired by grace, makes exercise of matrimonial love certain.[45]

Love is at the root of the performance of duty which manifests companionship. This is the Puritan explanation of the way in which God continues his original purpose for marriage.

Gouge approaches the matter differently, but the result is substantially the same. In one place he argues that since marriage is like Christ's union with the church, then the husband must be like Christ. The meaning of this particularly is that he is given grace so to guide his wife that she will live a godly life and be accepted into salvation.[46] In a second place Gouge takes up the idea that man and wife are one flesh and interprets this to mean that their spiritual love makes no distinction between the one's or the other's good. Each loves the other as himself, not because of the commandment to love the neighbor but because it is natural to love one's own flesh and grace has made the two one.[47] In a Christian marriage love is inspired by grace. This in turn means that the duties of marriage are known internally and not externally. The same thing that happens to the law for the elect in Calvin's theology here happens to the duties of marriage for those who have received grace. Love is the source of duty in a Christian marriage. When providence puts two persons together in wedlock, they are given grace to be what is necessary for each other.

Companionship requires performance of duties; duty requires inspiring love; continuing love requires the blessing of God on the marriage. This is the formula received by Milton, and he asks the most pertinent question: Where there is no companionship, is God's blessing on the marriage?

Divorce

The question of divorce also arises among the men being discussed here. Since being married directly implies the performance of certain

[44] Whatley, *A Bride-Bush*, p. 7.
[45] *Ibid.*, p. 8.
[46] Gouge, *Domesticall Duties*, pp. 30 ff.
[47] *Ibid.*, p. 116.

duties and suggests many others, it is proper to ask what happens if the marriage duties are ignored. Does failure to act according to the roles given in marriage mean that the marriage dissolves or never was to begin with?

Even though Thomas Gataker emphasizes the companionable purpose of marriage almost to forgetting there is a procreative purpose, he does not go so far as to argue that failure to perform duties of help and assistance is cause for divorce. He can admonish wives sharply when they fall short of perfection: "A bad Wife is no Wife in Gods account." [48] Yet he does not carry this reasoning to the point at which it would require him to argue, as Milton does later, that an incompatible marriage has never been a true marriage. Rather Gataker holds throughout his writings to the position taken in *Marriage Duties,* his earliest published work on matrimony: the husband is to continue loving his wife in spite of all difficulties, because he has taken her for his "perpetuall companion . . . at boord and in bed," and he is "glewed . . . inseparably" to her. [49] And on her side the wife's task is so to love her husband as always to "draw love from him," in spite of adverse circumstances or his perversity. Gataker's view is that marriage is no ordinary form of contract but has a third partner who holds the two earthly partners to their agreement and, in the case of Christians, enables them to live up to that agreement. This is his meaning when he tells a couple he has just joined, "There is a knot of God betweene you, that cannot be unknit." [50] The only remedy for a bad marriage, in this view, is not to make it in the first place.

Gataker nowhere discusses possible grounds for divorce. The grounds allowed by Perkins and Cleaver, whose views his otherwise resemble, are not even mentioned in his published sermons on marriage. But too much can be made of this. It would be rash to make Gataker an indissolubilist because he does not discuss divorce in the sermons he originally preached at weddings, where to speak of the dissolution of marriage would be out of place.

A more complex position is William Whatley's. This divine moves in the space of seven years from a position a little freer than Perkins' to

---

[48] Gataker, *A Wife in Deed,* p. 6.
[49] Gataker, *Marriage Duties,* p. 31.
[50] Gataker, *A Wife in Deed,* p. 17.

that of an indissolubilist, not allowing any grounds for divorce. In his first sermon on marriage (*A Bride-Bush,* 1617) Whatley argues that failure to perform the two main marital duties (chastity and cohabitation) is an outright severing of the marriage bond. Failure to keep chastity is of course adultery, and failure to cohabit is desertion.[51] But Whatley is willing to go a bit farther as well. Though he will not quite admit that anything less than adultery or desertion will break the marriage bond, he avers that failure to perform the lesser duties of wedlock "stretch" this bond, sometimes to the point at which one of the main requirements is broken. These lesser duties are, insofar as they are mutually directed, love and "secondly, faithfulnesse and helpfulnesse, joyned together, a faithfull helpfulnesse and an helpfull faithfulnesse."[52] Of the same rank in importance are duties owed the rest of the family, which largely have to do with the proper government of the household. Thus failure to take charge properly is as great a fault in the husband as failure to love his wife, and a wife's incompetence in managing the family food budget is of the same order as irreverence toward her husband.

Two observations on Whatley's early view of divorce are appropriate. First, he is scrupulously orthodox according to the standard set down by Perkins. What difference there is in the outlines of Perkins' and Whatley's positions is in the latter's more direct reliance on the category of failure of duty. Second, Whatley's admission that the marriage bond can be stretched by chronic failures of a lower order is, in my judgment, a slightly wider opening of the door to the radical position of divorce for incompatibility than Perkins makes. Whatley at this point is willing to make considerable concessions in the way of marital nonindissolubility in order to reinforce his concept of duty. It is ironic that his emphasis on duty and discipline is what ultimately requires that he go so far in what he says about divorce. Nevertheless, no one should understand Whatley as categorically and unambiguously expanding the number of grounds for divorce. In the outline of his position he adheres to the model of Perkins: divorce for adultery and desertion with remarriage for the innocent, but admonition to bear up under the strains of lesser breaches of the marital agreement.

[51] Whatley, *A Bride-Bush*, p. 5.
[52] *Ibid.*, pp. 6-7.

What there is of a liberal attitude toward divorce in *A Bride-Bush* is completely wiped away with the publication of *A Care-Cloth* seven years later in 1624. In a preface to this latter work Whatley admits that he was in error in what he earlier said about divorce. In his recantation he refuses to admit any grounds whatsoever for the ending of marriage. It is difficult to imagine a more complete change of position. His emphasis in this later sermon is on "the cumbers and troubles of marriage," not its duties, and the advice he gives is that in the face of difficulty the husband and wife should try to love each other more. For "this makes life sweet, & all the comforts of life comfortable." His final judgment on marriage is that of an indissolubilist: "[T]he husband & the wife [must] resolve to conquer the troubles of marriage together." [53]

Another writer who sees no contradiction in denying divorce where there is no companionship is Daniel Rogers. His *Matrimoniall Honour,* published only a year before the first of Milton's divorce tracts, extols companionship inspired by love as the chief purpose of marriage:

Husbands and wives should be as two sweet friends, bred under one constellation, tempered by an influence from heaven, whereof neither can give any great reason, save that mercy and providence first made them so, and then made their match; Saying, see, God hath determined us out of this vast world, each for other.[54]

Yet Rogers refuses the solace of divorce to those who cannot see themselves so placed together by providence. When two who are married are not "sweet friends" but bitter enemies, they should see it as their task to conquer enmity with more love. Rogers permits divorce *a mensa et thoro* for adultery and desertion, but even the innocent is not granted remarriage because this divorce is only a separation.[55]

A final example, more notable because of its obvious attempt to be a voice of orthodoxy, is that of William Gouge's *Domesticall Duties.* Gouge purports to follow Bullinger, but his treatise is reminiscent of the later parts of Cleaver's *A Godlie Forme of Household Government*

---

[53] Whatley, *A Care-Cloth,* pp. 78, 80.
[54] Daniel Rogers, *Matrimoniall Honour* (London, 1642), Wing STC 1797, p. 200.
[55] *Ibid.,* p. 121.

also. According to Gouge, marriage is the best state there is, and for this reason it must be entered into with great care. The proper mode of marrying is by now a familiar pattern: first there should be a contract, then a decent interval, then a public witnessing to the contract. This last is the wedding ceremony itself, and Gouge is indifferent as to whether it be a "religious consecration" or a "civill celebration." [56] Nevertheless, once marriage is entered into in any way, it is binding as "the covenant of God" as well as that of the two spouses. For this reason, Gouge states specifically, mutual consent of husband and wife is insufficient to break the tie.[57] But neither is desertion a breach of the bond. It removes the duty of subjection for the wife whose husband has left her, but they remain married. Gouge is conscious of different opinions on this matter, but he remains firm:

In many reformed Churches beyond the seas Desertion is accounted so farre to dissolve the very bond of mariage, as libertie is given to the partie forsaken to marie another. . . . Because our Church hath no such custome, nor our law determined such cases, I leave them to the custome of other Churches." [58]

He nowhere alludes to Perkins' admission of divorce on grounds of desertion.

Only adultery and death end a marriage in Gouge's judgment. He cites Jesus' words in Matthew 19 to the effect that adultery is the only ground for divorce and then adds, "For the adulterer maketh himselfe one flesh with his harlot. Why then should he remaine to be one flesh with his wife?" [59] The marriage bond is severed by adultery, which is a failure in the duty of chastity, and so the innocent is as free to remarry as if he had never been married.

The judgment of Puritan orthodoxy at the end of the first quarter of the seventeenth century follows the lines laid down at the beginning of that century by Cleaver, Perkins, and Ames. The view of Cleaver and Ames, that only adultery (besides death) breaks the marriage bond, is

[56] Gouge, *Domesticall Duties*, p. 203.

[57] *Ibid.*, pp. 232-33.

[58] *Ibid.*, pp. 215-16.

[59] *Ibid.*, p. 218. Though the quotation I have given is one-sided, the context shows clearly that Gouge takes the same view of a wife's adultery as of a husband's.

reproduced by Gouge, while Whatley before his remarkable about-face reproduces closely the reasoning of Perkins. One can only guess what grounds Gataker might have allowed for divorce, but his tone seems to place him near the position of Perkins and the early Whatley. The only significant difference between the earlier and the later groups of writers on the question of divorce is that the latter approach it via an investigation of failure of duty, while the former have no such well-developed category to serve as a bridge and so move directly from the concept of marriage to that of what breaks marriage.

Companionship in Marriage and the Importance of Love

What really differentiates these later writers from their better-known predecessors is not their approach to the divorce question but first their understanding of the nature of marriage and second their use of the category of discipline. If Perkins and Cleaver are ambiguous about the prime purpose of matrimony, Gouge, Whatley, Gataker, and Niccholes are not. For these latter the purpose of the institution of marriage is above all for companionship. In explaining the meaning of a proper companionship in marriage they are led to speak of duty and in turn love. The tension between the primacy of propagation and that of companionability which exists in Perkins and Cleaver is here resolved in favor of the latter, which is understood in terms of a disciplined life of duty inspired by love. It is both the absence of ambiguity about the purpose of marriage and the hard-headed reliance on the category of duty which distinguish the later writers from their predecessors.

Though the disciplined life is the ideal for the men we have been discussing, the balance between duty and the love which inspires it is so delicate that an easy simplification is to move directly from companionship to love. This is what happens in Milton's hands, but in the period now under discussion it was already taking place among more radical Puritans.

John Wing, a separatist preacher, gives in two sermons of 1620 an example of the advance of this simplified understanding of companionable marriage.[60] His general topic is how a wife may bring honor and

[60] John Wing, *The Crowne Conjugall; or, The Spouse Royall* (Middelburgh, 1620), STC 25844. Both sermons in this book have the same title.

happiness to her husband and thus to their marriage; therefore his sermons may be compared to Gataker's *A Wife in Deed* and *A Good Wife Gods Gift*. In Gataker's sermons there is an emphasis on marital love, but it is always set in the context of marital duty. Furthermore, these sermons include a discussion of children as a blessing of marriage, though this blessing is secondary to the prime one, a good wife.

In Wing's sermons both discipline and offspring receive scant treatment. The entire first sermon makes no mention of either while extolling loving companionship. If this sermon stood alone as an example of Wing's position, it would mean that mutual love, God's chief blessing on a marriage, is the sole referent for what the spouses do in their relationship. In the second sermon, however, Wing treats duty briefly (in one fifteenth of the total space of the sermon). While no antinomian, Wing is not concerned to advance the model of the duty-bound marriage. His emphasis remains on God's gift of love and its direct contribution to companionship. Children are again not mentioned in the second sermon, though Wing creates the opportunity for a defense of the propagatory aim of marriage when he briefly takes up the matter of parenthood.

On the positive side, Wing puts considerable weight on the idea that marriage is a peculiarly important trial run for salvation. His language is similar to that of Gataker:[61] all who are married should bow before God and look to him for direction so that

he will please to glorify himself, soe in our naturall matrimony one with another, that in it, we may be furthered in the mysticall match between him and us; that Husband and Wife, may in such sort manage their marriage, that this Crowne matrimoniall may be (as it were) the harbinger of that which is immortall to the wife; and that to the Husband, the being of the King of a family, may be the fore runner, of being a King (with the King of Kings) in glory; that the union of each to other during naturall life, may be the earnest penny, of the eternall union of both to the Lord of life, for ever and ever.[62]

Neither the absence of mention of discipline or offspring nor this emphasis on love in marriage as preparative for life in salvation would

---

[61] See p. 98.
[62] Wing, *Crowne Conjugall*, p. 145.

be significant alone. Together, however, they suggest that as early as 1620 at least some Puritans were beginning to revise the views of the Puritan fathers in the direction of greater freedom in marriage and a heightened concept of the role of love in this freedom. Of the writers of the main line of orthodoxy only Gataker comes close to Wing's position, and even he chooses to stress the life of duty in marriage to an extent that is far beyond Wing's. While Gataker, Whatley, and Gouge speak first of duties internal to marriage which arise out of the nature of marriage, Wing begins with an exhortation to look to God for guidance.[63] Thus Wing's concept of the loving companionship which is the prime reason for marriage goes considerably beyond the position of Perkins, Ames, and Cleaver, further than any of the more orthodox writers were prepared to go.

The most notable feature of the writings we have been considering in this chapter is their emphasis on companionship over offspring as the purpose of matrimony. In place of the ambiguity and tension which characterize Perkins' and Cleaver's treatments of the ends of marriage, it is clear here that the Prayer Book's order of the ends of marriage is precisely reversed. According to the liturgy, it will be recalled, the reasons for marriage are (in order) procreation, restraint and remedy of sin, and mutual society. It is the result of the Puritan emphasis on companionship in marriage that the first and last reasons change place. Another way of saying this is to note that the Puritans normally look to a verse from the second chapter of Genesis—"God said, It is not good that the man should be alone; I will make him an help meet for him" instead of the one normally cited from the first—"Be fruitful and multiply—for their explanation of why marriage was instituted by God in the first place. They explain this by arguing that the second chapter is a commentary on the first, clarifying the underlying meaning of the first.

To say that for Puritan writers on marriage the companionable purpose of marriage becomes higher in importance than the procreative is not to say that for them these two ends should be sought in temporal order, so that a couple should first seek companionship in their marriage, then turn to producing offspring. The possibility that having children might be put off until forgotten while the couple seeks more and more to

[63] *Ibid.*, p. 79.

have a loving marriage would be regarded as incredible by all the writers treated here. The priority of companionship over procreation is logical and theological, not temporal. All the ends of marriage are sought at the same time, yet the highest in rank is the companionable end. The reasoning of the Puritans in this: man and wife are to act toward each other so as to help each other to live well in this life and achieve salvation in the next; some of their actions curb and rechannel the drives of sexual desire, so that what might be lust outside marriage becomes benevolence in marriage; finally, it is these particular helping actions to restrain and remedy sin which lead to the production of offspring. The three ends of marriage stand, but the order of the liturgy is reversed as the companionable end of marriage is increasingly understood as the expression of the soul of God's original meaning for this union of man and woman.

As I have argued before, the underlying structure of the ends of marriage is a dichotomy between the procreative end and the companionable, with the restraint and remedy of sin becoming a subtopic of whichever is placed higher. Thus Whatley supports my interpretation of the Puritan way of seeing the marriage ends when he writes as follows of the reasons for marriage: "The Author of Nature hath appointed this union betwixt one man, and one woman (as for the comfort of themselves, and increase of mankind, so) for the preventing of inordinate desires.[64] In Gataker's treatment also, "In the first place commeth the Wife, as the first and principall blessing, and the children in the next." [65] A similar point is expressed by Samuel Hieron, who writes first that "the wife was made to be a remedy against the lonelinesse and solitarines of the man" and then adds that the wife's fruitfulness "is the blessing which God promiseth to the man which feareth him." [66] But Hieron obviously expects marriages to produce children; his position is just that children should not be begotten out of lust but out of mutual love and for the upbuilding of the church.[67] A blessing on a level with having children is to have a calling in life, and raising children to be godly is analogous to a godly pursuit of one's calling. But both these,

[64] Whatley, *A Care-Cloth,* p. 22.
[65] Gataker, *A Good Wife Gods Gift,* p. 12.
[66] Samuel Hieron, *The Marriage-Blessing,* in *All the Sermons of Samuel Hieron* (London, 1614), STC 13378, pp. 406, 408.
[67] *Ibid.,* pp. 408-9.

Hieron says, come from the first blessing of marriage, a help to relieve man's loneliness.[68]

The only sign that any of the ambiguity present in the positions of Perkins and Cleaver still persists into this later period is found in Niccholes' *Discourse*. Even though he writes first of the companionable end of marriage, saying that God gave Adam his wife as "a companion for his comfort" and later explaining further that in marriage "thou . . . unitest unto thy selfe a friend, and comfort for society," [69] Niccholes can also speak highly of the procreative end:

The chief end of Marriage is *proles*, Issue, yet there are other respects in that covenant, that no doubt may tollerate the most ancient in this kinde: God saw that it was not good for Adam to be alone therefore hee made him an helper, . . . and as it is in another place; Vae solus: Woe to him that is alone, for if he fall hee hath not one to helpe him up. . . . Age is most prone to scortch it selfe in the flames of that fire [of hell], & therefore may lawfully partake the remedy against it.[70]

In these words spoken in connection with the question of whether those past child-bearing age may marry, Niccholes seems at first to espouse the conventional doctrine to the detriment of his words exalting companionship. But in fact he does not do so. The old may marry for purposes of companionship and for avoidance of lust, even though they may not have offspring. Niccholes may only be admitting that companionship is the good which remains after the "chief end" is no longer possible of fulfillment, but another interpretation fits his argument better. Exalting companionship over procreation does not mean for the Puritans that procreation has less place in marriage. Rather a Christian marriage is expected to produce offspring as a result of companionable life. Though Niccholes cites the traditional doctrine in this one place (and nowhere else), the emphasis all through his work is on companionship in marriage. The reason the old may marry is the same one as that for marriage of the young: they are lonely if they have to live single. Children are an added blessing for the young, but for the old the main blessing, companionship, is enough to warrant their marriage.

[68] *Ibid.*, pp. 411 ff.
[69] Niccholes, *Discourse of Marriage and Wiving*, pp. 1, 5.
[70] *Ibid.*, p. 29.

Gouge's prohibition of polygamy is a final witness in favor of our interpretation. While Niccholes could approve the polygamy of at least Abraham, Gouge sees no good in it. Of the patriarchs he writes that their polygamy "was their sinne, & a great blemish in them." The reason is simple: polygamy and bigamy "are . . . both of them against the first institution of mariage." Were the production of children the first end of marriage, polygamy would be preferable as a more efficient means of increasing and multiplying so as to fill the earth. But Gouge shows that such is not in his mind by reasoning further that love is less in a polygamous marriage: "Whereas God at first made a wife to be as an helpe unto man, two, or more wives cannot but be a great grief and vexation unto him." [71] Love is not possible, he reasons, to all the wives in the same degree within a polygamous marriage. Dividing affection means that no one wife can be loved so much as the one wife in monogamous wedlock. It is only within a monogamous union, furthermore, that husband and wife can help each other in the ways intended by God. For Gouge it is not the greater number of offspring made possible by polygamy which is more important; it is the greater love and helpfulness possible in a marriage of one man and one woman. Thus companionship grounded in love takes precedence once more over procreation among the ends of matrimony.

This chapter has examined two trends, one toward a definite statement of the main purpose of marriage as companionship, the other toward a description of that companionship in terms of love-inspired duty. But it has also been noted that this second trend becomes in more liberal writers a statement of the necessity of God-given love for there to be companionship proper according to God's ordinance. It is this version of the Puritan marriage doctrine which is taken up and romanticized by Milton.

But while there is on the one hand a movement toward asserting the loving companionship of two spouses as necessary for theirs to be a true marriage, there is also in this period a movement toward closing off all recourse to divorce. Whatley here stands as a beacon. A tension results which comes to plague men like Milton. If a marriage is no

---

[71] Gouge, *Domesticall Duties,* p. 115.

marriage without loving companionship, the question is, Why not declare it no marriage and give the partners freedom? But in this period precisely the opposite tack begins to be taken, as exemplified notably by Whatley but also by Gouge and Rogers.

When duty is deemphasized in favor of a direct linking of love and companionship, the result is a romanticized view of marriage and a requirement that in some sense mutual love between the spouses must continually renew the marriage contract. In Christian marriages God keeps a marriage solid by inspiring each party's love by grace. But in the case of a marriage not made in accord with providence, the natural attraction of the spouses for each other, shallow to begin with, cannot stand the strain. This is a problem the Puritans are less and less concerned to address the more they move toward a less liberal view of divorce. What begins with Perkins as the assertion that God's charity inspires loving performance of mutual duty in a Christian marriage becomes with the later Whatley and Rogers an assertion that all who are married are commanded to love each other (not just do their duty) if they would do God's will. The free movement of love to inspire performance of duties of companionship has become the command to love. What was internal for Perkins and could only be described as God's act has become external, a human act to be evoked by a preacher's exhortation.

Before turning to Milton's doctrine of marriage in the following chapters, it is convenient and may be helpful to set up here a brief comparison on the subject of love in marriage. For all Puritans it is God's love, charity, which renders a marriage indissoluble. Perkins characteristically speaks descriptively: God gives his charity to Christians so that they may persevere in their mutual duties in a loving way. Whatley and Rogers (though certainly not Gataker) in the middle period use the language of command: God *wills* that husband and wife show his love in performing their mutual duties. Milton does not use duty language at all. But in what he says about love he is closer to Perkins than to Whatley and Rogers, though Rogers is his own contemporary. For Milton it is only when charity is present as an internal factor that husband and wife can love each other with a mutual love. He, like Perkins, begins with a descriptive statement: God's love, a gift, inspires the love between husband and wife. But he draws a negative conclusion

118

from this, usually expressed conditionally: if partners in a marriage do not love each other and indeed cannot do so, then it is because God's love is not present in them. It is this second statement which most sets Milton off from Perkins. But their common understanding that charity cannot be commanded, only given, differentiates them both from the duty-oriented writers of the period between them.

IV
John Milton's Marriage Doctrine

John Milton's divorce tracts are neither completely in continuity with earlier Puritan writings on marriage nor totally apart from them. In the first place, when Milton addressed the problems inherent in the official doctrine of marriage, the Puritan-Anglican marriage controversy had been dormant for at least a decade. During William Laud's tenure as Bishop of London and Archbishop of Canterbury Puritan opinions were suppressed, and after 1626, when writing and preaching on controversial matters were prohibited, debate on the essence of marriage and the possibilities of divorce largely ceased. The matter of matrimony, of course, was but one of the points at issue between the two principal parties in the English Church, and the suppression of the marriage controversy but one part of a more extensive attempt to snuff out heterodox opinions. When the dampened coals of controversy began to blaze again in the 1640s, Milton's was the only major voice to reopen the debate on marriage.[1]

---

[1] Cf. Powell, *English Domestic Relations*, pp. 84-86.

This renewal of the marriage controversy cannot properly be called a Puritan-Anglican controversy because in his radical advocacy of divorce for incompatibility Milton found himself opposed by his Puritan friends as well as by the official doctrine of marriage. Both Milton and his Puritan opponents regarded themselves as standing in the same tradition on matrimony, and this recalls the ambiguity with which many of the writers considered above expressed their opinions. While Milton stands apart from his predecessors among Puritan marriage theorists first of all because he was a decade and more removed from the controversy in which they were involved, he stands apart also because of the radical implications for divorce he drew out of their considerations on the essence of marriage and the possibilities of dissolving the marital bond.

Continuity is also evident, however, between Milton's arguments and those of earlier Puritan writers. Especially is Milton's position in the divorce tracts reminiscent of Perkins', and a flavor like that of Gataker's writings also appears. Important as it is to note that Milton drives the argument for divorce to its radical extreme, it is also necessary to see that the basis for his conviction that incompatible spouses should be allowed divorce is the doctrine that the essence of marriage is a covenantal society of mutual helpfulness and companionship. It is this doctrine, developed as early as Cleaver and Perkins, which occupies a central place in Milton's explanation of the essence of marriage. Furthermore, even on the question of divorce there is some continuity, for Milton's argument that incompatibility is worse than adultery recalls Perkins' denunciation of "adulterie of the heart" and Whatley's list of failures in marital duty which "stretch" the bond of marriage.

This chapter and the following one explore Milton's conception of marriage and the resultant argument for divorce in both their continuity and their discontinuity with earlier Puritan marriage doctrine. Milton's position in the divorce tracts is not merely or even mainly one on divorce; it is largely a positive assertion, supported by careful argument, of a conception of the nature of marriage as well. The question of divorce is not the main one asked; primarily Milton is seeking to discover what marriage is as ordained by God. Knowing what is no marriage implies for him knowing first what is marriage. This in turn requires development of such themes as the nature of man (both natural and

Christian), Christian love (charity) as an ethical precept, and human liberty (both natural and Christian).

With these themes now set out as questions to be answered, Milton's argument in the divorce tracts can be explored and evaluated.[2]

[2] There are essentially two editions of Milton's first divorce tract that must be here considered. *The Doctrine and Discipline of Divorce: Restor'd to the Good of Both Sexes* was initially published in 1643 and was in all likelihood chiefly the result of Milton's bad experience with his wife. To admit this autobiographical connection, however (which is general among authors of lives of Milton), is not to detract from its scholarly worth or its general pertinence to the society of Milton's day. The second edition, bearing the date 1644, was over the first considerably "revis'd and much augmented, in Two Books," in it Milton, to clarify his position, takes the argument away from its modest beginnings, showing its relation to others' opinions and replying to his critics. Two later editions of this tract published during Milton's lifetime are unchanged in content from the second edition.

At a glance the title pages of the first two editions of *Doctrine and Discipline* suggest that the emphasis has shifted in the time between their respective printings. The title of the first edition in full is "The Doctrine and Discipline of Divorce, Restor'd to the good of both Sexes, From the bondage of Canon Law, and other mistakes, to Christian Freedom, guided by the rule of Charity." The title of the second edition omits reference to Christian freedom and charity and concludes, "to the true meaning of Scripture in the Law and Gospel compar'd." Thus the titles suggest that at first Milton was concerned with Christian love and human freedom, while a year of thought made him more interested in showing how scripture supported his point of view.

But to judge these two editions of *Doctrine and Discipline* by their titles would be to misjudge gravely the scope of the arguments advanced in these tracts and the others Milton published on marriage and divorce. The titles are most misleading. Milton does not neglect scripture in the first edition, nor does he neglect charity and liberty in the second. These latter, if anything, grow more important for his argument in its augmentation. What is, in fact, the most notable feature of the second edition is the connection of charity with law and the introduction of a strong view of nature with its own law and its proper love. Liberty likewise in the second edition comes to be thought of on two levels and is in each case the name of love's action in fulfilling the law.

Milton wrote three other tracts on the problem of marriage and divorce. *The Judgement of Martin Bucer Concerning Divorce,* published in 1644, is a translation of part of the second book of Bucer's *De Regno Christi,* first published during the reign of Edward VI, to whom it was dedicated. *Tetrachordon: Expositions upon the Foure Chief Places in Scripture, Which Treat of Mariage, or Nullities in Mariage,* published March 4, 1644 (old style) or 1645 (new style), is Milton's most systematic attempt to find scriptural warrant for his position. Finally, *Colasterion: A Reply to a Nameless Answer Against the Doctrine and Discipline of Divorce,* published simultaneously with *Tetrachordon* in 1645, adds nothing to Milton's position on marriage and divorce but defends it with vigor.

Of these four tracts only *The Doctrine and Discipline of Divorce* and *Tetrachordon* are directly discussed in this and the next chapter. *The Judgement of Martin Bucer* and *Colasterion* have, however, been consulted in order to amplify Milton's position as stated in the two more systematic tracts.

References to the above works are cited from the Yale University Press edition of Milton's works, vol. II, as cited on p. 22, n. 9. Page numbers run consecutively throughout this volume, and to avoid confusion below I cite the name of the tract before the page number on which a given reference is found.

The Problem

"This therefore shall be the task and period of this discourse to prove," writes Milton near the first of *Doctrine and Discipline of Divorce,* "first that other reasons of divorce besides adultery, were by the Law of Moses, and are yet to be allow'd by the Christian Magistrate as a peece of justice, and that the words of Christ are not hereby contraried. Next, that to prohibit absolutely any divorce whatsoever except those which Moses excepted, is against the reason of Law."[3] With these words Milton sets his intent before his readers. Though this particular statement appears first in the second edition (where Milton takes care to make his argument as clear as possible), its gist applies equally to the first. But there is one pregnant phrase which indicates the direction Milton's thoughts are heading: "the reason of Law." This is to be a theological argument, but that does not rule out the use of the reason that is naturally available to man. Milton has taken this tack after reading Fagius, and he is now consciously aware of the part natural reason can play in discerning the truth of this matter. An important concomitant of the introduction of conscious reasonableness is that Milton can now speak to all men.

Milton states the position he plans to support in this way:

That indisposition, unfitnes, or contrariety of mind, arising from a cause in nature unchangable, hindring and ever likely to hinder the main benefits of conjugall society, which are solace and peace, is a greater reason of divorce then naturall frigidity, especially if there be no children, and that there be mutuall consent.[4]

He then goes on to give, as enumerated in the second edition, eight reasons for accepting this position. What is more important than the enumeration of reasons, however, is that in defending this proposition Milton has to say what he means by marriage and by divorce; he has to enter the field of disputation over kinds of divorce, reasons for divorce, annulments, remarriage after divorce; he has to develop a theory of human life which supports his notion of marriage; he has, in short, to

[3] *Doctrine and Discipline,* p. 239.
[4] *Ibid.,* p. 242.

develop a theology of marriage, a doctrine and discipline of marriage, from which the doctrine and discipline of divorce will follow.

It does not take long to discover that the key to Milton's understanding of marriage is the first two chapters of Genesis, in which the primal society of marriage, that of Adam with Eve, is described. Here Milton finds the (to him definitive) words declaring "what is mariage, and what is no mariage": "It is not good that man should be alone; I will make him a help meet for him" (Gen. 2:18, Milton's translation). Milton continues, "From which words so plain lesse cannot be concluded, . . . then that in Gods intention a meet and happy conversation is the chiefest and noblest end of mariage; for we find here no expression so necessarily implying carnall knowledg, as the prevention of loneliness to the mind and spirit of man."[5] The marriage of Adam and Eve is archetypal; God set Eve before Adam to relieve his loneliness, a loneliness he has in his nature as man even before the Fall. Thus marriage is not to be seen as existing primarily for the remedy of lust or for the the procreation of children, for Adam was given Eve by God before they knew lust, and likewise the injunction to fill the earth comes after the gift of a meet help. It is the concept of Eve as meet help to Adam to which Milton returns again and again and which sets the tone of all that he has to say about marriage.

To understand what is at stake in Milton's definition of marriage by the concept of meet help, it is useful to note that he, like Gataker,[6] plainly reverses the usual order of the reasons for the institution of marriage. The marriage service of *The Second Prayer Book of King Edward VI* puts the reasons this way:

One [cause] was for the procreation of children, to be brought up in the fear and nurture of the Lord, and praise of God. Secondly, it [marriage] was ordained for a remedy against sin, and to avoid fornication. . . . Thirdly, for the mutual society, help, and comfort, that the one ought to have of the other, both in prosperity and in adversity.[7]

For Milton "mutual society, help, and comfort" are the reasons for

[5] *Ibid.,* p. 246.
[6] See pp. 95-96.
[7] Parker Society, *The Two Liturgies,* p. 303.

which God ordained marriage in the first place, and a look at Gen. 2:18 proves it. The other two reasons given in the Prayer Book follow from this one, which expresses the essence of marriage. Milton's Ramist logic allows him to make this derivation: from the principal end of marriage come the others in orders of precedence (see Appendix B for more on this point). Thus his reversal of the order given in the liturgy is of considerable significance.

In *Tetrachordon* Milton is much more explicit about the ordering of the marriage ends than he is in *Doctrine and Discipline of Divorce*. Commenting on Gen. 1:27-28 and 2:18-24, he asserts, God has "treatably and distinctly . . . heer taught us what the prime ends of marriage are, mutual solace and help."[8] The preferred order of the three ends is expressed in Gen. 1:27-28: "So God created man in his own image, in the image of God created he him." This Milton finds to refer to the idea of meet help. For man images God, and woman in turn images man; man is subject to God and woman to man, while God through Christ is head of man and man similarly is head of woman. The image of God is not totally destroyed in the Fall, but rather there are some "remains" of it in man "as he is meerly man." Milton finds this idea of man's imaging God to describe the proper (meet) relation of mutuality which is still normative for fallen humanity.[9]

Verse 27 continues, "Male and female created he them." This Milton takes to explain the second end of marriage, that called in the Prayer Book a "remedy against sin." "This [clause]," he writes, "contains another end of matching man and woman, being the right, and lawfulness of the marriage bed; though much inferior to the former end of her being his image and help in religious society."[10]

Finally God's blessing, "Be fruitful, and multiply," for Milton "declares another end of Matrimony, the propagation of mankind."[11]

These three ends are taken up again in Milton's comments on Gen. 2:18, the "help meet" passage. Here Milton is forceful in his opposition to the notion that it is copulation which makes marriage—a conception which he associates with his opponents and especially with Roman

[8] *Tetrachordon*, p. 601.
[9] *Ibid.*, p. 591.
[10] *Ibid.*, p. 592.
[11] *Ibid.*, p. 593.

Catholicism. Woman is to remedy man's loneliness, and "by loneliness is not only meant the want of copulation." Indeed,

God is no deceitfull giver, to bestow that on us for a remedy of lonelines, which if it bring not a sociable minde as well as a conjunctive body, leavs us no lesse alone then before; and if it bring a minde perpetually averse and disagreeable, betraies us to a wors condition then the most deserted lonelines.[12]

Warming to his subject, Milton turns to the ecclesiastical courts, which gave full divorce only in case of adultery, asking, "What courts of concupiscence are these, wherein fleshly appetite is heard before right reason, lust before love or devotion?" He accuses the canon law of turning nature upside down, of making "the minde of man wait upon the slavish errands of the body." [13]

In *Doctrine and Discipline of Divorce* Milton does not go quite so far as to accuse the church courts of being "courts of concupiscence," but he points in several places to the evils that result from not allowing divorce where there is no mutually helpful society. Far from restraining sin and avoiding fornication, to require two incompatible persons to remain married is to create sin. For dislike of one's spouse creates wandering thoughts, and the body soon follows. Allowing divorce on the grounds Milton cites will have such results as these: "Places of prostitution will be less haunted, the neighbours bed lesse attempted, the yoke of prudent and manly discipline will be generally submitted to, sober and well order'd living will soon spring up in the commonwealth." [14] Should "the most honest end" of marriage (meet help) be lacking, the man will "piece up his lost contentment by visiting the stews, or stepping to his neighbours bed." [15] Milton would avoid this by permitting divorce in cases of incompatibility.

For Milton marriage is instituted for the prevention of loneliness to the mind and soul of man. The other goods or ends of marriage follow from the spouses' providing meet help to each other. Understood properly, this reasoning means that sin will be restrained and remedied

[12] *Ibid.*, p. 598.
[13] *Ibid.*, p. 599.
[14] *Doctrine and Discipline,* p. 230.
[15] *Ibid.*, p. 247.

and children will be begotten in marriages in which man and wife are meet helps for each other. Though Milton reads the ends of marriage in precisely the opposite way from the official listing in the marriage liturgy, he nowhere denies that the second and third ends (in his order) are goods to be aimed at in marriage; he only sets them in correct relation to the principal good, companionship.

Marriage if first of all, then, a union of two persons who are helps meet for each other. This is a doctrine which Milton derives directly from scripture, but his arguments and conclusion evince influence from earlier Puritan writers. The union of mutual meet helps is effected by a covenant made between them and witnessed by God, Milton next argues, and this too is a clear restatement of earlier Puritan marriage doctrine, though Milton once more makes much of drawing the idea of covenant from the Bible.

The archetypal marriage is that of Adam and Eve. But it is not God's gift of Eve to Adam which makes their marriage, Milton argues; it is rather Adam's taking her for his wife, the answer to his loneliness. That the woman is God's gift is important for Milton, as is shown below, but what makes the marriage is the acceptance of the gift. When Adam consciously takes Eve to be his wife with the words, "This is now bone of my bones and flesh of my flesh" (Gen. 2:23), and she acquiesces in some unrecorded way, this is their mutual covenanting which ratifies God's gift. In this way Milton finds the marriage covenant to be given in the marriage of the archetypal pair.[16]

From this exegesis two characteristics of the marriage covenant follow: the covenant must be mutual, and it must be in response to God's gift. The latter point is discussed below under the rubric of the call to marriage. The mutuality of the covenant, however, can best be considered at this time.

The mutuality of the covenant to marry consists in that husband and wife each consent together to be meet helps and companions to each other. Milton goes to great lengths to show that this covenant between man and wife is not essentially different from any other human covenant and that even persons without the grace of Christ may validly covenant to marry, not only the righteous. It would be tedious to cite all Milton's

---

[16] *Tetrachordon*, pp. 601-2.

illustrations of this point; three of different kinds will suffice. First, the Roman civil law (and by inference all equitable pagan law) defines a marriage which to Milton is true marriage, even though it can be ended.[17] The consent is mental, not physical, in this case. Milton quotes, "Consent alone, though copulation never follow, makes the marriage." [18] Second, Hebrew marriages were true marriages, and the consent there valid consent.[19] That Milton would affirm this is obvious to anyone who recalls Milton's dependence on the Old Testament in framing his understanding of marriage. Third, even an unbeliever and a believer may have a true marriage so long as their consent to be man and wife is mutual. For authority Milton cites Paul (I Cor. 7:12) : "If a brother have an unbeleeving wife, and she joyn in consent to dwell with him, . . . let him not put her away for the meer surmise of Judaicall uncleanness." [20] In these cases and others similar it is the consent of the spouses together which makes the marriage. In anticipation of a later discussion it can be noted that the other side of this is that when there is no more mutual consent, there is no more marriage, and divorce should be granted.

It is the continuation of mutual covenanting for a lifetime that makes marriage permanent. There is no external bond which holds the covenanting pair together in wedlock, and similarly their covenant does not itself bind them for any longer than they are able mutually to renew it. In this way Milton attacks the understanding of marriage of the Roman Church and High Anglicanism and also the arguments of those Puritans who maintained that the covenant of marriage is a special kind of covenant which has an unbreakable character.

First of all, the consent to marry which is mutually given in the marriage covenant is consent to provide meet help through life and to salvation.[21] This recalls the Thomist doctrine of marriage, in which the consent to marry is consent to live married for life, for "consent to take a woman for a time is no marriage." [22] But for Milton there is an important new factor which implies modification of this position.

[17] *Doctrine and Discipline*, pp. 326-27; *Tetrachordon*, pp. 610-11.
[18] *Tetrachordon*, p. 611. Milton cites the Roman *Juris Civilis*.
[19] *Ibid.*, p. 619 and *passim*.
[20] *Doctrine and Discipline*, p. 267; cf. *Tetrachordon*, pp. 685-86.
[21] *Tetrachordon*, p. 599.
[22] See p. 46 above.

The covenant is to provide meet help, and it must be mutual. Milton argues that it is the continuing mutual renewal of this covenant in acts of meet help and companionship which makes marriage everlasting though life.[23] The Thomist doctrine is quite correct in maintaining that consenting to take someone for a time only is not consent to marry. But Milton draws different conclusions about the consent from this assertion. For him the consent can be known as an everlasting consent only as it is shown to be so. In the Thomist doctrine the consent is to an everlasting bond, and once the consent is made originally, the bond is tied fast. Because Milton stresses the continuation of the act of consenting, or covenanting, the bond is fast only so long as the consent continues to be given in deeds of mutual meet help. The factor of mutuality, furthermore, requires that both partners to the covenant together renew their consent, and failure on one side breaks the covenant. In distinction from the Thomist doctrine that consent to marry must be everlasting because "consent to take a woman for a time is no marriage," Milton argues that the everlasting character of marriage lies not in the object of the consent, everlasting life together, but in the character of the consent, a continuing mutual covenanting for meet help the one to the other. So long as the marriage covenant is mutually given, it is binding.

Against the Puritan position that the marriage covenant is a special kind of mutual agreement that cannot, once made, be broken, Milton argues that it is not special even though it is called "the covenant of God." It remains no more than human in spite of this appellation; it has no more sanctity than any other agreement between men of whatever stamp.

For so the covnant which Zedechiah made with the infidell Kind of Babel is call'd the covnant of God, Ezech. 17.19. which would be strange to be counted more than a human covnant. So every covnant between man and man, bound by oath, may be call'd the covnant of God, because God therin is attested. So of mariage he is the author and the witnes; yet hence will not follow any divine astriction more then what is subordinate to the glory of God and the main good of either party.[24]

[23] *Tetrachordon*, p. 603.
[24] *Doctrine and Discipline*, p. 276; cf. *Tetrachordon*, p. 624.

Milton is not at all ambiguous on this point, and he stands in direct opposition to the opinion of such men as William Ames, who state unequivocally that the covenant of marriage is a special kind because it, unlike other covenants, cannot be broken. The reason for this, argue Ames and others among Milton's Puritan predecessors, is that God witnesses the covenant to marry and thereby grants it an everlasting approval. To this Milton makes two responses. The first is that just quoted: to call the marriage covenant "the covnant of God" does not distinguish it from other human covenants which are witnessed by God. His second response is that God's presence as witness to the marriage covenant cannot be assumed but can be known only after the fact, through recognition of God's helping the spouses to continue in giving mutual meet help to each other.[25]

This second response allows Milton to distinguish between Christian and other marriages. Though the covenant of marriage may be entered into validly by non-Christians, Christian marriages have the added blessing of God's help in the continuing mutual renewal of the covenant. God's role in a Christian marriage is not to make it something supernatural nor to impose upon it some external bond of everlastingness; it is to foster the love that is expressed mutually in marriage. God works in the realm of the mutual self-giving of the spouses, not alone in the more sterile world of the original agreement to marry. The passage quoted on the preceding page continues:

For as the glory of God & their esteemed fitnes one for the other, was the motive which led them both at first to think without other revelation that God had joyn'd them together: So when it shall be found by their apparent unfitnes, that their continuing to be man and wife is against the glory of God and their mutuall happiness, it may assure them that God never joyn'd them; who hath reveal'd his gratious will not to set the ordinance above the man for whom it was ordain'd.[26]

What makes a Christian marriage different from a pagan is that God has, as in the case of Adam and Eve, made ths woman to be the wife of this man, ordaining it by his providence, *and they know it*. Because

[25] *Tetrachordon*, pp. 598, 608.
[26] *Doctrine and Discipline*, pp. 276-77.

they know God has joined them, they give glory to God in their mutual covenanting in marriage. Milton does not deny that God has a hand in effecting Christian marriages, though he does not treat this as much as some other writers. But for him the hand of God is the hand of charity, which makes spouses to be for each other, helps them in their search for happiness together, and guides them in presenting a mutual front to society at large. It is neither the institution of marriage nor the original covenant which is holy here; it is the mutual love of the spouses which is a holy love because it is directly inspired by God's love. The image of God in man is also recalled in this context. When Milton declares "that Piety and Religion is the main tye of Christian Matrimony," he is affirming that the love of God and marital love are for the Christian inseparably linked. The covenant of mutual love between husband and wife is like that between God and man.[27]

The Solution

A. Theory of Divorce. Marriage for Milton is that society of a man and a woman who mutually covenant to live together as meet helps for each other. Christian marriage differs from pagan not in the character of the covenant but in that God joins with the marriage partners in helping them to maintain the covenant by inspiring their mutual love. By loving and helping each other the spouses glorify God and attest to his blessing on their marriage, and so long as this love lasts, God's presence is assumed, and the marriage is binding. Divorce is for Milton the declaration that the covenant of mutual love has been broken; it is the recognition that there is no marriage; it is the realization that God's blessing is not on a particular marriage to keep it.[28]

The doctrine of divorce is the other side of the doctrine of marriage. There are persons living together, Milton argues, who are no longer mutual meet helps for each other, whose acts toward each other do not express the covenant they have made together. These persons Milton declares to be already divorced in fact and deserving of being granted a divorce in law. But the institution of marriage, supported in England

[27] See p. 126.
[28] Milton makes this point often, but see esp. *Doctrine and Discipline*, p. 242, and *Tetrachordon*, p. 600.

by the canon law, binds them together in a "forced yoke." Milton thus advocates divorce for incompatibility, and his posture toward divorce fills out his doctrine of marriage.

A passage from Book II of *Doctrine and Discipline of Divorce* will serve to take us from the positive conception of marriage to the negative side, divorce. This passage is lengthy but central to Milton's thought.

Lastly, Christ himself tells us who should not be put asunder, namely, those whom God hath joyn'd. A plain solution of this great controversie, if men would but use their eyes; for when is it that God may be said to joyn, when the parties and their friends consent? No surely; for that may concurre to the leudest ends, or is it when Church-rites are finisht? Neither; for the efficacy of those depends on the presupposed fitnes of either party. Perhaps after carnall knowledge? lest of all: for that may joyn persons whom neither law nor nature dares joyn; tis left, that only then, when the minds are fitly dispos'd, and enabl'd to maintain a cherfull conversation, to the solace and love of each other, according as God intended and promis'd in the very first foundation of matrimony, I will make him a help meet for him; for surely what God intended and promis'd, that only can be thought to be of his joyning, and not the contrary. So likewise the Apostle witnesseth I Cor. 7.15. that in marriage God hath call'd us to peace. And doubtles in what respect he hath call'd us to marriage, in that also he hath joyn'd us. The rest whom disproportion or deadnes of spirit, or somthing distastfull & avers in the immutable bent of nature renders unconjugall, error may have joyn'd; but God himself never joyn'd against the meaning of his own ordinance. And if he joyn'd them not, then there is no power above their own consent to hinder them from unjoyning; when they cannot reap the soberest ends of beeing together in any tolerable sort. Neither can it be said properly that such twain were ever divorc't, but onely parted from each other, as two persons unconjunctive, and unmariable together. But if, whom God hath made a fit help, frowardnes or private injuries have made unfit, that beeing the secret of mariage God can better judge then man, neither is man indeed fit or able to decide this matter; however it be, undoubtedly a peacefull divorce is a lesse evil and lesse in scandal then a hatefull hard-hearted and destructive continuance of mariage in the judgement of Moses, and of Christ.[29]

The following propositions may be distilled from the above passage.

[29] *Doctrine and Discipline*, pp. 328-29.

First, only when there is a compatibility of mind—which for Milton includes both intellect and volition—can there be a marriage, for only then will the prime reason of matrimony, that spouses should be meet helps for each other, be realized. Second, God wills no unions of persons not thus compatible. Third, if any two not thus compatible join in matrimony, theirs is no true marriage but a joining of error. Fourth, if there be any married couple who are "unconjugal," they ought to be allowed to divorce by mutual consent. This divorce is no putting asunder; it is rather a recognition that the pair were in truth asunder from the first. Now let us discuss these propositions in turn.

Compatibility for Milton is essentially what he calls "mental," but moderns should understand the word in a broader sense than they are used to. For Milton this is a rubric for just about everything else but physical, sexual compatibility. The reason is that "all human society must proceed from the mind rather then the body, els it would be but a kind of animal or beastish meeting." [30] When Paul counsels marriage rather than burning, Milton understands him to mean the "rationall burning" which is distaste with solitude.[31] Not to have such compatibility or not to exercise it where it does in fact potentially exist is worse than adultery in leading to the destruction of a marriage.[32] [N]atural hatred whenever it arises, is a greater evil in marriage, then the accident of adultery, a greater defrauding, a greater injustice." [33]

Christians, who know that God is governing his world, confess that he will "call" together those who will satisfy for each other the main end of marriage, the provision of meet mutual help and the prevention of solitude. But the matter of such a call is difficult. Certainly some marry who have heard no call or who have heeded a false call. Further, not all men are believers, and it may be asked how God rules in their lives. Milton is sure that it is possible to ascertain at least when there is no true call: this is when two married persons simply cannot get along together in fulfilling the prime end of matrimony. His argument smacks of the Calvinist logic surrounding election: it is never certain whether individual persons are elect or not, but it behooves them to act

[30] *Ibid.*, p. 275.
[31] *Ibid.*, pp. 250-51.
[32] *Ibid.*, p. 269.
[33] *Ibid.*, p. 332.

as if they are if they can, and if they are not elect, the fact will soon show itself. If two persons have been set apart for each other in marriage, they should act so as to fulfill the best ends of their union, and God will give them the charity to attain their goal. But Milton suggests also that it is possible that two such persons may frustrate the will of God. Again, this is a tenet he likely learned from his Calvinist teachers. Finally, only God can know who is elect, and only God likewise can know whom he has called to marry each other. The point Milton is trying to make is that it is impossible to legislate such a call into existence when two persons have married who do not have compatible personalities.

A natural marriage is a real possibility, that is, a marriage based on natural attraction. What is lacking here is God's aid in ensuring the mutuality of the union.[34] But the important thing to note about Milton's whole marriage doctrine is that what certainty there is about the validity of any particular marital union is known by *ex post facto* reasoning. Even this is unsure, however, for the reason already noted: man may act so as to frustrate God's will. (This point is discussed in the following chapter.) The result of this reasoning that is perhaps the most perplexing to moralists is that it is impossible to say in the making of it whether any particular union of two persons in what society, the church, and they themselves call marriage is in truth a marriage. Thus Milton is simply not arguing on the same ground as those theologians who are certain that marriages are made in the present-tense consent of the partners once and for all time. They have to keep consenting, according to Milton, and only time will indicate whether they have grace—help from God's love—to do this. Only time will indicate—never with certainty, but with a fair reliability—whether a particular match is ordained by God or not.[35]

[34] This brings to mind Kierkegaard's cynical remark about lovers who swear by their love to love each other eternally. For Kierkegaard such an oath is meaningless. For Milton too the oath would have no binding power, but he looks more positively than Kierkegaard on the possibility of real love in marriage. If God has given the mutual love, then swearing on it would certainly have meaning for the lovers; if God is not author, it may still be sufficient to keep two persons married. Most important, however, is that knowledge of whether the love was of God and therefore binding eternally is only *ex post facto,* and, moreover, it is never fully certain.

[35] One familiar with Karl Barth's special ethics may recognize in Milton's position a similarity to that taken by Barth in his section on "Man and Woman" (sec. 54.1) in *Church Dogmatics,* III/4. For Barth marriage between two persons consists "essentially in

What Milton calls divorce, then, might perhaps more properly be termed annulment. If annulment is taken to mean a declaration that there never has been any marriage between two particular persons, then the term divorce as used by Milton has the same meaning. That is, it is impossible, on Milton's terms, that a truly God-inspired, loving, companionable marriage has ever existed if the partners fall away from each other. One can only guess why Milton does not call what he describes annulment, but a likely reason is that this word had fallen into disuse among Puritan writers. Furthermore, since Milton's argument is essentially a movement from earlier Puritan statements about divorce, perhaps he wishes to show continuity by his use of the term divorce.

When Milton speaks of a marriage as being in truth no marriage, he is always thinking in terms of the forum of conscience, specifically the consciences of the married pair. The church thinks it can legislate divorces and annulments, but in fact it cannot; this is in the province only of the particular two persons. An annulment certifies a marriage to have been null and void from the first, never, in fact, to have existed. Milton is describing exactly this situation when he writes of "unconjugal" spouses who are "unmariable together" by their natures. It seems that what he is arguing for is a broadening and internalizing of the category of annulment. But whichever term is used, divorce or annulment, a more significant factor in Milton's argument for divorce is that he would have the separation of parties badly matched to come about by mutual consent, just as mutual consent brought them together in the first place. The only intrusion of law into this matter of mutual consent is to ensure that the terms of separation are equitable. This was in fact accomplished in the Mosaic law governing divorce.[36] Milton's position is that "the law can to no rational purpose forbid divorce, it can only take care that the conditions of divorce be not injurious."[37] This position recalls that of William Perkins, who stipulates that while one or both partners break

---

the life-partnership established and subsisting between these two. As such it is the consumption of what is sought and striven for in genuine love. Marriage as a life-partnership is the touchstone *whether or not this seeking and striving was and is that of genuine love.* Marriage as life-partnership is therefore the proof of love." (Italics supplied.) See Karl Barth, *Church Dogmatics* (Edinburgh: T. and T. Clark, 1961), III/4, p. 187. For other points of similarity see pp. 217-18, 221-22.

[36] *Doctrine and Discipline,* pp. 343-44.

[37] *Ibid.,* p. 350.

the bond of marriage by their sin, it is the magistrate who grants divorce, following the custom of the land.[38]

Milton's theory of divorce can be summed up in this way. Providence works through nature to put together two persons who are mutually suited to help each other in the chief work of man, namely to glorify God and serve him in this life. When two come together, they form a mutual help contract, to which they have been directed by God, and in this sense—a sense primarily "mental" in Milton's language—they become "one flesh" (only in a derivative sense do they become "one flesh" through coitus, since the physical act follows the mental consent). But if it should be discovered later that these two are not able to aid each other toward the chief end of man and provide meet helps each for the other in their life together, what has put them together is not providence but the "error" of men—themselves, their parents, or whomever. They are in such a case known after the fact of the marriage vows never to have meant those vows, even though they may have thought they did at the time. They have never been "one flesh." The marriage is only external, and so divorce should be granted. As for the internal forum, there was never any true marriage, for there could have been no true consent: "No covnant whatever obliges against the main end both of it self and of the parties covnanting." [39] Thus this divorce is not at all man's putting asunder what God has joined; it is a signification that there never was any acquiescence of God in this particular matter at all. And who, in the Puritan view, can know this better than the individuals involved? Thus divorce ought to be granted when there is mutual consent to it.

Milton's argument does not aim primarily at making divorce easier; its main intent is to remove external restrictions on what is essentially internal, the marriage bond.

B. Grounds for Divorce. According to the Mosaic law (Deut. 24:1), a man may divorce his wife if she finds no "favour" in his eyes or if he finds some "uncleanness" in her. In order that there can be some rule of law, even if the law seeks only to ensure equity, Milton discovers that

[38] See p. 76.
[39] *Doctrine and Discipline,* p. 245.

he must explain what is meant by the Mosaic conditions. First of all, he is adamant that neither Moses nor he wants arbitrary, capricious divorce on scant grounds. It is because the Pharisees interpreted the law of Moses in a capricious way that Jesus has such harsh words for them in Matthew 19, as Milton points out at length in *Tetrachordon* and more briefly in *Doctrine and Discipline of Divorce*,[40] where he finds Jesus' answer to "nonplus" the Pharisees because of their "license" and their "supercilious drift." [41] But Milton is also sure that more grounds for divorce must be granted than adultery only, for adultery is not the only or even the worst breaker of the marriage tie. The canon law of his day allowed remarriage of innocent parties divorced for adultery of the other spouse. Milton finds this unrealistic and unrelated to what marriage actually is. The intent of Jesus' words to the Pharisees was not to abrogate the law of Moses, for it is inconceivable, Milton reasons, that God would have given this law permitting divorce if it had not been good. Jesus does not do away with the law of God. If God had simply given a dispensation to the Jews as a whole because of their hardness of heart, he would be convicted of giving in to sin. This Milton cannot admit.

This cannot be lesse than to ingraft sin into the substance of the law. . . . Nay, this is, which I tremble in uttering, to incarnat sin into the unpunishing, and well-pleas'd will of God. . . . A law wholly giving license cannot upon any good consideration be giv'n to a holy people for hardnesse of heart in the vulgar sense.[42]

The point is that God's charity cannot be exercised in the giving of an evil law to his people. It is not the case that marrying one spouse is good and divorce and remarriage is permitted only as a necessary evil because of God's merciful love. Rather his love must be somehow already present in the law given. This is precisely the case, argues Milton, and Christ's words, far from abrogating a law which was less than good, serve to bring the charity that is in it into the open. Marriage was ordained for the good of man because God's charity was awakened

---

[40] *Tetrachordon*, pp. 642 ff.; *Doctrine and Discipline*, pp. 308 ff.

[41] *Doctrine and Discipline*, pp. 310, 311, 331 respectively.

[42] *Ibid.*, pp. 295-96.

when he saw man's loneliness. Divorce likewise is a work of charity. "[I]f we mark diligently the nature of our Saviours commands, wee shall finde that both their beginning and their end consists in charity: whose will it is that we should be so good to others, as that wee be not cruel to our selves." [43] Divorce was and is not only permitted but commanded by God as a work of charity for the good of man.

Far from being the only or even principal grounds for divorce, adultery for Milton is near last on the list of grounds. "Natural hatred, when it erises, is a greater evil in marriage, then the accident of adultery." [44] Mutual love is the end of marriage; where there is none, there should be a divorce.[45] Idolatry is a worse breach of matrimony than adultery, but "frigidity of self" and "numnesse of minde" [46] are at least as evil in marriage as idolatry. These are not reasons primarily theological; Milton assigns them to the realm of nature. "[I]f the noysomnesse or disfigurement of body can soon destroy the sympathy of mind to wedlock duties, much more will the annoyance and trouble of minde infuse it self into all the faculties and acts of the body, to render them invalid, unkindly, and even unholy against the fundamentall law book of nature." [47] It is man's nature to be lonely without a meet help; this remains unchanged after the Fall. What has been impaired is the ability to provide meet help, but only charity can be of force in this regard, not an enforced institution of marriage. Milton even goes to the brink of saying that a union which persists in spite of obvious mutual unfitness or "hatred" is adulterous. Speaking of the status of children of a second marriage, he writes:

And because some think the children of a second matrimony succeeding divorce would not be a holy seed, it hinder'd not the Jews from being so, and why should we not think them more holy than the offspring of a former ill-twisted wedlock, begott'n only out of a bestiall necessitie without any true love or contentment, or joy to their parents, so that in some sense we may call them the children of wrath and anguish, which will as little conduce to

[43] *Ibid.*, p. 330.
[44] *Ibid.*, p. 332.
[45] *Ibid.*, p. 258.
[46] *Ibid.*, pp. 268-69.
[47] *Ibid.*, p. 272.

their sanctifying, as if they had been bastards; for nothing more then disturbance of minde suspends us from approaching to God.[48]

The significance of the line of argument in the above paragraph is that Milton would have divorce be allowed when there is some longstanding and profound incompatibility between the spouses. When inability to join in conjugal love and helpfulness is habitual, then divorce ought to be allowed, for the partners are in truth not man and wife, though they may be living together and producing children. Habitual incompatibility means that there could have been in the first place no true consent to live together as meet helps. In contrast to thoroughgoing, habitual incompatibility Milton places the accidental, chance character of adultery.[49] The canon law "dares to tutor Christ to be more strict then he thought fit," as Milton phrases his criticism in *Tetrachordon*.[50] "Man only puts asunder when his inordinate desires, his passion, his violence, his injury makes the breach: not when the utter want of that which lawfully was the end of his joyning, when wrongs and extremities, and unsupportable greevances compell him to disjoyne."[51]

Milton takes another tack when commenting on Matt. 19:9.[52] ("And I say unto you, Whosoever shall put away his wife, except it be for fornication, and shall marry another, committeth adultery: and whoso marrieth her which is put away, doth commit adultery.") He attempts to show that "fornication" does not just mean copulation with someone not one's spouse but has a much broader meaning:

[T]he language of Scripture signifies by fornication (and others besides St. Austin so expound it) not only the trespas of body nor perhaps that between maried persons, unlesse in a degree or quality as shameless as the Bordello, but signifies also any notable disobedience, or intractable cariage of the wife to the husband, as Judg. the 19.2.[53]

Both in *Doctrine and Discipline of Divorce* and in *Tetrachordon* Milton

---

[48] *Ibid.*, pp. 259-60.
[49] *Ibid.*, p. 332.
[50] *Tetrachordon*, p. 641.
[51] *Ibid.*, p. 651.
[52] *Ibid.*, pp. 667 ff.
[53] *Ibid.*, p. 672.

advances this interpretation. Divorce is not the biblical punishment for fornication in the narrow sense. A fornicator in the narrow sense is punished not by divorce but by death.[54] Always this was the understanding of the Mosaic law until the time of the Pharisees. Jesus set this straight, and his words were understood properly by the early Christians, only to be perverted into a Christian Pharisaism by the Roman Church. The Reformed churches have rediscovered the sense of Jesus' and Moses' words, and this is what Milton advances as his argument.[55]

What Milton says on divorce remains theoretical. He gives no precise grounds for divorce. As he puts it in many ways in many places, divorce is not a matter for law to decide but a matter of conscience. The law ideally serves not to bind but to set man free to serve his and his neighbor's (that is, his spouse's) good. Thus the end of civil divorce law should be to preserve charity. This is perhaps an unexpected result, but on this point Milton is coming to express his understanding of how the state ought to allow religious liberty as well as individual liberty. Of this more will be said later in the section on liberty. Now let it simply be noted that Milton wants as little law as possible in something which by rights is a matter of conscience.

As a footnote to this we need to answer the question of what Milton says about remarriage. He is not so concerned with this problem as he is with that of marriage and divorce per se, nor is he really concerned with the children of serial marriages or with such secondary yet important impediments to divorce as property. But the logic of his position is clear, and so are what words he does have on remarriage. The reason for complete divorce and not just separation *a mensa et thoro* is to allow the parties involved—both of them—to marry again, hopefully to someone who will be a compatible help.

This reveals once again just what kind of divorce Milton is advocating. Above it was suggested that he is really arguing for annulment, since a divorce is simply a declaration that a supposed marriage never was. The parties themselves make this decision, according to Milton, and the courts only confirm it and see to the equity of the divorce settlement. But such a divorce is a complete one; there are no bonds remaining

---

[54] *Doctrine and Discipline*, p. 337.
[55] *Tetrachordon*, pp. 693 ff.

between those who once called themselves husband and wife. Thus Milton cuts across all the conditions set forth in canon law for divorce and annulment. Does he not know that these were there for some reason? Frankly, if he does know it, he seems to think that the reason no longer is reasonable. The heart of his doctrine is the relocation of the marriage bond from the fleshly union of the married couple to the mental (i.e., intellectual, volitional, spiritual) acceptance each of the other as his meet help.

C. Law and Gospel in Marriage and Divorce. It might be argued that Milton does not understand law, or even that he is confusing law with gospel. These two criticisms, each of which has a certain validity, need to be explored.

There is a certain frustration that comes from reading Milton on marriage and divorce not unlike that which comes from reading some Christian contextualists of today. Always there is the polemic against the bondage of laws promulgated by the church. The exposition of the argument against this bondage takes the form of an interwoven fabric of theoretical foundation-building (in this case Milton's emphasis on what marriage is in its first institution) and a listing of the evils that come from the bad law (even salvation can be put in jeopardy by a bad marriage held together by force, as well as the normal bad results: ill temper, nights spent in other beds, "unholy" children). But there is nowhere any successful attempt to fill the gap that remains between the quite ideal theory and the quite perturbing reality of many marriages. Yet it is precisely to fill some such gap as this that the church and society make laws in the first place. Should not Milton offer some sort of approximation to law at least, some sort of concrete guidance to those caught or about to be caught in the reality of marriage? Does he not need some kind of "middle axiom" to apply the ideal of marriage to actual marriages? And if he did this, would not the result turn out not unlike the very laws he is protesting against?

Let us attempt to illustrate this difficulty. Milton counsels that temporary, "accidental" incompatibilities should not be taken as grounds for divorce but only those which are "perpetuall." [56] Now in order to insure

---

[56] *Doctrine and Discipline*, p. 331; cf. p. 309, *Tetrachordon*, pp. 670-71.

equity, the court granting a divorce would have to have some standard by which to judge when the latter and not the former is the case. And if equity is to obtain from one case to another, not just in a particular one, and from one court to another, then there must be some minimum standard for perpetuity of incompatibility. Again, in a given case how would a judge decide with equity how to grant terms of divorce, *even though there be mutual consent* (Milton's main stipulation), if each of the pair wishing to divorce feels the more wronged?

Is it not precisely the strength of the law existing in Milton's time that it set standards of equity for such decisions? In the case of divorce for adultery even Milton would admit that adultery normally follows on some mental incompatibility. And the law he is combating allows for punishment of the guilty and grants permission to remarry to the innocent on the basis of this external matter, adultery. Desertion is another case in which the courts could decide on the basis of the law and an external act of one of the parties how to grant terms of divorce.

Milton is not ignorant of problems such as these; this much may be said for him. When he calls for divorce to become a matter for decision by the conscience and not by the courts, he may not offer any help to legislators faced with drafting an equitable law of the sort he would accept, and he may be too naïve in expecting that those who could not agree on how to live together can agree on how to cease living together. It is quite obvious that he does not understand the problems to be faced in framing any law. But at the same time he does have a firm grasp on the problems posed by the existing laws governing marriage and divorce. They do not fill the gap between the ideal of marriage and the realities of many marriages either. And his attempt should not be dismissed lightly as offering no workable alternative in law, for Milton's concern is to set the record straight on what marriage is and what the persons married to each other ought to bring to it and get from it. It is his contention that the existing laws do not proceed from a proper basis (i.e., from a proper appreciation of what marriage ought to be) and so perversely keep together persons who should be allowed to separate and marry others. Milton seeks to provide a proper basis for marriage and divorce; he will leave the formulation of law to others. But the lawmakers must keep in mind that no law ought to oblige against the good of man, as Milton argues. Law should aim at allowing charity to operate.[57]

To accuse Milton, then, of an unrealistic attitude toward law because he does not advance any concrete suggestions as to how positively to frame a law regulating divorce is a criticism partially valid and partially invalid. It is valid for all the reasons given above; it is invalid, however, if it implies that the existing law of Milton's day was any more helpful in bridging the gap between ideal and real. The strength of Milton's position lies in his going back to the institution of marriage as the basis of what he says about actual marriages which should or should not be. His critique of the canon and civil law of his day is not made on the level of law but on the level of the essence of the institution behind the law. It is perhaps correct to say that Milton does not offer much positive, concrete advice as to what a workable divorce law might be, but no matter how correct such a statement may be, it does not help toward understanding the actual argument advanced by Milton, which is at bottom an attempt to show what marriage is and what, in particular cases, makes it, so as to allow everything else to follow logically in train and be worked out in its implications by legal minds more competent than his.

The other criticism mentioned above is that Milton confuses law and gospel. It is without doubt that he does, at least on one level. In order to

[57] Some similarity may be noted between Milton's reasoning here and that of William Perkins in *A Treatise of Christian Equitie and Moderation* (*Workes*, II, 502-20). Perkins distinguishes between the "extremitie of the law" and the "mitigation of the law," arguing that not only magistrates but also individuals may and must on the basis of conscience interpret law so as to serve the end of the law and not the words of a specific legal injunction. The example he uses in this place is that of a starving boy who steals bread. The magistrate, Perkins argues, ought to "mitigate" the punishment ordained by the "extremitie of the law," because the law does not seek to keep bread from the starving but ensure it to all. In such mitigation the magistrate is conforming to the will of God expressed in his mercy toward sinful man. Since God "mitigates" the death penalty incurred by man through sin, man ought to do likewise for offenses against other men. Another example is cited by David Little in *Religion, Order, and Law* (p. 125). Little writes, summarizing Perkins: "An individual citizen may even disobey the law of the land if *in his judgment* the end of the law (the purpose of God) is advanced by his action! For example, says Perkins, a person is quite justified in opening the gates of the city to allow citizens in, even though the magistrate had declared absolutely that no man shall open them, because he has not hindered the *end of the law*, which is to protect citizens' safety." Since Milton's criticism of the divorce law rests on its failure to promote the end of marital union, it follows that he is not exceeding the bounds traced out by Perkins in arguing for the right of conscience to act in accord with the end of marriage, even though this may mean breaking existing statutes.

explore this criticism fully, it is necessary first to examine briefly his doctrine of nature and grace to see how fallen man makes use of the institution of marriage given to Adam and Eve before the Fall. The intent here is to discern what if any difference there is in the working out of a marriage according to nature and one aided as well by God's grace. In the course of this investigation it will become apparent how, according to Milton, law and gospel begin to work and what their relation is.

Whatever else may have happened to man and woman as the result of the Fall, Milton leaves no doubt that the loneliness which leads toward marriage is a natural part of the human condition both before and after the Fall. So far as Milton is concerned, the desire to have a helper is at basis the same whether before the Fall or after. Speaking of the (to him "rationall") burning which a man should avoid through marriage, he asserts the unity of man over all time with Adam before being given Eve:

What is [that burning] then but that desire which God put into Adam in Paradise before he knew the sin of incontinence, that desire which God saw that it was not good that man should remain alone to burn in; the desire and longing to put off an unkindly solitariness by uniting another body, but not without a fit soule to his in the cheerfull society of wedlock. Which if it were so needfull before the fall, when man was much more perfect in himself, how much more is it needfull now against all the sorrows and casualties of this life to have an intimate and speaking help, a ready and reviving associate in marriage.[58]

As this passage shows, not only does Milton understand the desire for a mate as being essentially the same before and after the Fall; he also believes that the desire can be satisfied with a meet mate after the Fall as well as before. There is a natural need for a spouse which was in the beginning and remains at the center of the institution of human marriage.

Milton supports what can be called his natural-law argument for marriage in various connections. Prohibition of divorce is "respectles of human nature," he argues in Book I, Chapter X of *Doctrine and Discipline of Divorce,* where he uses scriptural injunctions about not sowing with different seeds in the same vineyard and not plowing with an ox and an

---

[58] *Doctrine and Discipline*, p. 251.

ass yoked together to show that purely natural incompatibilities arise in quite ordinary circumstances such as sowing and plowing. Shortly thereafter, in a passage already quoted, he writes that mental incompatibility leads to physical acts "unholy against the fundamentall law book of nature, which Moses never thwarts, but reverences." [59] Again, "shee who naturally & perpetually is no meet help, can be no wife." He writes that a "fit and perfect marriage" is the result of nature's joining the spouses. The love which binds man and wife in marriage is "most ancient and meerly naturall." [60] Such arguments find expression also in *Tetrachordon*. Marriage is a relation which "cannot take place above the prime dictats of nature." It is "the first and most innocent lesson of nature" which teaches man to stay away from what harms him and so leads him to divorce an incompatible spouse.[61]

Many other loci for this kind of connection between marriage and nature both pre- and post-Fall could be given, but the above are sufficient. Further, as soon as it has been said that nature continues Adam's burning in all his progeny, it must also be said that there is a fundamental difference between how he responds to that burning and how his progeny do so. Essentially the same position is taken in both *Doctrine and Discipline of Divorce* and *Tetrachordon,* but the following passage from *Tetrachordon* states Milton's belief best:

In the beginning, had men continu'd perfet, it had bin just that all things should have remain'd, as they began to Adam & Eve. But after that the sons of men grew violent & injurious, it alter'd the lore of justice, and put the government of things into a new frame. While man and woman were both perfet each to other, there needed no divorce; but when they both degenerated to imperfection, & oft times grew to be an intolerable evil each to other, then law more justly did permitt the alienating of that evil which mistake made proper, then it did the appropriating of that good which Nature at first made common.[62]

Things are not what they were before the Fall. Man and woman have "degenerated to imperfection" because the first man and woman

[59] *Ibid.,* pp. 270, 272.
[60] *Ibid.,* pp. 309, 319-20, 345.
[61] *Tetrachordon,* pp. 621, 623.
[62] *Ibid.,* p. 665.

made a "mistake" which made evil "proper." The propriety of the wrong binds mankind after the Fall to repeating the mistake. Milton does not in the divorce tracts give any systematic account of what has happened to man as a result of the Fall, but his position can be gleaned from the above passage and its context and further filled out by turning to those frequent passages which praise reason and deplore blind passion. The companionship which Eve gave Adam remedied his "rational burning," and even after the Fall marriage aims primarily at quenching this flame. If mental compatibility is lacking in marriage, the marriage is a "beastish meeting." In short, the "degeneration" resultant from the Fall arises from that "mistake" which first allowed passion to rule over reason. It is the disorder of reason and passion which is characteristic of fallen man. But in a Christian marriage, the disorder is removed by God's help through the inspiration of mutual conjugal love through charity. Milton's doctrine of the Fall is thus essentially Augustinian even though his position on marriage departs somewhat from Augustine's.[63]

[63] The interpretation given above of Milton's doctrine of the Fall is supported by a reading of his later treatment of this subject in *Paradise Lost* and *De Doctrina Christiana*. Though both these works follow much later in Milton's life than the divorce tracts, there is no radical change in Milton's conception of fallen humanity from the earlier to the later writings.

In *Paradise Lost*, Denis Saurat writes, man "is a double being, in whom co-exist desire and intelligence or passion and reason. The two powers ought to be in harmonious equilibrium, desire being normally expressed, but remaining under the leadership of reason. Evil appears, the Fall takes place, when passion triumphs over reason." Saurat supports this analysis with a citation from *Paradise Lost*:

> Since thy original lapse, true liberty
> Is lost, which always with right reason dwells
> Twinned, and from her hath no dividual being:
> Reason in man obscured, or not obeyed,
> Immediately inordinate desires
> And upstart passions catch the government
> From reason, and to servitude reduce
> Man till then free. (XII, ll. 83-90.)

If the general character of the Fall is passion rulling over reason, the particular characteristic of the fallen state is sensuality, argues Saurat. He writes, "Sexual desire is, so to speak, essentially 'desire.' It is most capable of obliterating reason completely and of leading man to the worst folly. And in such obliteration is the abstract trait typical of the Fall." See Denis Saurat, *Milton: Man and Thinker* (rev. ed.; London: J. M. Dent & Sons, 1944), pp. 124-28.

Milton's position in *De Doctrina Christiana* parallels that just outlined. There he states explicitly that the sinful condition of fallen humanity "consists, first, in the loss, or at least in the obscuration to a great extent of that right reason which enabled man to discern the chief good." But vestiges of the image of God, man's original righteousness,

Man's nature remains after the Fall, but it has become disordered. The passionate, physical burning which once was a subordinate part of the rational, mental burning has come, through sin, to be the senior partner. And the supreme irony of this is that the civil law and even the church enshrine this result of sinfulness as the normal and best relationship man and woman should have. To base Christian marriage on procreation of children and restraint and remedy of sin is to surrender to the disordered nature of man.

The alternative to this is for Milton to base marriage on its original institution, God's gift of a meet help to remedy not lust but loneliness. Again Milton is Augustinian. He insists that marriage ideally is a union of those perfect for each other, as Adam and Eve were. But after the Fall and after Christ "the rule of perfection is not so much that which was don in the beginning, as that which now is nearest to the rule of charity. This is the greatest, the perfetest, the highest commandment." [64] There is a new perfection, and that is the rule of charity. It is to this rule that marriage now should conform. But it is significant that Milton calls this "the highest commandment." Charity is for him, at least in some respects, a law. And this begins at last to take us back to the criticism advanced some pages ago, that Milton confuses law and gospel, or as now phrased law and charity. Let us see what he says about their relationship.

Charity has some concrete meaning for Milton, as he knows that "love only is the fulfilling of every commandment." [65] At the very least he sees that in law "it is not the stubborn letter which must govern us, but the divine and softning breath of charity which turns and windes the dictat of every positive command, and shapes it to the good of mankind." [66] In this way charity is to be seen behind the entire body of legislation which God gave the Jews through Moses. But Milton occasionally goes far beyond this position on their relation. While denying that it is possible "to command love and sympathy, to forbid dislike" in marriage, he insists that where conjugal love and sympathy are impossible, charity

---

remain in man's understanding. See *De Doctrina Christiana,* in Frank Allen Patterson, general ed., *The Works of John Milton* (New York: Columbia University Press, 1933), XV, 203 ff.

[64] *Tetrachordon,* p. 667.

[65] *Doctrine and Discipline,* p. 258.

[66] *Tetrachordon,* p. 605.

commands divorce.[67] It is not simply that the Mosaic law has to be viewed through charity's spectacles; rather charity in Milton's conception seems almost to seek out the ill-wed and separate them. Charity sets right what sinfully disordered nature has made wrong. Commenting on Prov. 30:21-23, Milton writes, "[A] hated woman when she is maried, is a thing that the earth cannot beare. What follows than but that the charitable law must remedy what nature cannot undergoe." [68] In the case of marriage with an unbeliever, "If . . . the conceived hope of gaining a soul come to nothing, then charity commands that the beleever be not wearied out with endles waiting under many grievances sore to his spirit.[69]

The full matter of Milton's understanding of the role of charity will be taken up in the next chapter. The quotations just given suggest that he was making charity into law, but that is not the point immediately at issue. The present question is whether Milton was confused as to the respective roles of nature and grace or charity, and the answer seems to be that he was. The very fact of ambiguity on this matter suggests confusion. I shall return to this question of nature and grace, of law and charity, in the following chapter. Hopefully the systematic discussion of the themes of charity and liberty there will cut through some of Milton's ambiguity and make possible a clearer statement of Milton's position.

Sexuality is for Milton a good, not an evil, aspect of man's nature. God created man and woman sexually different, thereby approving sexuality, and though the Fall has intervened, this basis in creation persists, and sex remains good. But this is not to condone sensuality, the disordered, sinful response to sexuality which is man's since the Fall. The desire man and woman have for each other is after the first sin no longer a properly ordered desire. The rational burning that was Adam's loneliness has been replaced by the passionate burning that is human lust. This inordinate desire draws man and woman together even when they are not fit for each other. In a society like that of Milton's England the result of such unions often is bad, and yet a strict nondivorce policy in law makes it impossible to break such unions for better ones. Milton sees this as a perversion of God's will: God intended marriage as remedy for man's

[67] *Doctrine and Discipline*, pp. 346, 355.
[68] *Ibid.*, p. 307.
[69] *Ibid.*, p. 267.

loneliness, but man has made marriage into a lonely bondage for the procreation of children. Another result, and by no means an unimportant one, is that this latter sort of marriage promotes evil and increases sin, making the godly to sin while not affecting the wicked, who merely go on taking no account of the law, canon or civil. With his usual eloquence Milton makes a point which is none the less valid because it seems to reflect his personal experience with marriage:

And lastly, it is not strange though many who have spent their youth chastly, are in some things not so quick-sighted, while they hast too eagerly to light the nuptiall torch; nor is it therefore that for a modest error a man should forfeit so great a happiness, and no charitable means to release him. Since they who have liv'd most loosely by reason of their bold accustoming, prove most successfull in their matches, because their wild affections unsetling at will, have been as so many divorces to teach them experience. When as the sober man honouring the appearance of modestie, and hoping well of every sociall vertue under that veile, may easily chance to meet, if not with a body impenetrable, yet often with a minde to all other due conversation inaccessible, and to all the more estimable and superior purposes of matrimony uselesse and almost liveles: and what a solace, what a fit help such a consort would be through the whole life of a man, is lesse paine to conjecture then to have experience.[70]

The laws against divorce make the righteous suffer and do nothing to keep the wicked from their sin. Some of the righteous may be able to bear their troubles; indeed there may be something of God's will in attempting to make a seemingly incompatible pair learn to live and love together. But Milton is frankly not optimistic; he thinks that more evil than good comes from restraining divorce. This restraint, this bondage of the flesh,

drives many to transgresse the conjugall bed, while the soule wanders after that satisfaction which it had hope to find at home, but hath mis't. Or else it sits repining even to Atheism; finding it self hardly dealt with, but misdeeming the cause to be in God's Law, which is in man's unrighteous ignorance. . . . It also unties the inward knot of mariage, which is peace & love (if that can be unti'd which was never knit) while it aimes to keep

[70] *Ibid.*, p. 250.

fast the outward formalitie; how it lets perish the Christian man, to compell impossibly the maried man.[71]

The law of God is the law of charity, which aims always at man's good. Man's law instead produces evil for man, and the more righteous the man tries to be, the more evil the law makes for him. This law (of men) is not the way of charity, not the way of perfection.

Him I hold more in the way of perfection who forgoes an unfit ungodly & discordant wedloc, to live according to peace & love, & Gods institution in a fitter chois, then he who debarrs himself the happy experience of all godly, which is peaceful conversation in his family, to live a contentious, and unchristian life not to be avoided, in temptations not to be liv'd in, only for the fals keeping of a most unreal nullity, a mariage that hath no affinity with Gods intention, a meer toy of error awing weak senses, to the lamentable superstition of ruining themselves; the remedy whereof God in his law voutsafes us. Which not to dare use, he warranting, is our infirmity, our little faith, our timorous and low conceit of charity: and in them who force us, it is their masking pride and vanity, to seem holier & more circumspect then God. So far it is that we need impute to him infirmity, who thus divorces: since the rule of perfection is not so much that which was don in the beginning, as that which now is nearest to the rule of charity. This is the greatest, the highest commandment.[72]

It is nothing less than God's charity which not only permits but commands divorce of incompatibles. This follows directly from the meaning and prime end of matrimony, the provision of meet helps to remedy man's loneliness. The fact that charity works to dissolve an unreal marriage recalls that it is also charity working through God's providential rule over nature that provides meet spouses in the case of good, true marriage. This might seem to suggest failure on God's part when two incompatible persons marry, but Milton resists this conclusion. In such cases it is the two parties themselves who, through their own error and disregard for God's will for them, have contracted their match, a possibility which remains to man because God's guidance is not rigidly deterministic. God watches over true covenants of marriage to keep them,

[71] *Ibid.*, p. 269.
[72] *Tetrachordon*, pp. 666-67.

but when there is no true covenant, he first of all declares the marriage not to be. If man does any less, he is trying to be more righteous than God himself; he is in rebellion; he is increasing sin in the name of God. This is the germ of Milton's "restored" doctrine of divorce.[73]

[73] Milton does not see or at least does not admit that the accusation of attempting to be "holier & more circumspect then God" might be laid on him as well. If it may be argued, as Milton does, that to have a law which seeks to state God's will for man is to elevate the law to the place of God, then similarly it can be advanced that such exaltation of the conscience as Milton performs puts the individual conscience in the place of God. Since in Milton's doctrine of marriage the will of God works through the conscience-based mutuality of love of the spouses and since the presence of the will of God in a marriage is known only after the fact of a godly married life, then before and during the fact the only bond would seem to be that of mutual willing between the spouses. God logically has no more place in Milton's theology of marriage than he has in the position Milton opposes. But this is not a difficulty unique to Milton's treatment; it is a continuing problem in conscience-law debate. Little discerns this very problem in Perkins: "Who is it, in Perkins' scheme, who grasps the end of the law? Who is it who perceives that toward which all laws drive? It is, of course, the genuine Christian. He stands above the law with a special capacity to judge it, because he stands in a new order toward which all earthy law points and in which it is fulfilled. In the new elite, he has become a law unto himself." (*Religion, Order, and Law*, p. 125.)

Milton misses the point in his criticism, if the point is that logically he leaves God room to act while his opponents do not. The difference is really deeper and is expressed better in Milton's understanding of charity. It is not whether God has room to act which is the real issue; it is *how* God characteristically acts so as to communicate his charity to man. Here Milton follows Perkins in conceiving the activity of charity as having special reference to individual consciences. But this is something any orthodox Puritan would admit. Milton interprets Perkins' position radically, however, to argue that the working of charity in the individual conscience is, in the case of marriage, an indictment of existing law.

V
The Liberty of Charity

The judgment of history on Milton is that his understanding of marriage and divorce was decidedly un-Puritan. Arthur Barker calls him an "antinomian";[1] Paul N. Siegel argues that he was a humanist in the tradition of Sir Thomas More;[2] his contemporaries thought he was dangerously libertarian. Antinomian, humanist, libertarian, all these in some sense Milton was; yet simultaneously he was decidedly a Puritan. Haller discerned this nearly thirty years ago,[3] but his argument has not convinced everyone. For Milton is certainly not a textbook example of what the popular mind takes to be a Puritan. There is similarity between Milton and his Puritan forebears, to be sure; Haller demonstrated it, and earlier chapters of this book attempt to do so as well. But what of the discontinuity which is also present? Is this aspect of Milton's thought derived from humanistic sources and training?

[1] *Milton and the Puritan Dilemma*, p. 323.
[2] Paul N. Siegel, "Milton and the Humanistic Attitude Toward Women," *Journal of the History of Ideas*, XI (1950), 42-53.
[3] In "The Puritan Art of Love."

The assumption must be challenged that there is an element in Milton's thought on marriage which is radically anti-Puritan. It is this assumption which underlies attempts to make of Milton *either* Puritan *or* humanist, with no middle ground. This assumption obscures the strong influence of humanism on the English Reformation and covers over the fact of the classical education, stressing Greek and Latin, offered Cambridge Puritans as well as Oxford High Churchmen. Though there are elements in Milton's marriage doctrine which can rightly be called humanistic, this should not detract from the essential Puritanism of the divorce tracts. The concept of man as a free moral being before God is a common theme of the Renaissance, but when Milton describes freedom in marriage, he carefully derives whatever liberty man has from the presence of charity in his heart. Human freedom comes from both nature and grace, working subtly together. This subtle mixture is also present throughout Milton's writings on marriage.

Still there is no denying Milton's opposition to the marriage doctrine of the orthodox Puritanism of his day. For most midcentury Puritans the key to a life of service and glorification of God was an all-encompassing discipline drawn from the Bible and administered both internally, by the conscience, and externally, by the church and the Christian state. In his divorce tracts Milton implicitly advocates overthrow of church discipline. He does not mount a frontal assault on discipline itself, but rather he undermines its import by exalting Christian liberty, flowing from charity, as the fundamental fact of life in Christ. The writers treated in Chapter III typically define marriage, then describe at length the duties which flow from the definition. Milton, however, defines marriage and then enters a discussion of the subject of charity and its implications for Christian life in wedlock. What he says about the institution of marriage and the goods toward which it aims is perfectly orthodox, but his rejection of the disciplined life as the Christian life goes counter to accepted Puritan doctrine at the time of the writing of the divorce tracts. It is at this point, the exaltation of freedom over discipline as more essentially Christian, that real divergence from midcentury Puritan orthodoxy occurs. It is also at this point that writers begin calling Milton "antinomian," "humanist," "libertarian," and worse.

Among the positions discussed in this book, those of William Gouge and the later Whatley stand most diametrically opposed to Milton's.

It must be admitted that their emphasis on discipline over freedom in the Christian life is much more characteristic of Puritanism in the 1640s than any position stressing charity. Gouge subordinates all aspects of marriage to categories of discipline, and if charity is maintained in some guise (mainly God's merciful forgiveness for breaches of discipline), free mutual self-giving is lost. Gouge sharply separates adherence to "godlie discipline" from the workings of charity. Delineating God's law in the manner of a biblical literalist, he presents duty as externally imposed law, not charity-inspired inward knowledge of God's will.[4]

To see men like Gouge and Whatley—both firm advocates of the carefully regulated life as alone Christian—as purely definitive of Puritanism is, however, not to appreciate the considerable diversity marking Puritan opinions prior to the Laudian repression. As was shown earlier, Thomas Gataker, contemporary with these two men, describes marriage as a free gift of the spouses to each other by God. The character of this relationship is seconded by the Christian couple, who freely give of themselves in love to each other. The duties of marriage (to which Gataker devotes an entire sermon) are guideposts to aid in channeling the spouses' free mutual self-giving.[5] This is a position not too far from Milton's.

The most fundamental statement of the balance among charity, discipline, and freedom (and one which Gataker follows closely) is that of William Perkins, writing just before the turn of the century. The idea of charity has a role in Puritan marriage doctrine at least from this time forward. But Perkins puts much weight on discipline as well. Thus it is possible to see both Gouge and Milton as deriving from Perkins, though they represent quite opposite positions on marriage and divorce, indeed holding mutually contradictory conceptions of the Christian life.

For Perkins charity is the link between God and man; it is how God manifests himself to man. To manifest charity the Christian acts in certain ways. These are largely set out in the Scriptures, but biblical law is not externally binding because charity causes it to be internally ratified. In general the Christian will follow scriptural discipline, which can be codified and administered externally but nevertheless is inspired in the heart. Thus Perkins stresses both charity and the disciplined life

---

[4] See pp. 110-12; see also Gouge, *Domesticall Duties, passim.*
[5] See pp. 94-100.

while maintaining that discipline proceeds from charity. The change that occurs as the seventeenth century advances is essentially a de-emphasizing of the role of charity in inspiring discipline. This change is virtually complete in Gouge's *Domesticall Duties,* and the resulting position becomes orthodoxy when Laud drives the Puritans toward conservatism. If godly discipline is set out in the Bible, the reasoning goes, man need only look there to find out how to please God. A biblical fundamentalism ensues which places the letter of the law over the charitable meaning of it.

In Perkins' conception only those with charity can act so as to please God, but they do so in carefully prescribed ways. The literalist position turns this around: if one can act in this carefully prescribed manner, he is pleasing to God and has charity. It is this latter position against which Milton's exaltation of charity stands out most sharply. In many ways his argument recalls that of Perkins' more liberal passages. Milton too insists that charity is prior to any action pleasing to God. He too insists that a reader with the eyes of charity can find in the Bible rules of conduct to aid in the ordering of life. But Milton also differs importantly from Perkins, notably in stressing the freedom that comes from charity in place of the disciplined life inspired by charity. To avoid the pitfalls of a literalistic legalism Milton detours far in the other direction, replacing the disciplined life with the free life of grace. In avoiding the one extreme he takes the other, and so he, like the literalist disciplinarians, diverges from the carefully balanced position of Perkins on charity and duty.[6]

Milton never completely discounts law for the Christian life, but in the place of a "godlie discipline" he places the freedom of a Chistian man. God's gift of charity and man's response to that gift in freedom—these are twin themes around which Milton's arguments in the divorce tracts center.[7]

[6] For a fuller discussion of Perkins see pp. 65-86. See also the following works by Perkins for treatment of the themes of charity, law, and freedom: *An Exposition upon . . . the Epistle to the Galatians,* in *Workes,* II, 356-57, 372; *A Treatise of Christian Equitie and Moderation, ibid.,* pp. 502-20; *An Exposition of Christs Sermon in the Mount, ibid.,* III, 1, 33-37.

[7] Charity and freedom do not occupy a ruling position in Milton's writings from the first. Barker writes: "It is not uncharitable, and it is certainly instructive, to consider what view would probably have been taken of such a situation as his own bad marriage by the author of *Comus, Lycidas,* and the anti-episcopal tracts, if it had been hypothetically

Charity, the Root of Law

Discipline can be understood in two ways, according to whether it is imposed internally or externally. In Puritan thought self-discipline is the result of charity, which points to duties and also provides the strength to do them. External discipline is imposed and administered by the church with the minister and elders at its head. In Perkins' writings conceptions of internal and external discipline exist side by side. For Gouge the latter is primary, with charity-inspired self-discipline deemphasized. Milton's position in the divorce tracts is that in grave matters of conscience minister and elders may admonish but nothing more. Final responsibility rests with the individual believer, who decides what he must do on the basis of the charity he has.[8] This self-discipline is for Milton the manifestation at once of liberty and adherence to law, though the law is internal. Charity is the root of law.

Milton's objective in the divorce tracts is not the negative one of casting out discipline from Christian life; it is the positive one of providing room for charity to work to restore the righteous who have sinned. And charity can, in fact, work through law. The Mosaic law is a vehicle for charity, Milton argues; may Christian laws be less? Even after Christ mankind is characterized by sin; this is the fact that has to be reckoned with.

What is more or lesse perfect we dispute not, but what is sinne or no sinne; and in that I affirm the Law requir'd as perfect obedience as the Gospell: besides that the prime end of the Gospel is not so much to exact our obedience, as to reveal grace and the satisfaction of our disobedience. What is now

---

proposed to him in 1641. He might have offered such charitable observations on human frailty and the incapacity of innocence to defend itself at all points against the world as now occur in the divorce pamphlets. But he would certainly have added, I think, that such an experience must be the consequence of a mind insufficiently guided, restrained, and protected by virtue, and that the reformed church could provide the spiritual discipline by which alone such mistakes could be prevented. . . . The weight of emphasis in the divorce argument by no means falls on such ideas. The burden of that argument is not the prevention of mistakes through discipline but the freedom of divorce necessary if the unhappy consequences are to be avoided; and the argument is supported, not by the citation of inflexible decrees of divine authority . . . but by an insistence on the infinite mercy of divine charity and a defence of the legitimate (if frail) inclinations of human nature." (*Milton and the Puritan Dilemma*, pp. 65-66.)

[8] *Doctrine and Discipline*, p. 353.

exacted from us, it is the accusing Law that does it ev'n yet under the Gospell; but cannot bee more extreme to us now, than to the Jewes of old: for the Law ever was of works, and the Gospell ever was of grace. . . . If the Gospel require perfecter obedience than the Law as a duty, it exalts the Law and debases it self, which is dishonourable to the work of our Redemption. Seeing therefore that the cause of any allowance that the Jews might have, remain as well to the Christians, this is a certain rule, that so long as the causes remain the allowance ought.[9]

That is, since man is still as much a sinner as ever, he still needs the allowance of divorce; moreover, since God's grace ought to be manifest by all Christians, charity demands divorce. These two points are at the heart of Milton's argument for divorce, and the role of charity is thus seen to be that of a sinner's last resort, a declaration of the mercy of God. A rule of life for perfect people is the last thing charity is; rather it is in fact the most conscientious followers of the legalistic path to righteousness who stand most in need of charity.

Though charity is the underpinning of Milton's entire divorce argument, it is frequently linked with the notion of law. The position within Christian theology which Milton sees as most antithetical to his own is that one which sets up charity as a more perfect law. As the selections quoted above show, Milton will have no part of this doctrine.

Central to his opponents' position is their interpretation of Christ's words to the Pharisees in Matthew 5. This section of the Sermon on the Mount the conservative Puritans take to support their revocation of the Mosaic permission to divorce. To this line of reasoning Milton in one place responds with three observations:

First, that this saying of Christ, as it is usually expounded, can be no law at all, that a man for no cause should separate for adultery, except it be a supernatural law, not binding us, as wee now are. . . . Secondly, this can be no new command, for the Gospel enjoyns no new morality, save only the infinit enlargement of charity, which in this respect is call'd the new Commandment by St. John; as being the accomplishment of every command. Thirdly, it is no command of perfection further than it partakes of charity, which is the bond of perfection.[10]

[9] *Ibid.*, pp. 304-6.
[10] *Ibid.*, pp. 330-31.

Milton's first point arises from his conviction that Christian man is not perfect man. The Augustinian strain in his theology and in Puritan theology in general continues to assert that sin remains even in believers, that sainthood is a state of dependency on God rather than straight-forward ability to do good things. Thus "as wee now are" a law forbidding divorce cannot bind. Milton is willing to admit that it might be "a supernatural law," but such laws have no place among men, for even in Christians sinful nature is still mixed with the supernatural. And although Milton will grant for the sake of argument that there might be a kind of supernatural law contained in Christ's words, he nowhere returns to the theme of supernature and its laws. He is not here concerned with the Thomistic distinction between nature and supernature, between "precepts of morality" and "counsels of perfection." The immediate foe is a misrepresentation within Protestantism, within Puritanism, which has made of grace a law, of discipline an iron rule enslaving those who would be faithful.

Milton is not actually against law; he is rather for charity and the law which proceeds from it. He argues here that the Mosaic law contains the charitable command (not just the grudging permission) to divorce for incompatibility, and that Christian law should certainly allow charity no less room to work. If the Jews were sinners, so are Christians; the difference is not one of perfection but of knowledge of grace. Charity is no new level of perfection for Christians alone; it is God's healing and forgiving mercy to all sinners.

The notion of sinfulness must be rightly understood. Milton is most concerned with the plight of those who are conscientious in fulfilling their Christian duties in marriage but who through some inavoidable "error" are caught in a trap of incompatibility. He argues that even the act of adultery does not so readily break the marriage bond as does habitual coldness and incompatibility. The sin that charity heals and forgives, then, is not this or that act or many acts taken separately; it is a habitual state of rebellion against God. For Milton's purposes in the divorce tracts sin is first the penchant for doing evil to the self and to others by failing to follow God's providential will, which aims at man's good. This means in particular that two persons may decide to get married even though they are not meet helps for each other. And

159

second, sin is the inability to continue in charity which even the most righteous experience when bonded to an incompatible mate. In this case charity itself provides the remedy: "Charity commands that the beleever be not wearied out with endles waiting under many grievances sore to his spirit, but that respect be had . . . to the present suffering of a true Christian." [11]

"As wee now are," then, we cannot be bound by Christ's supposed prohibition of divorce, even if it be a supernatural law. Man is just not capable of such perfection. Milton's first point against the conservative interpreters of Matthew 5 is thus to dispose of the idea of perfect men and the law given for them.

The second point is that the coming of Christ is for "the infinit enlargement of charity." Milton does not speak of the *introduction* of charity, and this is significant. In the first point he sets himself against those who would make charity a new law more stringent than the old; in the second he shifts his attack slightly to answer those who argue that charity is in fact a new morality discontinuous with the old. To deny that charity was in God's law from the beginning is to make God inconsistent, Milton argues. Charity is God's will for sinful man, not some high perfection which can be codified for the benefit of pseudo-Christian Manichees or Catharists.[12]

God's will is in essence charitable. It is not the case that a law without charity was given to the Jews while a new law with charity added has been given to the Christians. For Milton the original institution of marriage was a charitable act, when God saw the loneliness of man and gave him a meet help for his good. Divorce was originally allowed as a charitable act after the Fall, when God gave his law through Moses to bind up the self-inflicted wounds of a sinful humankind. Thus the argument Milton advances for divorce is no new argument, as he sees it; it is rather a conclusion drawn from the history of God's actions with his people. This history reveals charity at work in all of it, working in God's providential dealings with his people.

If it be affirm'd that God as being Lord may doe what he will; yet we must know that God hath not two wills, but one will, much lesse two con-

---

[11] *Ibid.*, p. 267.
[12] Cf. Perkins, *Sermon in the Mount,* in *Workes,* III, 35 (on Matt. 5:18).

trary. If he once will'd adultery should be sinfull, and to be punish't by death, all his omnipotence will not allow him to will the allowance that his holiest people might as it were by his own Antinomie, or counter-statute live unreprov'd in the same fact, as he himself esteem'd it, according to our common explainers. The hidden wayes of his providence we adore & search not; but the law is his reveled will, his complete, his evident, and certain will; herein he appears to us as it were in human shape, enters into cov'nant with us, swears to keep it, binds himself like a just lawgiver to his own prescriptions, gives himself to be understood by men, judges and is judg'd, measures and is commensurat to right reason; cannot require lesse of us in one cantle of his law then in another, his legall justice cannot be so fickle and so variable, sometimes like a devouring fire, and by and by connivent in the embers, or, if I may so say, oscitant and supine.[13]

Or as Milton makes the point in another place, "As without charity God hath giv'n no commandment to men, so without it, neither can men rightly beleeve any commandment giv'n. For every act of true faith, as well that wherby we beleeve the law, as that wherby we endeavor the law is wrought in us charity." [14]

It is to the enlargement of charity that Christians are called, following God's will made known most lately in Christ. The fulfillment of the law is the theme Milton assigns most usually to the work of Christ, and he sees this as the increase of mercy in God's dealings with his people. The law itself is charitable because it reveals God's will, and the fact that it is God's will is in no way abrogated by the law's being "as it were in human shape." It is through the law that God makes his charitable will accessible to man's reason. As noted before, it is not law per se that Milton sets himself to oppose; he is no antinomian. Rather it is wrong law, law that obstructs the working of charity in the name of charity. Milton wants that law which will most allow the working of God's charity among men.

Charity is to be enlarged from a base in the charitable law of God to the Jews. This is one aspect of Milton's second point against his critics. The other aspect is that the enlargement of charity is to be accomplished by setting men free to follow their consciences. Full treatment of this theme of human freedom in its relation to God's charity will

[13] *Doctrine and Discipline,* p. 292.
[14] *Ibid.,* p. 340.

be deferred until later in this chapter. At this point it is simply noted that Milton's understanding of the mechanics of charity's working among men requires that God and man be left free. Milton's major objection against strict antidivorce laws is that they obstruct God's purposes for men. The corollary of this objection is the positive assertion that the best laws are those which leave God's grace as free as possible to act in men's consciences.

Remembering that we shall return later to a general consideration of the theme of human freedom and charity, we can now examine Milton's third point in commenting on the interpretations of Matthew 5. Jesus' statement to the Pharisees on divorce, Milton says, "is no command of perfection further than it partakes of charity, which is the bond of perfection." This point grows out of the second, even as the second grows out of the first, following good Ramist style. There are once again two aspects of Milton's statement, which complement each other and the rest of the argument. The first aspect is the obvious one: charity makes perfect, and the law is perfect only so far as it is charitable. But this is true only because, in the second place, charity is the "bond of perfection" in the human spirit connecting man with God. It is through charity that God has his dealings with men.[15] Charity is not grafted onto law; it is the substance of law (if we are speaking of God's law). It does not rule externally but makes itself known internally. Conscience is the province of charity, and reason is the tool which conscience uses to clarify the charity which inspires the law.

Expansion of these two aspects of Milton's third point will amplify our understanding of Milton's concept of the work of charity.

The law is perfect only insofar as it is charitable. But is this a meaningful statement? It might only be a tautology, such as "God is good," when goodness is defined by the idea of God. But Milton has something more enlightening in mind than a subtly disguised tautology. First of all he limits himself to speaking of God's law. This law, then, "is his reveled will, his complete, his evident, and certain will" by which God "measures and is commensurat to right reason." In the law, man can discern by his reason God's will for him. The law is in essence charitable since it is God's complete will. But this means that charity can be known by reason.

---

[15] Cf. Perkins, *Sermon in the Mount,* in *Workes,* III, 34.

This does not mean, however, that it is known as charity. Instead, God's charitable will for man is known by reason as what is good for man. God's will in creating Eve for Adam was to remedy his loneliness: "It is not good that the man should be alone." Everything God has done for man since he made him has been for his good, a good which is accessible to man through his reason. It is Milton's conviction that what is God's charitable will for man, namely to do that which is good for him, can be known by man through the operation of natural reason. But what is known, the object of reason, is simply the good for man. The Christian, so far as he has reason, knows no more than the natural man. Yet the Christian knows in addition, because of grace, that it is God, the author of charity, who wills that things should be thus.[16]

The laws of nature and charity coalesce because God is the author of both. One cannot approach Milton with the notion that the two are distinct from each other. When Milton writes "that the charitable Law must remedy what nature cannot undergoe," [17] he is not to be seen as setting the two in opposition. Rather it is God's charity which has made human nature what it is, and when this nature cannot "undergoe" something, it is because that something is against charity. The law of nature is the charitable law; the law which God gave to Moses was a dispensation of charity to aid fallen human nature to its good.

To push the above line of reasoning to its conclusion would be to argue that man can ultimately do nothing against his own good if he follows the dictates of his own nature. But Milton will not go so far; in fact, he does not place as much reliance on human nature as a guide as one might think from making a count of his uses of the word "nature." He seldom goes beyond "the first and most innocent lesson of nature," [18]

---

[16] Support for my interpretation on this matter is found in the chapter "Christian and Human Liberty" in Barker's *Milton and the Puritan Dilemma*, pp. 98-120. Barker writes (p. 113): "The eternal morality and equity underlying the Mosaic Law and made plain by the Spirit in the hearts of believers is, it appears, immediately related to the law of nature. The right of judgment Milton demands for the individual is thus both Christian and natural. It is a part of the liberty of the Gospel and is 'engraven in blameless nature.' In fact it is 'so clear in nature and reason' that divorce was left to conscience 'not only among the Jews but in every wise nation.' That 'God and the law of all nations' so leave it is abundantly demonstrated in 'that noble volume written by our learned Selden, *Of the Law of Nature and Nations.*' "

[17] *Doctrine and Discipline*, p. 307.

[18] *Tetrachordon*, p. 623.

which is to seek what is good for us and to avoid what does us harm. Man has, after all, fallen. A primary fact of his fallenness is that he does not cling to what is good for him. The Mosaic law is an external restraint on fallen man, therefore, though it aims at man's natural good.

The charity which is present in the law is God's attempt to deal with the fact of man's condition after the Fall. It is not something alien to the notion of law, nor is it alien to the nature of man. It is indeed the base of both law and nature.

There are of course laws which do not partake much of charity. Such laws are those of the "courts of concupiscence" about which we have already spoken. The divorce law does not partake of charity if it forces man to do something against his good, even if the forcing is done in the name of charity.

The perfection of law, then, lies in its aiming at man's good, for this is what charity means on the human level. "The great and almost only commandment of the Gospel, is to command nothing against the good of man, and much more no civil command, against his civil good." [19] So far as law is conformed to God's will, it aims at the good of man. And it is within the province of right reason to know what is good law and so measure any given law. It must now be explored how this is possible for fallen man.

In the section of *Tetrachordon* which treats Matt. 5:31-32, Milton takes up the assault begun in *Doctrine and Discipline of Divorce* against those who take Christ's words to be a "new precept." The law of Christ is not such, he insists.

If the law of Christ shall be writt'n in our hearts, as was promis'd to the Gospel, Jer. 31, how can this in the vulgar and superficiall sense be a law of Christ, so farre from beeing written in our hearts, that it injures and dis-allowes not only the free dictates of our nature and morall law, but of charity also and religion in our hearts. Our Saviours doctrine is, that the end, and the fulfilling of every command is charity; no faith without it, no worship, no works pleasing to God but as they partake of charity.[20]

It is in the heart of Christian man that charity makes itself known.

[19] *Ibid.*, p. 639.
[20] *Ibid.*, p. 637.

It is this charity in the heart that is the "bond of perfection" of which Milton speaks in *Doctrine and Discipline of Divorce*. And this is the doctrine with which he hopes to carry the day over his opponents. Milton refutes those who would have Christ's words give a "supernatural" law by pointing out that man the sinner is not himself supernatural; therefore such a law would not apply to him. Further, he answers those who make of Christ's words a new morality distinct from that of Moses by finding charity in the creation and in the dispensation from Sinai. In the passage quoted above he begins to give his own understanding of the meaning of Christ's words. Milton is not against law but against laws which deny charity room to work. And laws which do this are those laws which bind the heart (or, alternatively, the conscience), the place in which charity makes itself known and felt in Christian men.[21]

It is not law in itself which Milton opposes in the name of charity, but rather a specific kind of law, a supernatural perfectionism ostensibly drawn from the gospel. In fact Milton and his opponents share belief in the fundamental orderliness of the world, an orderliness expressed in terms of a God-given natural law. God governs the world in an orderly fashion by his providence, but his government is carried out by his self-imposed law of nature. Although they agree on this particular doctrine, Milton and his opponents differ widely in their respective understandings of it. To understand Milton's argument for divorce, then, it will be helpful to explore this idea of the orderliness of the world.

Precisely because the world is under the orderly rule of God, Milton

[21] "What was ever in all appearance lesse made for man, and more for God alone than the Sabbath? Yet when the good of man comes into the scales, we hear that voice of infinite goodness and benignity that Sabbath was made for man, not man for Sabbath. What thing ever was more made for man alone and lesse for God then mariage? And shall we load it with a cruel and senceles bondage utterly against both the good of man and the glory of God? Let who so will now listen, I want neither pall nor mitre, I stay neither for ordination, nor induction, but in the firm faith of a knowing Christian, which is the best and truest endowment of the keyes, I pronounce, the man who shall bind so cruelly a good and gracious ordinance of God, hath not in that the Spirit of Christ." (*Doctrine and Discipline*, pp. 282-83.)

What Milton states so forcefully here with "neither pall nor mitre" is reminiscent of Luther but more directly of Perkins. The position is not one the Presbyterians found attractive, but in Milton's time Puritans of the independent stamp were advocating freedom in various areas on such similar grounds and in such like language that there is no reason to go to classical notions of man to get the source for Milton's opinion.

argues, divorce ought to be allowed. In spite of sin God still rules, and his charity therefore is the law of the world to which all human laws ought to conform. This is all the more true for Christians, who of all people ought to be able to recognize God's charity as it comes into the world to work for man's good. Sin separates from charity, but there is a "residue" of the charity of creation which remains in man the natural being. In addition to this there is the charity of Moses' law and the charity of Christ. Man can benefit from charity either by using his "residue" of creation—reason—or by adhering to Moses' law, which charitably spells out what is good for man. But he does not recognize what his reason tells him is good and what the law holds up as good as the will of God for him until he receives the charity of Christ. The grace of Christ does not change man's good; it rather makes man aware that what he can naturally know to be his good is God's will for him. Milton's concept of the orderliness of the world is unique in that for him the providence governing the world is nothing other than charity, since God manifests himself through charity to man. This is a clear modification of the general Puritan notion of God's orderly rule of the world.

When Milton quotes from authorities generally revered within Puritanism, he finds support for his arguments, but without the heavy emphasis on charity he makes characteristic of his own position. In *The Judgement of Martin Bucer Concerning Divorce* the word charity is not used even once, though Milton delights in pointing out that Bucer is advancing the same argument as his own. Calvin, though he speaks of God's mercy in connection with his rule, does not stress the working of charity. Perhaps Milton takes this idea from Luther, whose doctrine of Christian freedom he seems at times to follow closely. Another possibility is Grotius' commentary on Matthew 5. Milton writes:

When I had almost finisht the first edition [of *The Doctrine and Discipline of Divorce*], I chanct to read in the notes of Hugo Grotius upon the 5. of Matth. whom I strait understood inclining to reasonable terms in this controversie: and something he whisper'd rather then disputed about the law of charity, and the true end of wedlock.[22]

A possibility not to be overlooked is, of course, the works of William Perkins.

[22] Milton, *The Judgement of Martin Bucer Concerning Divorce*, II, 434.

Wherever his idea of charity comes from, Milton stresses it from the very first in his writings on divorce. The first edition of *Doctrine and Discipline of Divorce* uses the word charity or its derivatives seventeen times; in later editions the number is insignificantly increased to twenty. More important is that from the first the concept of charity as God's ruling will in the world, aiming at man's good, is integral to Milton's argument. When he amplifies his argument in the later editions of *Doctrine and Discipline of Divorce* and in *Tetrachordon,* he builds upon a firm structure in charity. Charity underlies the whole of Milton's argument for divorce. It is, as he sees the matter, the reason for marriage in the first place, and it continues to rule after the Fall in marriages and in unions which should not be called marriages.

Charity is the essential characteristic of God's dealings with man, and thus it may be said without exaggeration that charity is Milton's doctrine of providence. It is charity working in the individual's conscience that causes him first to take a meet help as spouse. Only because of the Fall does charity not have full sway. But even after the Fall charity makes itself felt through nature. And the opposite is also true: where there is no mutually meet helpfulness, charity commands divorce, whether it be known as charity or not. This is the reason for Milton's parallel statements that charity commands divorce and that nature commands divorce. It is charity that first worked in creating the world; it is charity that now works to redeem it. And insofar as the world after the Fall and before redemption has any order, it is charity which provides that order. Thus Milton tells his readers that "Moses never thwarts, but reverences" the "fundamentall law book of nature" and continues:

And certainly these divine mediating words of finding out a meet and like help to man, have in them a consideration of more then the indefinite likenesse of womanhood; nor are they to be made waste paper on, for the dulnesse of Canon divinity: no nor those other allegorick precepts of beneficence fetcht out of the closet of nature to teach us goodnes and compassion in not compelling together unmatchable societies, or if they meet through mischance, by all consequences to dis-joyn them, as God and nature signifies and lectures to us not onely by those recited decrees, but ev'n by the first and last of all his visible works; when by his divorcing command

167

the world first rose out of Chaos, nor can be renew'd again out of confusion but by the separating of unmeet consorts.[23]

It is to the doctrine of creation that Milton again and again returns for the first principles of his argument. But creation is always interpreted through the doctrine of charity. It is in the creation that God and nature are inseparably joined; if there seems after the Fall to be a separation between them, that is the result of sin's distorted perspective. Because of the fact of sin Milton can speak alternatively, as his argument progresses, of charity commanding divorce and of nature commanding divorce; the fact that the two are used so often in parallel should not be missed. What Milton is in fact saying is that charity does not have to be known as such in order for law to embody its precepts. The general run of mankind can know the direction in which charity tends by right reason just because they are men, creatures of God. The lesson taught by nature and that of charity are one and the same. Milton's phrasing in the passage just quoted is significant: "God and nature signifies and lectures to us not onely by those recited decrees, but ev'n by the first and last of all his visible works." The verbs in the singular are not by accident, and the linking of God, nature, and creation strikingly brings home the point that it is God with whom man has to deal even after he thinks he has escaped from him by leaving Eden. It is because God's will and man's natural instincts concur and because both are expressions of God's charity that Milton can argue for the divorce of those "whom God and nature in the gentlest end of marriage never joyn'd" on the basis that to keep them together means that "the supreme dictate of charitie is hereby many wayes neglected and violated." [24]

Finally, Milton thinks that charity has not always been recognized as such in God's dealings with his creatures. Milton is clear that it is only through Christ that the law of Moses and the law of nature can be seen to be instruments of charity. It follows that it is most incumbent on the Christian, who recognizes God's dealings for what they are, to endeavor to have civil laws made which will not constrict the activity of charity. The law of Moses was known as an external constraint by the Jews, but it is not so to the Christian.

[23] *Doctrine and Discipline*, pp. 272-73.
[24] *Ibid.*, p. 250.

It is anough determin'd, that this Image of God wherin man was created, is meant Wisdom, Purity, Justice, and rule over all creatures. All which being lost in Adam, was recover'd with gain by the merits of Christ. For albeit our first parent had lordship over sea, and land, and aire, yet there was a law without him, as a guard set over him. But Christ having can-cell'd the hand writing of ordinances which was against us, Coloss. 2.14. and interpreted the fulfilling of all through charity, hath in that respect set us over law, in the free custody of his love, and left us victorious under the guidance of his living Spirit.[25]

Milton writes these words near the beginning of his comments on Gen. 1:27 and 2:18, 23-24. And so far as he is concerned, he avers, all that is really necessary is to look at the institution of marriage in creation from the point of view of one who has benefited from Christ. He goes on only because he wants to answer any opposition in advance:

Thus wee have seen, and if wee be not contentious, may know what was Mariage in the beginning, to which in the Gospel wee are referr'd. And what from hence to judge of nullity, or divorce. Heer I esteem the work don; in this field the controversie decided; but because other places of Scripture seem to look aversly upon this our decision, although indeed they all keep harmony with it, and because it is a better work to reconcile the seeming diversities of Scripture, then the reall dissentions of neerest friends, I shall assay . . . to perform that office.[26]

In the preceding chapter it was shown that Milton's understanding of marriage and the position on divorce which grows out of it come from his interpretation of the institution of marriage as God's gift of Eve to be a meet help to Adam and a remedy for his loneliness. There it was demonstrated that Milton draws out the implications of the critical passage, Gen. 2:18, by asserting that man and wife must be mutual meet helps since Adam was perfect for Eve even as she was for him. Further, on the basis of this doctrine divorce is to be allowed for incompatibles since no marriage can be said to be a true marriage, that is, conformable to the will of God in the institution of marriage, if there is no mutual meet helpfulness. Milton's position has now been explored more fully

[25] *Tetrachordon,* pp. 587-88.
[26] *Ibid.,* p. 614.

by considering the role of charity in his thought. It is charity which makes it possible for Milton to make the claims he does. His entire argument in the divorce tracts becomes an assertion that God is working in the world in spite of Man's sin and that Christians should promote laws that will not oppose his redeeming activity.

What is most notably missing thus far is an insistence on the transforming work of charity in the will of the individual Christian. So far this discussion of charity has focused on God's work in the world at large, among men in general. Does not Milton see what many of his opponents see, that charity can transform a Christian so that he is capable of new things those without charity cannot do?

Milton in fact does argue that charity works the will of God in the Christian. "Every act of true faith, as well that wherby wee believe the law, as that wherby wee endeavour the law is wrought in us by charity," he writes.[27] But Milton's understanding of how charity works is quite different from what other Puritans in his day were saying. It has been shown that according to Milton there can and ought to be structures of law which are in accord with the working of charity. Now it must be added that these structures are those which promote the greatest freedom of conscience in the individual, and especially in the Christian, who is the only man capable of being truly free. The difference between Milton and his opponents is in how they conceive of charity as working in the individual. Those advocating a strict position on divorce could conceive of charity as working only to enable man to fulfill a perfectionist law. Milton does not deny that charity works for good in the saints, but he maintains that it does so by setting them free, by making them each a law to himself. Charity cannot be bound by humanly imposed laws; man's laws must leave charity free to work. And what this actually means is that laws must allow free decision in matters of conscience. Milton sees the advocates of discipline as trying to second-guess God, as trying to legislate for him—not only in his name, as deputies, but as lawgivers to the Almighty—and therefore he accuses them of trying to be "holier & more circumspect then God."[28] The alternative to setting up laws which will hinder the work of charity is to make laws which will allow charity

[27] *Doctrine and Discipline*, p. 340.
[28] *Tetrachordon*, p. 667.

free rein in the individual conscience. Charity requires a high level of individual liberty. This is what law should ensure.

Christian and Human Liberty

A. Liberty in Law. Arthur Barker writes:

With Luther's commentary on Galatians and his letter *Concerning Christian Liberty,* Calvin's chapter on the doctrine in the *Institutes* provided the source for orthodox opinion. Theologically the two treatments differ very little, though it is possible to distinguish between the effects on English Puritanism of Luther's mystical enthusiasm and Calvin's legalistic logic. The *Institutes* fixes the meaning of the doctrine with exactness. Christian liberty consists of three parts: (1) "The consciences of the faithful, when the assurance of their justification before God is to be sought, may raise and advance themselves above the Law, and forget the whole righteousness of the Law." . . . (2) Christian consciences "obey the Law, not as compelled by the necessity of the Law, but being free from the yoke of the Law itself, of their own accord they obey the will of God." . . . (3) "We be bound with no conscience before God of outward things which are by themselves indifferent, but that we may indifferently sometime use them and sometime leave them unused." All things concerning which there is no gospel prohibition are sanctified to the Christian's use.[29]

Barker continues by pointing out that it is this orthodox opinion among Puritans on which Milton builds, his most significant alteration of the orthodox interpretation being his treatment of the third type of liberty. With regard to divorce, it is a thing indifferent, neither specifically prohibited nor specifically commanded by the gospel; it is rather entirely in the domain of the conscience. But going beyond the narrow matter of marriage and divorce, Barker asserts that "the consequence of Milton's handling [of the received doctrine] is the assertion of personal liberty not only in the indifferent matter of divorce but from all external authority." [30] Thus Barker sees Milton's roots as nourished by orthodoxy, though the branches and foliage of his position are heresy to the Presbyterians.

[29] Barker, *Milton and the Puritan Dilemma,* pp. 100-101.
[30] *Ibid.,* p. 105.

This is the essence of Milton's doctrine of Christian liberty. It at once maintains true freedom and denounces license. The weight of emphasis fell either on the first or on the second of these consequences according to circumstances; but from the divorce tracts to the final pamphlets both were implicit in his doctrine at every point. The difference between his interpretation and the orthodox did not lie in any breaking down of the force of moral law which binds man, but in his description of its manifestation in the personalities of regenerate men. For those who are not regenerate, the works of the moral law, whether revealed by Moses or nature, are "matters of compulsion"; the regenerate "bring forth good works spontaneously and freely," under faith and through the Spirit.[31]

But Barker accuses Milton of antinomianism, arguing, "Since neither the law of God nor one's neighbor can be forced, laws must not be imposed either on the regenerate or the unregenerate to compel them to act in conformity with the scriptural letter."[32] We have already disputed such a position in regard to the general working of charity among men, and we shall have occasion to do the same below in reference to charity in the individual conscience. Milton is not an antinomian; he rather would restructure law so as to allow charity its fullest reign.

Barker's interpretation of Milton's doctrine of Christian freedom is based on his reading of the whole Milton corpus, from the divorce tracts and *Areopagitica* to *De Doctrina Christiana*. Thus his conclusions must be taken with this in mind. Our task here cannot be so large; this discussion will be confined to the concepts of liberty in the divorce tracts and their relation to the controlling concept of charity.

Milton certainly does not see himself as an antinomian when he writes the divorce tracts. The first of these deals with "the doctrine and *discipline* of divorce," as readers are informed from the title. And we have noted that even though the Christian life is conceived ideally as one of the free spirit moving in the light of charity, Milton nevertheless has room for discipline in his understanding of Christianity. Mainly he is pessimistic about its leading to sanctity, since he eschews even the Puritan form of works-righteousness, that is, not so much a doing of good works as the avoidance of bad. Further, as is shown in the above dis-

[31] *Ibid.*, pp. 320-21; cf. Arthur Barker, "Christian Liberty in Milton's Divorce Pamphlets," *Modern Language Review*, XXXV (1940), 155-56.
[32] Barker, *Milton and the Puritan Dilemma*, p. 323.

cussion of charity, law occupies Milton's mind in various ways. Thus, far from being an antinomian, Milton hopes to fill out the content of the meaning of Christ as the fulfillment of the law.

In true Ramist fashion Milton lists the causes of marriage, which must all be present:

First therefore the material cause of matrimony is man and woman; the Author and efficient, God and their consent, the internal Form and the soul of this relation, is conjugal love arising from a mutual fitnes to the final causes of wedlock, help and society in Religious, Civil and Domestic conversation, which includes as an inferior end the fulfilling of natural desire, and specific increase.[33]

[33] *Tetrachordon,* p. 608. Milton's dependence on Ramism is pervasive throughout the divorce tracts. It is especially striking, however, in the definition of marriage in *Tetrachordon.* The passage quoted above serves as an introduction to a lengthy discussion of definitions of marriage, in which Milton discards those given by Paraeus, Ames, Hemingius, and Justinian for some lack or some disordering of the four causes. At last he gives his own definition: "Marriage is a divine institution joining man and woman in a love fitly dispos'd to the helps and comforts of domestic life" (p. 612). Following this Milton discusses the parts of his definition, drawing attention to the presence of the four causes in proper Ramist order: efficient, material, formal, final. After a section on the implications of these causes in this order, he concludes, "Heer I esteem the work don" (p. 614). That is, if the definition given, since it is a proper one, is understood in all its implications, there is no need to argue further. The conclusion is implicit in the beginning.

One of the most important conclusions which follow from this definition of marriage is the reversal of the ends of marriage from the order given in the Prayer Book. If Milton's definition and method are accepted, it is impossible to treat the marriage ends other than he does. Since he gives a Ramist definition and uses Ramist method, the list of the ends of marriage is a Ramist list. Ramist method is to put the most important, by which is meant the most comprehensive or general, first, following it by the next most important, and so on until all implications are exhausted. In the case of human marriage the most important characteristic is that of community. This differs sharply from the Aristotelian Anglicans and Catholics who, following Thomas Aquinas, set forth a definition of marriage based on its generic and specific nature. Generically, that is, considered as something common to all animals, the union of male and female is directed to offspring; this is thus the first end of marriage for this tradition. Specifically, that is, considered only as concerning the species man, the marital union is directed toward community; this end is for Thomas and his tradition always secondary (*Supp.,* Q. 65, A. 1; see also Q. 41, A. 1, A. 2). The difference with Ramist Puritans and with Milton in particular is partly one of logic and partly one of judgment. Logically, the Ramists are notably unconcerned with definition by *genus,* excising it by means of Occam's razor. With this accomplished for marriage, the most general characteristic becomes what was for Aristotle second, its peculiarly *human* end, community. The results of this logical move precisely coincide with the purely *judgmental* decision by Puritan marriage theorists to weigh the donation of Eve to Adam for companionship more highly than the injunction, a few verses earlier in the text, to be fruitful and multiply. Procreation, no longer treated first as generically

This listing is significant here because it illustrates how God and man cooperate to effect marriage within the structures imposed by the other causes. The consent is free, and yet it is bounded by law (the other causes). Man and woman consent freely, but God somehow is the author of their covenant together.

Earlier Milton has argued, "For ev'n the freedom and eminence of mans creation give him to be a Law in this matter to himself." [34] Again, commenting on Paul, he asks, "And how adds it to the word of the Lord (for this also they [Milton's opponents] object) when as the Apostle by his christian prudence guids us in the liberty which God hath left us to, without command?" [35]

In all these cases Milton's tendency seems to be away from law and toward freedom. The question we shall have to answer is whether this freedom is lawless or, if it is not, what character of law it possesses. The phrase "a law to himself" has different implications depending on whether the emphasis is placed on "a law" or on "to himself." And since the Fall it is further necessary to examine the changes made necessary by man's being other than his created essence because of sin. "The Gospel indeed tending ever to that which is perfetest, aim'd at the restorement of all things, as they were in the beginning." But "the rule of perfection is not so much that which was don in the beginning, as that which now is nearest to the rule of charity. This is the greatest, the perfetest, the highest commandment." [36]

---

good, must now be reinstated as a specific good, one somehow implicit in the good of community. To put procreation first is, in Milton's words, to make "the minde of man wait upon the slavish errands of the body." Putting mutual helpful society first sets matters right. God gave Eve to Adam as a meet help to remedy his loneliness; it is in an act of mutual meet help that they conceive children. Put another way, the divine command to multiply must logically follow the divine gift of woman to man. It is no accident that the element of mutuality is present in all the four causes of marriage in the passage from p. 608 quoted above, nor that the other ends of marriage, "the fulfilling of natural desire, and specific increase," come up only as *included* in the final cause, "help and society in Religious, Civil and Domestic conversation."

Much more could be said about the significance of Ramism for Milton's thought on marriage, but there is no space here to do so. The most complete study of Milton's Ramism is Franklin Irwin's "Ramistic Logic in Milton's Prose Works" (Ph.D. diss., Princeton University, 1941), but the subject is also treated in Wilbur S. Howell's *Logic and Rhetoric in England. 1500-1700* (Princeton: Princeton University Press, 1956), pp. 146-47. See also the appendix on Ramism at the end of this volume.

[34] *Doctrine and Discipline,* p. 347.
[35] *Tetrachordon,* p. 684.
[36] *Ibid.,* pp. 665, 667.

The problem is not one of a simple dichotomy or even of two simple dichotomies. There is always a duality within any given act of man, a duality which reflects his existence as a fallen creature—but still a creature—of God and as a recipient of grace at the same time. And within Milton's statement of the doctrine of Christian liberty there is also a duality which comes from his unwillingness to surrender the external character of law while at the same time asserting its inwardness, both as natural inclination and as charity through Christ. Speaking perhaps overly simply, there is in Milton's doctrine an uneasy and perhaps unstable alternation between the classical Lutheran and Calvinist versions of human liberty under Christ.

Milton's own position on the relation of God and man to any act of man's is stated above (p. 161): "Every act of truth faith, as well that wherby wee beleeve the law, as that wherby wee endeavour the law is wrought in us by charity." So far as faith is concerned, so far as any act is one of charity, God is the author of it. But this is not such a clear statement of man's impotence as it seems. Significantly Milton links God and man together as the efficient cause of matrimony: "the Author and efficient, God and their [the man's and woman's] consent." Even when an act of charity is in question, man and God do it together. The cliché that the Reformation denigrates man in order to exalt God is tempting but untrue, at least for the Puritans, who assert over and over that man can oppose God's grace as it tries to work in his life. There is maintained a tension between the omnipotent God who decrees for eternity but remains inscrutable in essence and the God who reveals himself to man as the God of mercy who would win sinners to himself.

B. Liberty and Law in Covenant Relationships. God and man act together. This is expressed most consistently in the notion that God has entered into covenant with man, binding himself no less than man to follow certain rules. And as Milton tirelessly reminds his readers, this covenant and its rules are for the good of man. All covenants between man and man derive from this primal one and ought to be like it; they ought to aim at the end it tends toward, the good of man. If any given covenant does not do this, it is in fact no covenant, and its terms not binding: "Indeed no ordinance human or from heav'n can binde against the good of man." [37]

Freedom of conscience enters into marriage in the first place because of this general condition placed on all covenants. Because of the stipulation that there is no binding power in covenants made against man's good, it is possible that even what appears to be mutual consenting in marriage is not that at all. Moreover, marriages arranged by family or friends without the consent of the spouses are likewise void. But the above condition is only a general rule that applies to all covenants between man and man. When a covenant is made in which God is one of the partners, the binding power is a different sort. So far as true marriage is concerned, God is always present in the covenant between the spouses since the institution is God's own for man's good. Thus marriage is of a category in some way different from that of human covenants or agreements over property lines, water rights, or whatever. Because marriage is an institution of God, because he is at work both in man's nature and through active charity to ensure man's good in it, true marriages are between those "whom God hath joyn'd together." Yet his joining is not external; it works in their consciences so that when the spouses covenant together to be meet helps they really mean it. It is they who covenant, yet it is God who gives them the power to do so.

This position differs from the sacramental theory of marriage in that the action of God is relocated. For Milton, God works not primarily through the first moment of consent to the bond of marriage; he works prior to the parties' consent to marry and continues throughout their lifetimes to enable them perpetually to renew their bond.[38]

The general condition placed on all covenants is that they do not bind against the good of those covenanting. This is known through nature and also through the analogy with God's covenant with man.

[37] *Ibid.*, p. 588.

[38] See the discussion of the Thomist doctrine of marriage in Chap. I. Milton opposes not only the sacramentalist understanding of marriage but also that of the orthodox Puritans who maintained that marriage is everlasting by nature because it is "the covenant of God." *True* marriages are everlasting, but no union of a man and a woman can be known by an external observer to be a true marriage. Marriages are everlasting when both partners freely love each other as inspired by charity, but not all unions are so fortunate. Calling unions not inspired by charity "marriages" or "covenants of God" does not make them binding forever. (Cf. pp. 128-32 above.)

In marriage both apply; marriage is ordained by God in creation and brought about by natural inclination, while at the same time God has made laws regarding it in his agreements with his people. This requires, on both levels, that man and wife must individually and mutually covenant for the good of both; otherwise there is no marriage.

In addition to the general condition covering marriage as covenant there is a specific condition growing out of the "indifference" of divorce as a moral problem. This is the third of Calvin's kinds of freedom, freedom of choice concerning things indifferent to salvation. Milton states his position this way: "But divorce being in it selfe no unjust or evill thing, but only as it is joyn'd with injury, or lust, injury it cannot be at law, if consent be." [39] Specifically in the case of divorce the choices to be made are those of the supposed husband and wife only; God does not enter in, and the matter is not one in which salvation is at stake. God's presence has been lacking in this union from the first, for he has no part in covenants which bring two incompatibles together. This means that in the case of a marriage which has ended in divorce the mutual agreement entered into by the spouses to get married is precisely analogous to an agreement over property lines or any other agreement at law presided over by the civil courts. It is for this reason that Milton is happy to find Bucer arguing that "matrimony and divorce are civil things." [40] Milton himself places the matter of marriage and divorce in the hands of the magistrate and the civil law,[41] whose function it is to see that conditions of divorce be equitable and that there truly be mutual consent to divorce. "Which way soever we look the Law can to no rational purpose forbid divorce, it can only take care that the conditions of divorce be not injurious. Thus we see the triall of law how impertinent it is to this question of divorce, how helplesse next, and then how hurtfull." [42] What is neither impertinent, helpless, nor hurtful is the question of conscience.[43]

[39] *Tetrachordon*, p. 646.
[40] *The Judgement of Martin Bucer*, p. 456.
[41] *Doctrine and Discipline*, p. 343.
[42] *Ibid.*, p. 350.
[43] Lowell W. Coolidge writes in a note to Chap. XIII of *Doctrine and Discipline*: "Cf. William Ames, *The Marrow of Sacred Divinity* (1638; HEHL), p. 323: 'Neither doth this marriage perpetually depend upon the will only and covenant of the persons contracting: for then by consent of both parts, a covenant so begun may be unloosed again, as it useth to be between master and servant: but the rule and bond of this covenant is the institution

Even though God made marriage, he did not institute it in such a way as to impose on Adam's free will nor on that of his descendants. Instead the picture is of Adam's recognizing what is good for him and calling Eve therefore "bone of my bones, and flesh of my flesh." Thus Adam initiates the covenant with his wife. In the same manner Christ does not impose any new requirements on man which violate man's natural duty to do that which is good for him. Milton sees strict anti-divorce laws as doing precisely what God does not, however, and therefore he calls them no laws. It is in this sense that he is the antinomian Barker would make of him: he is against laws which tend to make man do what is against his natural good. But he is not against law in general; it is in fact through law that God furnishes the occasion for man to exercise his free choice, to covenant freely.

The way Calvin divides the uses of the law is apparent in Milton's treatment of law and Christian freedom. The third use of the law is here the appropriate one. Calvin's and Milton's treatments might have been written by a single hand. The following is Calvin's statement of the third use:

The third use of the Law (being also the principal use, and most closely connected with its proper end) has respect to believers in whose hearts the spirit of God already flourishes and reigns. For although the Law is written and engraven on their hearts by the finger of God, that is, although they are so influenced and actuated by the Spirit, that they desire to obey God, there are two ways in which they will still profit in the Law. For it is the best instrument for enabling them daily to learn with greater truth and certainty what that will of the Lord is which they aspire to follow, . . . and to confirm them in this knowledge. . . . The servant of God will derive this further advantage from the Law: by frequently meditating upon it,

---

of God, whence also it is in the Scriptures sometimes called the covenant of God. Prov. 2.17.' " (*Doctrine and Discipline*, p. 275, n. 1.)

The editor here calls attention to something Milton often denies, that the marriage covenant is a special sort of covenant unlike those of business and such relations as that of master and servant. I have discovered no one among the Puritan writers consulted who agrees with Milton on this. Not only Ames, but also Perkins, Dod, Cleaver, and others of less influence all say that the marriage covenant is with God as well as with the marriage partner. It is not the covenant with the partner that is binding for these writers; it is the covenant each partner makes with God at the same time they covenant with each other. Milton's departure from the tradition is striking; the logic of his position, however, forces him to deal thus with this matter.

he will be excited to obedience, and confirmed in it, and so drawn away from the slippery paths of sin.[44]

To understand Milton's insistence on retaining—or rather restoring —the Mosaic law on divorce in Christian society it is necessary to see that he regards its primary purpose as being a guide to Christians, not a restraint to sinners. It directs Christians toward God's will for them, that they should live in peace. The restraint of sin is accomplished in a roundabout fashion. In the first place Milton does not think that the unregenerate are going to be restrained in any meaningful way; this is behind his poignant picture of the righteous man who falls into a bad marriage through ignorance while a playboy happens into a happy marriage through experience gained in many affairs, "which are as so many divorces." His real concern is that the law should not drive the righteous into sin; he wants no law that will violate conscience by requiring a badly married person to search for companionship outside wedlock. Thus the kind of law he wishes to have on the books of England is to be permissive in its externals so that the consciences of Christians can stay free of conditions of sin.

It is significant that Milton makes this point in a chapter which is directed against "Familisme, Antinomianisme, &c." His immediate opponent is excessive literalism in the interpretation of scripture. He fears

lest the soul of a Christian which is inestimable, should be over-tempted and cast away, considering also that many properties of nature, which the power of regeneration it self never alters, may cause dislike of conversing even between the most sanctify'd, which continually grating in harsh tune together may breed some jarre and discord, and that end in rancor and strife.[45]

So what Milton is trying to avoid, as we have seen repeatedly, is that kind of law which, far from restraining sin, actually promotes sin among even the most righteous. Law itself he does not find to be evil.

If this be so, what is it in Milton's doctrine that causes Barker to apply the name antinomian to him? In the first place, Milton would put to the

[44] John Calvin, *Institutes of the Christian Religion* trans. Henry Beveridge, I (Grand Rapids: Eerdmans Publishing Co., 1957), 309.

[45] *Doctrine and Discipline*, pp. 279-80.

decision of conscience a matter which had been governed by law: divorce. However, Milton would still have there be a law, though a permissive one. The fact that he sees the permission to divorce by mutual consent as taking the form of law is indicated by his insistence that it is a command for such to divorce as cannot be meet helps to each other.

Second, and the heart of Barker's position, is Milton's making what begins as a matter of conscience to Christians a permission to all, re-generate and unregenerate alike. Here we return to the distinction be-tween Calvin's second and third uses of the law. Since those who have charity are bound only by it, no external law can bind them unless it be in accord with charity. Thus the kind of divorce law Milton wants obviously would be for the good of the regenerate, since they might slip into an incompatible marriage, no matter how "sanctify'd" they might be. But such a law would govern the rest of the citizenry as well, and the choice Milton makes is not to set up a strict divorce law so as to restrain their sin.

The first reason for Milton's choosing thus is that he sees the gospel as aimed at the good of the saints, not the restraint of the wicked. But underlying this is a presupposition shared throughout Calvinism that only God and perhaps the elect individual know of the individual's election. Law should not be set up on the basis of who can be imagined by others to be a saint. God has his own way of dealing with the wicked. The sin of the wicked and the sanctity of the elect, furthermore, are not primarily matters of what they do or do not do in this life. Thus a law which aims at the restraint of a few "sins" while causing the righteous to stumble is a bad law.

The second reason for this choice is the more profound. Not only does it illuminate Milton's attitude toward law; it also shows how such a law as he desires can apply to the good of both sorts of men. This reason is that by leaving the matter of divorce to the consciences of those involved, God's providence (charity) will have opportunity to work in all the ways proper to it: nature, law, gospel.

Critical Recapitulation

The structures of human liberty are analogous to those of charity. Charity is God's essential character as he works in the world and especially with men. It is present as the basis of creation, and it remains after the Fall implanted in human nature. It is God's charity which is made known verbally in the Mosaic law, and this law in no wise contradicts the natural impulses still in fallen man as a residue of creation, even though the law stands in some way over against man and is felt by him as an external compulsion. The work of Christ was not to introduce a new law, for that would have been to make God the author of evil for not having introduced it before. Christ, rather, fulfills the old law. What this means for Milton is that through charity now, after Christ, the gulf between God's law poorly known in nature and God's law fully known but not felt inwardly through Moses' dispensation is bridged. The work of Christ in fulfilling the law is to effect the union of God's will for his creatures and the believing conscience, so that the law of man's nature implanted in creation and the external, verbalized law of Moses join together in the man of faith, becoming the internal knowledge that the will of God is that man do what is good for him.

Liberty is also a property of man's creatureliness, and in a different way it is a property of Moses' law. Again, it is a property of the work of Christ as manifested in believers. First of all, man's liberty is natural: Adam did not have to choose Eve, but in rightly seeing what was good for him, he ratified God's choice for him by the act of choosing her for his companion. A residue of freedom remains to man after the Fall, but it is the freedom to err, to make choices against God's implanted will, to choose what is not good for man. Milton is never clear about whether he thinks this choosing wrongly follows on some defect in freedom itself; he never in the divorce tracts states flatly whether he sees freedom itself as warped in the Fall or as merely following another warping or defect—perhaps that of knowledge of God's will in one's nature, which is impaired by the Fall. The judgment made in these two chapters is that his position is the latter. Man errs in his use of free will after the Fall because he no longer can see clearly what is God's will for him.

Second, liberty is a property of the Mosaic law. This law allows man to make choices within certain structures, though it sets off certain activities as not good in general for man. The freedom to divorce is given to man when his wife finds no favor in his eyes; this is freedom within structure. But man may not murder; this is a general prohibition. It

181

follows from this that a man is not free to divorce for trivial causes, and it is precisely this error in the direction of license of which Christ convicts the Pharisees. The use the Pharisees made of this freedom illustrates the gulf within fallen man between his natural freedom and the knowledge of what is good for him. When the law is external, no matter how close a copy it is of the implanted but badly known law of nature, man's tendency is toward the extremes: either to emphasize the restrictions of law till no freedom remains or to take the permitted choice in some matters as general license to do anything. The former tendency is exemplified by laws against divorce promulgated by those who would be "stricter than Christ"; the Pharisees—and even more obviously, the antinomians—exemplify the latter.

It might be proper to call the natural liberty which man has "human liberty," as does Barker, and thereby distinguish this sort from "Christian liberty," which only believers have. But the above exploration does not support this dichotomy. Rather the truth seems to be that the liberty of a Christian man consists in an internal ratification through charity of the Mosaic law, the verbalized law of God, as the expression of God's will in human nature. Christ fulfills the law by making it possible for man to interpret the law of Moses as God's will for him, which is in no way different from the best impulses coming from within his nature as man. To speak of a "human" and a different "Christian" liberty is to reintroduce in new guise the old and discarded dichotomy between the "old" and "new" laws of Moses and of Christ.

Working backward from this point it becomes obvious how Milton would apply to everyone, believer and unbeliever alike, laws which promote charity. First, a law which binds must, for Milton, have man's good as its aim. Otherwise it is no true, that is, binding, law. Thus positive law must agree with the law of nature still residually present in every man. The law of Moses is such a law. The portions of Moses' law which are "Judaicall" rather than "judicial" have been superceded by other civil laws, but the moral laws remains and binds because of its agreement with the imprint of charity on man's nature. The Christian knows why a law binds; he understands that if it aims at his good, it is God's will that he obey it. And yet even unbelievers are bound by such laws, for God's will does not have to be understood by man for it to be nevertheless his will for his creatures. Therefore a law supported by Christians, even legislated by Christians, can be binding on all, Christians and non-Christians alike, for it aims at man's good so long as it has charity as its end. And the reverse is likewise true: a law which does not aim at man's good is not binding even on those who do not know this, as Christians do.[46]

The end of man is that he should glorify God and do that which is God's will for himself and other men. Milton at times lumps these together under the rubric "what is good for man"; at other times he connects them by the term "charity." But charity, the good of man, is ensured by freedom. The Mosaic law does not leave loopholes for sin, Milton asserts adamantly; it leaves room for human choice, guided by right reason and the law of nature within, to choose among matters indifferent to salvation. Christ has made reason righter in the faithful; he has led men to a better knowledge of what is their nature and its good. At the same time he is the declaration of God's will that man should be forgiven in spite of his erratic ways, in spite of his misuse of his freedom. The Mosaic law embodies principles of freedom in itself, for one of man's created goods is to be free to choose. A Christian law will do at least the same, Milton insists. There will still be law, but the range of indifferent things narrowed by legalists will be broadened to

[46] Wolfe criticizes Milton's approach to legislative reform suggestively. Milton "thought of reform as an achievement possible with a few strokes of the legislative pen; he did not conceive of English society historically." He would not be content with offering his improvements on law as addenda; he wanted rather to abolish what existing laws he saw as bad and replace them with his own. The abstract idea of the end of the law is his model, not the law as it stands and offers itself for improvement. Thus Wolfe sees Milton as unrealistic in his proposals. This lack of practicality, however, is shared with Puritanism in general, as Wolfe notes, and it is one reason the Puritans failed to accomplish their ends when they had the power to do so, during the Commonwealth.

On the other hand, to follow out Perkins' emphasis on liberty of conscience and his understanding of law in its "extremitie" and its "mitigation" does not necessarily imply the above development. The development of English common law can easily be described in Perkins' categories. Wolfe's understanding of Milton on this point rests on his conception of Milton as essentially a product of the Renaissance. For this reason Wolfe emphasizes Milton's leaning toward the abstract idea of law. To place Milton within a Puritan framework, however, suggests another possibility. The Puritan failure to bring lasting reform to England comes not from reliance on abstract law but from their attempt to impose Hebraic structures on English life. This extensive graft did not take. Milton is guilty of the same mistake, not the one of which Wolfe accuses him. (Wolfe, *Milton in the Puritan Revolution*, pp. 334-36.)

allow free, conscientious decision in accord with that measure of charity a moral agent possesses.

Milton broadens the category of the "indifferent" far beyond the bounds given by Puritan orthodoxy in his day, and he is willing to broaden this category even further as charity dictates. For him there is ultimately no law for the Christian but that of charity. This means that the Christian is ultimately bound only internally if he has the fullness of charity. There is for such a person no need for external legal structures, since the law is written on his heart by faith. It is this reasoning which seems to lie behind the accusation that Milton is an antinomian. But never in the divorce tracts is this position pushed to its ultimate conclusion. While Milton is critical of uses of law to restrain sin when the freedom of charity is thereby also abrogated, he simply does not argue for the abolition of law. His position is always one of a reform of the law so as to restore it to a likeness with God's revealed will through Moses and in Christ. Though he makes claims which might seem antinomian for the Christian and even for natural man (so far as he is truly natural and not sinful), he does not go beyond orthodoxy in this, for Luther and even Calvin make equally liberal statements. Milton's admonition "to hold for truth, which accords most with charity" epitomizes his position; never does he issue millennial proclamations of the day when *full* accord with charity will be reached and no laws be necessary.

The most significant contribution Milton makes in this discussion of freedom is his broadening of the category of things indifferent beyond the scope usually allowed in his day. He is able to do this, not on the grounds of modern liberals who speak of individual rights as basic and communal rights as derived, but on the ground that God's charity to all men is known individually in two ways which are made one by Christ. The Christian knows what is indifferent and what is not, and thus he can support laws which accord with charity in leaving free the non-essentials. Thus the result of Milton's argument is to undercut the use of law to restrain sin, the primary function of Puritan discipline, and to elevate the third use, that of the pedagogue which leads men to the right. Even freedom does this, for it is the will of God that man should be free, as he was made in creation. Milton is no antinomian, for he would have law; but the law must be true, binding law, law which is in accord with charity and therefore aims at man's good. Milton opposes only those laws which do not fit these criteria. The uncharitably strict divorce laws of his day are of this latter character, he insists, and the only remedy is to replace them with laws leaving more room for conscientious choice in a matter which is essentially one of individual choice, according to its very institution by God in creation.

CONCLUSION

Enough has already been said to relate the positions of the men treated above to one another, so that to attempt to do so at any length now would be redundant.

In brief I have argued that the Puritan doctrine of marriage systematically stresses the mutual companionship of the spouses over the necessity to produce offspring. The origin of marriage, in the Puritan view, is to be found in the record of Gen. 2:18, "And the Lord God said, It is not good that the man should be alone; I will make him an help meet for him." From the primary good of marriage, provision of mutual companionship, flow all other goods of this primal society of man and woman, including offspring. The Puritan doctrine of marriage is clearly at an opposite pole from that view of matrimony which puts its main stress on the purpose of procreation and derives the good of companionship only because a continuing society of parents is required for the rearing of children.

The Puritans were aided in formulating their doctrine by the covenant theology, which provided a ready framework of theological language and societal analogies to marriage, and by Ramist logic, which gave a unique way of arranging and ordering theological and social data about marriage. The companionable society of wedlock is a species of covenantal society. It is entered into by a covenant (the archetype of which is indicated in Adam's words taking Eve for his wife: "This is now bone of my bones, and flesh of my flesh"), and it endures according to mutually endorsed rules for behavior like those spelled out in any other covenant relationship. The marriage covenant differs from other agreements between men only because it is in some way participated in by God, the maker of all true marriages. What form God's participation takes varies, however, from writer to writer. For Perkins, God inspires the performance of mutual duties of companionship; for Milton he gives husband and wife his love freely so that they may freely prove loving helps for each other. But for other writers God appears as the judge who seals the contract of marriage and provides the rules by which the spouses adhere to their agreement. In all these cases it is the Ramist logic which provides a way for relating God's and man's activities to each other. Furthermore, it is this dialectical system which aids Puritans of all stamps in giving order to the multiple needs and requirements which accompany marital life. Marriage is instituted by God; it is entered into by man and woman through a mutual covenant. But it is Ramist logic which draws together all the implications of marriage, God's institution and man's covenant, and arranges them according to priority. The emergence of companionship as the chief end of marriage is a notable result of the use of Ramist reasoning.

While the Puritan doctrine of marriage emerges in controversy with High Anglicanism over the correct theology of marriage, the development of the Puritan position is marked by controversy and conflicting interpretations as well. Though companionship replaces procreation as the primary end of marriage for all Puritans, this companionship is defined differently by different writers. The focal point of these varying interpretations is the relationship between charity-love and duty or discipline. I have argued that these are originally (with Perkins) united in a relation of cause and effect: God's charity produces in the spouses the desire to perform the duties of wedlock, which are also spelled out in the Scriptures. The spouses' acts of mutual love express themselves in a way which can be described using language of duty, but the source for their loving actions is God's own charity. Second, I have shown how the concept of disciplined life together increasingly comes to define marriage as the seventeenth century advances. The rules of life together, which first are expressed as results of charity, come to be taken as definitive of charity. If husband and wife show their companionship for each other in certain scripturally defined ways, then they have fulfilled charity's requirements. Finally, I have indicated that Milton's divorce tracts are a reaction against this rigidity in Puritan marriage doctrine even while they must be seen as a development within Puritan thinking on marriage. Milton's "restoration" (as he saw it) of the truth about marriage is essentially a restatement of Perkins' dictum that charity inspires mutual acts of love between spouses. But Milton adds a strong emphasis on freedom in love which removes all support for the legalistic definition of marriage as a disciplined society. In this view marriage remains dependent on God's charity for inspiration of mutual acts of love; what is changed is that no longer can those who have fulfilled the letter of existing laws governing marriage (whether scriptural or civil) be assumed to have received charity, the blessing of God on their marriage. From this point arises the argument for divorce of incompatibles: two who are experientially not able to be mutual meet helps are not married in God's sight and so ought to be allowed to divorce.

There are Puritans and there is a Puritan marriage doctrine after John Milton. In fact, had I continued the study of the development of this doctrine through the rest of the seventeenth century, a position close to the modern popular conception of Puritanism would have emerged. Richard Baxter stands as a signpost here, for his *Christian Directory* contains an influential statement of a conservative Puritan attitude toward marriage. For Baxter marriage is essentially companionable life together; the good of companionship remains primary in Puritan thought on marriage. But Baxter, following midcentury Puritan orthodoxy, defines this relation of meet helps in terms of sober duty. More importantly, while mutual companionship remains primary among the goods of marriage, there is in Baxter a new stress on that life toward which earthly life is but a preparation. This forward look toward glory is a feature of Puritan marriage doctrine from the first, but Baxter makes it the primary feature.[1]

By the time of Milton all the issues are clear in the Puritan approach to marriage. Baxter represents a continuation of the conservative tendency illustrated by Gouge and the later Whatley. The issues are those born in controversy: companionship versus procreation as the chief end of matrimony, and loving freedom versus disciplined loving as the proper way to express marital companionship. The question of divorce arises out of both these, but it is mainly as a result of the Puritan emphasis on meet help in marriage that various attempts are made to allow full divorce (and not that *a mensa et thoro* only) with remarriage rights for the innocent. When later Puritans like Baxter return to what had earlier been the Anglican position—divorce *a mensa et thoro,* with no remarriage for either party—it is because their gaze has shifted to the heavenly world and their concern for a warm mutual relationship between spouses in this life has suffered.

It should be most clear by now that the writers treated in this study are concerned to treat marriage as a phenomenon of life here and now. Though God made marriage, he made it for man, and married life should aim at the realization of those strictly human goods which only true mutual companionship can provide. The heavenly life will follow in good order, but marriage is for the bettering of this life. In contrast to the cold repression of the natural which is assumed today to have been characteristic of Puritanism, the writers treated in this paper exhibit a deep concern for the natural as the creation of God. Man and the world in which he lives are both tainted by the sin of primal man. But this sin is a disordering of the good of creation, not a displacement of it. Therefore true marriage is that in which husband and wife with God's help fulfill mutually the natural needs both feel. God's charity and God's discipline do not turn the spouses away from mutual love to thoughts of the hereafter; rather the partners in marriage are enabled to love mutually here and perform acts of meet helpfulness and companionship because God aids them with his love and the manifestation

[1] A full statement of Baxter's position is outside the scope of this study. See Richard Baxter, *The Practical Works of the Rev. Richard Baxter* (London: James Duncan, 1830), vol. IV, *The Christian Directory*, part II, "Christian Economics (or Family Duties)."

of his law. Though life here is a foretaste of the life hereafter, the natural life is good in itself because God is its maker.

Because of this emphasis on the natural John Milton's definition of marriage can stand as a general statement for all Puritans of the early seventeenth century: "Mariage is a divine institution joyning man and woman in a love fitly dispos'd to the helps and comforts of domestic life."[2]

But perhaps Henry Smith's words better express the flavor of Puritan thought on marriage: "For as God hath knit the bones & sinews together for the strengthening of mans bodies, so he hath knit man and woman together for the strengthening of their life, because two are firmer then one."[3]

[2] *Tetrachordon*, p. 612.
[3] Henry Smith, *A Preparative to Mariage*, in *The Sermons of Maister Henry Smith* (London, 1597), STC 22722, p. 11.

APPENDIX A
Two Polemical Authors on Marriage:
Edmund Bunny and John Rainolds

With the exception of Alexander Niccholes and John Milton, the writers treated in this study did not write polemically; they either, like Perkins, Cleaver, and Gouge, fueled theological debate over marriage by producing massive scholarly treatises on the subject, or else, like Gataker, Pricke, and Whatley, they nurtured the souls and minds of the Puritan laity by erudite homilies delivered at weddings. A great number of polemical tracts, however, date from the hundred-year period ranging roughly from Henry VIII to Milton. These tracts are of all levels of scholarship and of lengths from a hundred pages all the way down to one or two pages of print. Two characteristics unite this literature: the intended audience is somewhat wider than that of the theological treatises or even the sermons on marriage, and the polemical tracts generally limit themselves to one issue. Milton's divorce tracts are notable examples of polemical writings on marriage, but Milton uses the issue of divorce to bring into focus an entire doctrine of marriage. Other polemical writers are not so ambitious. The two tracts discussed in this appendix are more representative of the type, and furthermore they serve to show how two reasonably scholarly polemicists besides Milton treat divorce. That Bunny's pamphlet antedates the period explored in the above pages is of little consequence since both the issue and the method of argument persist for a hundred years after Bunny's writing. Rainolds is a rough contemporary of Perkins and Cleaver, and his argument can be compared to theirs.

Bunny's *Of Divorce for Adulterie, and Marrying Again* takes issue against what has become custom by inveighing against all kinds of divorce, even that granted for adultery. Bunny's purpose, as he states it, is to see whether divorce for adultery with remarriage rights for the innocent party "has any warrant at all in the written word."[1] Still, he does not content himself with biblical exegesis but engages directly in a polemical battle for his own position. It is readily apparent that his objectivity is but a veneer, for the first sentences raise the "Turkish peril" argument: if divorce is to be allowed with freedom to remarry, then England will be no better than Turkey, and every man might just as well have a harem. To allow full divorce with remarriage amounts to polygamy.[2] The flavor of the argument is intensified when, a few pages along, he assures his readers that divorce was never a very good thing: "Thou shalt not finde in the Olde Testament, any of the better sort of men to have used (the libertie of) divorce."[3] But while Bunny sticks to such arguments as these, he also probes deeper in order to refute Erasmus and Calvin, and when he does, it becomes apparent that his position rests on a sacramental theory of matrimony.

There are two places in the Bible which have most to be consulted: Deut. 24:1-4, the verses giving the so-called "Mosaic permission," and Matt. 19:1-9, Christ's midrash on this law of Moses.

Bunny takes a strange tack in his exegesis of the Deuteronomy passage. First of all, he argues that it represents a punishment of the husband if he has to put his wife away. He has to admit his own mistake in choosing her if he divorces her, and he certainly does himself no good in the community by such an action. Rather he shows himself to be weak and unable to control his wife.[4] Furthermore, such divorces were only permissions granted to make a mistake more livable, and they were

---

[1] Edmund Bunny, *Of Divorce for Adulterie, and Marrying Again* (London, 1542), STC 4091, p. 1.

[2] *Ibid.*

[3] *Ibid.*, p. 8.

[4] *Ibid.*, p. 36.

a last resort. God never approved of them; he only allowed them because of sin among his people. "Such divorces, although they were tolerated by the Civill Law, yet in court of conscience they were never lawfull." [5] Here Bunny finds himself on firm ground, for he even cites Calvin's *De Repudiis et Divortiis* as authority for his own position.

But the Deuteronomy passage is really not the crucial one for Bunny, for it does not treat of divorce for adultery directly. In fact, divorce for adultery was unnecessary in Moses' day, as adulterers were to be punished by death. Even Rainolds, as we shall see, does not argue for a "Mosaic permission" divorce law for England. It is only with Milton that this becomes a point of contention.

Matt. 19:6 is the crucial passage for Bunny, and the interpretation of that verse which he wishes to confute is Erasmus'. He represents the latter's position on Jesus' meaning thus: "For that, saith hee, did God joine together, which was rightly joined: and that doth God himselfe put asunder, which is well put asunder." [6] That is, Erasmus' view is that God himself is the author of divorce in certain cases, just as he is the author of real marriage. This is a position much like the one Milton later advances, and it is consonant with the views of many of the reformers. Bunny's answer does not go to the heart of what Erasmus is saying. It is not in the power of either of the spouses to break the marriage bond, he argues, nor can both do it together by mutual consent. Marriage is not just a matter concerning the husband and the wife.

Those others that joine with them therin, are, God himselfe, and his vice-regents on earth among us. . . . Every party that is marryed, is by the vertue of that marriage, bound fast to the other in foure severall bonds: one of his owne; the second, of his yokefellow; the third of the magistrate, or of the Government under which they live; and the last, of God, or of his holy ordinance.[7]

Bunny chides Erasmus for having never "espyed his former errour" [8] and for continuing in that error, but he never comes to grips with

[5] *Ibid.*, p. 40.
[6] *Ibid.*, p. 48.
[7] *Ibid.*, p. 50.
[8] *Ibid.*, p. 33.

Erasmus' point: that God himself is the author of some divorces. The position taken later by Cleaver and Perkins, that adultery itself breaks the marriage bond because that is the will of God, in fact the structure of his ordinance of marriage, is not even considered by Bunny. Rather, God joins in wedlock; after that, nothing can break the bond but death.

Bunny's position is sacramentalist: once the marriage has been made, nothing can break it. In the case of a bad marriage a separation can be granted, and this is the only recourse even in the extreme case of adultery. The analogy, he argues, is this: A man who has once been baptised is, for some evil act of his, branded a bad man and no Christian. Still, his baptism is in no way revoked. Likewise, separation from bed and board brands the guilty party or parties in matrimony, yet this does not revoke the marriage bond.[9]

Bunny is an indissolubilist. "In policie, I grant and for the hardnesse of our harts [divorce] may after a sort bee tolerated among us: and of the Jewes before: but where have we otherwise any one authority for it, when it is rightly examined?"[10] There is no scriptural authority for any kind of divorce but separation *a mensa et thoro*, even for adultery. And there are no allowances for remarriage of even the innocent party after such a separation for cause of adultery. Marriage once blessed is dissolved only by death.

John Rainolds' *A Defence of the Judgment of the Reformed Churches* (on adultery and remarriage) represents itself on the title page as an answer to Bellarmine and "an English pamphlet of a namelesse author." Rainolds comes straight to the point: Jesus in Matt. 19:9 says it is lawful to divorce for adultery. Paul assumes this in I Cor. 7:27-28, when he writes, "Art thou loosed from a wife? If thou marrie thou sinnest not."[11] Divorce for adultery and remarriage afterward are permitted by scripture.

As Bunny was concerned to refute Erasmus, Rainolds wishes to refute Bellarmine, whose position he states: "The Marriage of the faithfull is a singe of Christs conjunction with the Church, as St. Paule teacheth. But that conjunction is indissoluble, and cannot be loosed, The band of

---

[9] *Ibid.,* p. 54.

[10] *Ibid.,* p. 96.

[11] John Rainolds, *A Defence of the Judgment of the Reformed Churches* (*Touching Adultery & Remarriage*) (London, 1609), STC 20607, pp. 2, 3.

Marriage is therefore indissoluble too." [12] Rainolds answers by setting up another comparison. Just as a rebel's head may be severed from the body it was justly attached to before his wrongdoing, so a wife's head (her husband) may be severed from her for just cause, namely adultery. The analogy with Christ and the church is false when pushed as far as Bellarmine pushes it because Christ can perservere with the church and fill her with "his gifts & graces" while the husband has no such power with his wife. [13]

Bellarmine's position is that marriage is a sacrament, that grace enters into it and makes it like Christ's union with the church. Rainolds simply asserts that this is not the case. Marriage is a social unity, and what grace is present operates through the persons married. Yet they are always only vessels, and grace is impeded by their sin. If Rainolds wanted to, he could make a similar argument for the kind of presence Christ has with the church, for his dissatisfaction with the sacramentalist position cannot be limited to the application of that theory to marriage. But the immediate target is marriage, and his language shows that he sees nothing of the sacrament in marriage.

Rainolds argues for full divorce only in the case of adultery, and then he would have remarriage allowed for the innocent. In this he follows lines laid down by Cleaver and Dod, as well as by Perkins. He would allow no divorce for lesser faults on either side.

For the first divorce which was made at Rome, was of a chast wife put away by her husband because she was barrein, & did not bear him children. Now to seperate husbands & wives for such causes (we graunt) it is unlawful: our Saviour allowing it for whoredō only. [14]

On the other hand, adultery itself would not have to be admitted as a cause for divorce if adulterers were put to death, as they were among the Jews and in heathen Rome. But the mercy of Christianity extends to giving them a time to repent; thus while they are not allowed to remarry, they are left with their life. The innocent, however, is set free when his partner is adulterous.

[12] *Ibid.*, p. 80.
[13] *Ibid.*, p. 81.
[14] *Ibid.*, p. 93.

When Christian faith came among the Heathens the Emperours did punish adulterie first by death: afterward Justinian mitigating that law did punish by divorcement. But in both these cases the man being severed from his adulterous wife was free to marrie againe.[15]

Rainolds' position is more liberal than Bunny's in that he allows full divorce and remarriage for the innocent in the one case of adultery. But he is really not stating a very revolutionary doctrine. He shows explicitly by his language that he thinks always of the man wronged by an adulterous wife; the contrary situation seems inconceivable. In this he does not match the charity of some other Puritans. Further, his conception of adultery is exclusively tied up with the physical act. Those others who wrote against adultery in more general works on marriage or in commentaries on various portions of scripture tended also to put weight on the sinfulness of those states of mind which led to actual adultery, though only the latter actually could break the bond of marriage.

But as has been noted, once Rainolds' basic position could be granted, its implications were many. In this he is interesting: he is a conservative Puritan in this essay on marriage, and yet he represents a position capable of much more radical interpretations than he would ever give. In this confrontation of Rainolds' and Bunny's tracts we can see the heart of the two theological positions that were at war in the issue of marriage. Is marriage a sacrament? Bunny says yes, Rainolds no. And once the latter answer is taken seriously, it proves impossible to stop at allowing divorce for adultery with remarriage for the innocent.

[15] *Ibid.*, p. 94.

APPENDIX B
Topics from Ramist Logic

That there is a connection between Ramist logic and the Puritan doctrine of marriage cannot be ignored. The place of Ramism in Puritanism as a whole is still being explored, but that it has a place is not a matter for doubt. Credit for major work in this chapter in the history of ideas belongs to Perry Miller, whose "Instrument of Reason" in *The New England Mind: The Seventeenth Century* continues to serve as a benchmark in studies of Ramism and Puritanism; to Wilbur S. Howell, whose *Logic and Rhetoric in England, 1500-1700* is the fullest study of Ramism in its English context; and to Walter J. Ong, whose *Ramus, Method, and the Decay of Dialogue* is the most complete study of the Ramist dialectic in the context of the development of logic. One who is interested in serious study of the relation between Ramist logic and Puritan thought is directed to these works (see the bibliography for full information). In the specific case of the development of a discrete Puritan marriage doctrine, I have argued for a particular kind of relationship, one not quite of causation but rather of complementation, between Ramism and Puritan thought. That is, it appears necessary to accord to

Ramism a role of supporting and complementing the Puritan drift toward a doctrine of marriage based on mutual love and companionability, though it would be going too far to argue that, given Ramistic modes of thought, a concept of marriage stressing companionship should be the only logical result. Similarly, to make a causal connection between Aristotelian logic and the High Church theology of marriage would be to overstate what the evidence warrants, yet it is possible to discern a correlation between Anglican predispositions and the scholastic version of Aristotelian dialectic inherited from Catholicism (and taught at Oxford while Ramism flourished at Cambridge). No system of logic produces theological content, yet given their theology, Puritan divines found Ramism an agreeable tool for expressing their beliefs, while the old Aristotelianism was less handy. The case is similar, though reversed, with the High Churchmen. In a given theological text of any period and on any subject, an understanding of the working of the author's mind helps toward a comprehension of what the data of faith are to him. In the case of the Puritans this task of the student is somewhat eased by the almost universal use of Ramist categories and method. As an aid in the understanding of Puritan marriage doctrine, then, this appendix offers a brief discussion of some terms and ideas both central to the Ramist system and directly pertinent to the development of a discrete doctrine of marriage within Puritanism.

Argument

"An argument," writes John Milton in his *Artis Logicae,* a work consciously based on Ramus' *Dialectica,* "is that which has a fitness for arguing something." [1] This term argument, as used in Ramist logic, has connotations unfamiliar in modern usage. The broadest possible meaning is that which Milton assigns it, but in practice the word argument in the Ramist sense can be applied to single terms, phrases, propositions, or extended discourses so long as there is a single idea adhering to each. An argument is the result of what the Ramist calls "invention," which is of two kinds, definition and description, respectively pertaining to the

[1] John Milton, *Artis Logicae,* in *The Works of John Milton* (Columbia University Press edition), XI, 23.

two kinds of argument, "artistic" and "nonartistic." An argument, then, is the carrier of a single, discrete idea which may be used to argue something and which has more precision, more uniqueness, in proportion as it is defined more carefully. An example may aid toward comprehension of this peculiarly Ramist notion of argument. One may believe that there is a moral law against killing. Someone attempts to convince him to do murder. He responds, "I may do no murder, *because there is a moral law against killing.*" Today's usage and Ramist usage agree that the underlined clause is an argument, in the sense of a reason why one may not kill. But to a Ramist the word "killing" and the phrase "moral law" are also arguments because they have a fitness to argue against something, namely the act of putting another person to death. Similarly, "murder" is an argument, which may be equal to "killing" if their definitions are the same, or which may be contained within the argument "killing" as a subclass or special case. In a Ramist argument everything rests on the precision of its definition.

The Invention of Arguments

A. Definition of Artistic Arguments and the Idea of Causality. An argument in Ramism is perhaps best understood not in itself but as the result of a unique process of invention. The most precise class of arguments, artistic arguments, is composed of those whose invention has been by the procedure of definition. Definition, then, is the first class or type of invention. To define, in Ramist terms, means exactly this: to list the four causes (which are taken from Aristotle) in the order: efficient, material, formal, final. The definition of marriage Milton gives in *Tetrachordon* is of this sort: "Marriage is a divine institution [efficient cause] joyning man and woman [material cause] in a love [formal cause] fitly dispos'd to the helps and comforts of domestic life [final cause]." [2] In light of this definition the nature of marriage is precisely known; marriage is, in the Ramist sense, now an argument. Moreover, it is an *artistic* argument, one which has the power (or artistry, hence the term "artistic") of itself to compel agreement. According to Ramus:

[2] *Tetrachordon,* p. 614.

Argument is then artistic or non-artistic, as Aristotle partitions it in the second of the *Rhetoric:* artistic, which creates belief by itself and by its nature, is divided into the primary and the derivative primary. Non-artistic argument is that which by itself and through its own force does not create belief, as for example the five types which Aristotle describes in the first of his *Rhetoric,* laws, witnesses, contracts, tortures, oaths. Thus it is always that these arguments are interchangeably called authorities and witnesses.[3]

The clear implication is that an artistic argument is one which is self-evidently obvious. This follows from the nature of its causes, which, when they are known and arrayed in proper order, allow no room for variability of interpretation. This explains Milton's self-righteous attitude toward marriage doctrine, at least in part: he is sure that he has the essence of marriage before him, and it is this clear and distinct idea of marriage (use of Descartes' phrase is intentional) which compels the conclusions he draws. His conclusions are implied in the argument marriage.

The Ramist concept of the proper order of causes requires attention. The four causes are Aristotle's, but the order is not that of Aristotelian logic. The latter puts final cause first in importance because it represents the perfection of the thing, that toward which the thing tends. Ramus places efficient cause first, however, emphasizing it as the original force of the thing's existence. There is no indication that Ramus intends to undercut the Aristotelian understanding of causality, but he does perform a deliberate and significant shift in emphasis. For Ramus the efficient cause gives rise to the others. It "procreates and maintains"[4] the thing; without it the other causes would have no existence. In this understanding the other causes are all included in the efficient; that is, they are all implications from the efficient cause. How Ramus can argue this way while also asserting the independence of the causes is a problem in Ramist logic which cannot be resolved in this appendix. I repeat, however,

---

[3] Quoted by Wilbur S. Howell, *Logic and Rhetoric in England, 1500-1700* (Princeton: Princeton University Press, 1956), pp. 155-56, from Ramus' *Dialectique,* pp. 5-6. This is a French version (not a translation) of the *Dialectica,* and according to Howell the two differ somewhat. I have not been able to locate a copy of Ramus' *Dialectique* for comparison.

[4] Milton, *Artis Logicae,* p. 33.

that Ramus' intent seems not to be to discount Aristotle's idea of causation but rather to shift the emphasis from one type of cause to another.[5]

The import for theology of Ramus' reordering of causation can be illustrated by two examples. The first is the ends of marriage as conceived in Puritanism. Puritans typically emphasize the efficient cause of marriage, God's giving Eve to Adam in Eden, with the result that in their marriage doctrine the mutual help (however defined) husband and wife give each other takes on primary importance. Milton, the most radical, even argues that when spouses can give no mutual help to each other, the efficient cause, God's will that they should be married, is lacking and there is no marriage at all. Anglican theorists, contrarily, emphasize what both they and the Puritans take to be the final cause of marriage, the procreation of children. Thus in their marriage doctrine the logical ordering of ends places mutual meet help after the injunction to procreate for the good of church and state.[6]

A more general example is that of the doctrine of God in Catholicism and in Puritanism. There are theological reasons for the logical priority of final cause in the former doctrine: putting final cause first when speaking of God emphasizes his purposiveness, and a doctrine of God stressing his omniscience, omnicompetence, and immutability implies the necessity of treating final cause as first in order of importance. But there are also important theological reasons for putting efficient cause first: the Puritan conception of God as creator and preserver of the uni-

---

[5] In Aristotle's *Physics* and *Metaphysics* the material cause, not the efficient or the final, is given priority. In biological growth only two causes are discernible, the material and the formal, with the latter including the efficient and the final. The material cause represents in biological growth the principle of motion, while the formal cause represents the teleological principle. Thus Aristotle's theory of causation is not so simple as it might seem from only the *Organon*.

For this reason Ramus' dependence on Aristotle becomes all the more interesting. While Ramus retains the quadripartite division of causes, he groups the four into two groups of two—an example of his love for dichotomy. Efficient and material causes are classified together, as are formal and final causes. The most remarkable feature of this grouping, now that another side of Aristotle is before us, is that it corresponds to Aristotle's description, though not his grouping, of the two biological causes according to their principles. It appears that Ramus might have been attempting to correct Aristotelian logic on the basis of Aristotelian science!

See Aristotle, *Physica,* trans. R. P. Hardie and R. K. Gaye (London: Oxford University Press, 1930), Bk. II, sec. 3; *Metaphysica,* trans. W. D. Ross (Oxford University Press, 1908), Bk. VIII, sec. 4-6 esp.

[6] Cf. Chap. V, n. 33.

verse through a forceful, active providence is best expressed by a logic stressing the priority of efficient causation. In this case, as in the one of marriage doctrine, a difference in logic reinforces real theological differences. This is particularly true in the seventeenth-century context, for the content of faith was then conceived by all Christians, Catholic and Protestant alike, to be positively given and rationally apprehensible. In this conception, all else being equal, the better theology is that one which is better informed by reason. Better logic makes for better theology. In a more mystical age the role of logic in theology would have had an entirely different cast.

B. Description of Nonartistic Arguments and the Idea of Testimony. The best arguments are the artistic, those which compel belief by their very nature, which are self-evident and obviously true. An argument of this class is said to be invented when its definition can be given in the form of listing its causes in the order: efficient, material, formal, final.

Nonartistic arguments have not the force to compel belief, but they serve as witnesses pointing to the truth. A nonartistic argument is incomplete relative to the artistic: specifically, all its causes are not known, so that it cannot be defined, and therefore its grasp of truth is never perfect. Invention of nonartistic arguments is accomplished by "description," not definition, by listing not causes but "testimonies." The force an artistic argument has is known when the force of its causes is known; similarly, the force of a nonartistic argument comes from the authority of the testimony which describes it. Inconclusive testimony or witnesses not known for veracity thus make for a weak argument, whereas concurrent testimony by unimpeachable witnesses makes for an argument approaching the artistic in force. In Puritan use of Ramism one specific kind of nonartistic argument is in fact the equal of artistic argument in having a complete grasp on truth and therefore being able to compel belief. That is nonartistic argument secured by *divine* testimony. An example will help to illustrate these relations. In Jonathan Edwards' famous metaphor from "Sinners in the Hands of an Angry God," the spider being dangled over the flames is an artistic argument: it is a ready-at-hand image and can be defined by all men in terms of its causes. While the pain the spider may feel has to be imagined, drawing on memories all have of being burned at some time, what happens to the spider is observable: it withers up grotesquely and is consumed. The vividness of this image indicates the force it has as an argument. Edwards' assertion that sinners will suffer a like fate to the spider's when an angry God takes hold of them is a nonartistic argument based on scriptural testimony. But because God speaks through the Scriptures and because God's word is literally true (two tenets of Puritan faith), this argument (Edwards' assertion) has a compelling forcefulness.[7]

Nonartistic arguments described by testimony other than divine have force corresponding directly to the authority of the testimony. Puritan writers prefer, however, the more compelling forms of argument already discussed. At the end of *Tetrachordon,* after his doctrine of marriage has been set forth by means of artistic arguments and nonartistic ones based on scripture, Milton appends a section summarizing the positions on marriage of certain church fathers and Christian emperors. This is nonartistic argument supported by human testimony; it has some force, but after the more certain kinds of argument it comes as an anticlimax. Milton recognizes this and prefixes to this section a short, chiding lecture on logic:

Although testimony be in Logic an argument rightly call'd inartificial [i.e., nonartistic; the particular word used to translate Ramus' concept into English varies], & doth not solidly fetch the truth by multiplicity of Authors, nor argue a thing false by the few that hold so, yet seeing most men from their youth so accustom, as not to scanne reason, nor cleerly to apprehend it, but to trust for that the names and numbers of such, as have got . . . the reputation among them to know much . . . it will not be amiss for them who had rather list themselves under this weaker sort, and follow authorities, to take notice that this opinion which I bring, hath been favour'd, and by som of those affirm'd, who in their time were able to carry what they taught, had they urg'd it, through all Christendom.[8]

Puritan marriage doctrine does not importantly depend on what men think of it (nonartistic argument based on human testimony), for it is based on nature (artistic argument) and the Bible (nonartistic argument

[7] The argumentive force which Edwards' analogy has derives ultimately from Ramist logic, but when Lockean psychology is added, the analogy becomes terrifyingly apt to Edwards' hearers. For a discussion of Edwards' use of Locke see Perry Miller, *Jonathan Edwards* (New York: Dell Books, 1967), pp. 142 ff.

[8] *Tetrachordon,* pp. 692-93.

based on divine testimony). Puritan writers on marriage thus conceive their doctrine to have a compelling obviousness about it and treat it correspondingly.

Distribution of Arguments and Ramist Method

Once an argument has been invented (in the Ramist sense), it must be "disposed" or "distributed" with other arguments so as to prove whatever it is desired to know. The disposition of arguments is the subject of the second book of the *Dialectica*. Here Ramus treats three forms of disposition: the axiomatic, the syllogistic, and the "methodical." [9] Overarching the whole discussion is Ramus' predilection for dichotomies, and the three forms just listed are in fact treated by dichotomization: axioms are "noetic" distributions, while syllogisms and "method" are "dianoetic." This division has to do with how immediately truth is comprehended, but structurally there is another difference: axioms are made up of what we might think of as "simple" arguments and are themselves "compound" arguments, on the analogy with the Lockean psychology of knowledge. In turn, axioms are distributed in syllogisms or according to what Ramus calls merely "method." Thus axioms are not like geometrical axioms; the closest analogy would perhaps be to Aristotle's propositions or perhaps to geometrical theorems. The essential feature of axioms is that they are sentences in which arguments are arranged so as to make a truth obvious. This truth is immediately apparent to anyone who hears or reads the sentence, and this is the reason for calling axioms noetic distributions.

The first form of dianoetic distribution is the syllogism. This is nothing more than the Aristotelian syllogism, and Ramus treats it at considerable length and with respect, but not with the thoroughness of a scholastic dialectician. Essentially a syllogism is an ordering of axioms (or in Aristotelian language propositions) so as to make apparent some truth which depends on the axioms. Ramus' treatment of the syllogism is not particularly significant for our purposes here so I shall go no further than this brief statement, which shows the place of the syllogism in Ramus' distribution of arguments. [10]

[9] "Method" has a technical meaning for Ramus, which is defined below.
[10] This slighting of the treatment of syllogistic distribution of arguments should

The most significant form of the distribution of arguments is what Ramus calls "method." Once more a technical term is encountered which must be explained. The term method means for Ramus the ordering of axioms (i.e., propositions) so that each one becomes clear because of the one before it. It is possible to feed knowledge reached through syllogisms in laterally, as it were, but the basic structure of method is independent of the syllogistic form of disposition of arguments. The working of method cannot be explained with precision because it varies from subject to subject and involves much that is intuitive. Put another way, there is a range of possibilities for the use of method. Most loosely conceived, it is what makes a speaker put one point first because he thinks his meaning is clearer in that order. Most rigidly conceived, method is that particular method Ramus uses in his *Dialectica:* successive dichotomization, proceeding from a definition to all the implications of that definition. This latter is what is meant in this book when mention is made of Perkins' or Milton's adhering to Ramist method, though Milton's procedure in *The Doctrine and Discipline of Divorce* is a good example of the looser sort of Ramist ordering. Sufficient examples are given in the text above to illustrate Puritan use of Ramist method in developing a doctrine of marriage. Here one point needs a final emphasis: the Ramist concepts of causation and method reinforce each other in their employment in Puritan marriage doctrine. Both require putting companionship first in marital union: in the first place,

---

not be taken as implying that Ramus sought to abolish syllogisms in logic. Rather his intent seems to be here as elsewhere to correct what he thought to be a misinterpretation of Aristotle. It is clear that he regards syllogisms as only one kind of valid dianoetic distribution of arguments, the other being "method," i.e., an ordering of axioms so that each one guarantees the truth of the next. I must here differ sharply with the opinion of P. Albert Duhamel that the Ramist dialectic systematically relegates the use of syllogistic reasoning to the place of last resort. Duhamel uses this judgment to argue that Milton is no Ramist because he uses syllogisms ("Milton's Alleged Ramism," *PMLA,* LXVII [December 1952], 1035-53). On this basis even Ramus is no true Ramist, nor is anyone who reasons otherwise than with an ordering of axioms according to certainty. It is true that the Puritan preachers stressed "method" in their sermons and eschewed syllogisms. But it is incorrect to say that Ramus or the English Ramists avoided syllogisms at all costs. A typical use of syllogisms is to clarify an axiom, which is then ordered according to "method," and this is precisely the use Milton makes of syllogistic reasoning in the passages cited by Duhamel. It is interesting to speculate why Ramus spent so much time explaining various kinds of syllogisms and their uses in clarifying and ordering incoherent facts (arguments) if he, as Duhamel thinks, sought to relegate syllogisms to the place of last resort.

it points to the efficient cause of the union—God—and includes in it all other causes; second, companionship is the most inclusive of the ends of marriage since the other two ends are in some sense implicit in this one. Ramist logic thus seconds a datum of faith and facilitates expression of that datum of faith in a coherent and discrete doctrine of marriage.

SELECTED BIBLIOGRAPHY

Primary Sources

Many of the works consulted for this book were available to me only on microfilm. When a microfilmed work is listed in this bibliography, only the date and place of publication are given, followed by the *Short-Title Catalogue* (STC) number.

Adams, Thomas. *A Divine Herball: Together with a Forrest of Thornes.* London, 1616. STC 111.

Ainsworth, Henry. *Annotations upon the Books of Moses.* London, 1626. STC 219.

Ames, William. *Conscience, with the Power and Cases Thereof.* London, 1639. STC 550.

Aquinas, Thomas. *On the Truth of the Catholic Faith.* 4 vols. Garden City, N.Y.: Doubleday & Co., 1955-57.

————. *Summa Theologica.* Trans. Fathers of the English Dominican Province. Vol. III: *Supplement.* New York: Benziger Brothers, 1948.

Baxter, Richard. *The Practical Works of the Rev. Richard Baxter.* London: James

Duncan, 1830. Vol. IV: *The Christian Directory,* part II: "Christian Economics (or Family Duties)."

Becon, Thomas. *The Goldē Boke of Christen Matrimonye.* London, 1542. STC 1723.

———. *The Principles of Christian Religion.* London, 1550. STC 1752.

Bradshaw, William. *See* Gataker, Thomas, and Bradshaw, William.

Bullinger, Henry. *The Christen State of Matrimonye.* Trans. Miles Coverdale. London, 1541. STC 4045.

———. *Decades.* Vol. VII: *First and Second Decades;* vol. VIII: *Third Decade.* Cambridge: The University Press, 1849-50.

Bunny, Edmund. *Of Divorce for Adulterie, and Marrying Again.* London, 1542. STC 4091.

Calvin, John. *Institutes of the Christian Religion.* Trans. Henry Beveridge. 2 vols. Grand Rapids: Eerdmans Publishing Co., 1957.

Cleaver, Robert. *A Godlie Forme of Household Government.* London, 1598. STC 5382.

———, and Dod, John. *Bathshebaes Instructions to Her Sonne Lemuel, Describing the Duties of a Great Man, and the Vertues of a Gracious Woman.* London, 1614. STC 6935.

Dod, John, and Cleaver, Robert. *A Plaine and Familiar Exposition of the Ten Commandments of Almightie God.* London, 1612. STC 6956.

Downame, John. *The Christian Warfare Against the Devill.* 4th ed., corrected and enlarged. London, 1634. STC 7137.

Gamon, Hannibal. *A Godly Womans Praise.* London, 1627. STC 11548.

Gataker, Thomas. *A Good Wife God's Gift, and A Wife Indeed: Two Marriage Sermons.* London, 1623. STC 11659.

———. *Marriage Duties.* London, 1620. STC 11667.

———. *A Marriage Praier.* London, 1624. STC 11669.

———, and Bradshaw, William. *Two Marriage Sermons.* By Thomas Gataker: *A Good Wife Gods Gift.* By William Bradshaw: *A Marriage Feast.* London, 1620. STC 11680.

Gouge, William. *Of Domesticall Duties Eight Treatises.* London, 1622. STC 12119.

Greenham, Richard. *The Workes.* London, 1599. STC 12313.

Hieron, Samuel. *All the Sermons of Samuel Hieron.* London, 1614. STC 13378. *The Marriage-Blessing,* p. 404; *The Bridegroome,* p. 467.

An Homily of the State of Matrimony. One of Certayne Sermons, or Homilies, Appointed by the Kynges Maiestie, to Be Declared and Redde by All Persones Vicars, or Curates, Every Sondaye in Their Churches, Where They Have Cure. London, 1640. STC 13639.

Hutchinson, Lucy. *Memoirs of the Life of Colonel Hutchinson.* 2 vols. London: Longman, Hurst, Rees, Orme, and Brown, 1822.

Milton, John. *The Works of John Milton.* General ed. Frank Allen Patterson. Vol. XI: *Artis Logicae,* vol. XV: *De Doctrina Christina.* New York: Columbia University Press, 1935, 1933.

―――. *The Complete Prose Works of John Milton.* General ed. Don M. Wolfe. Vol. II: *1643-1648.* Ed. Ernest Sirluck. New Haven: Yale University Press, 1959. *The Doctrine and Discipline of Divorce,* pp. 217-356; *The Judgment of Martin Bucer,* pp. 416-79; *Tetrachordon,* pp. 571-718; *Colasterion,* pp. 719-58.

Newstead, Christopher. *An Apology for Women.* London, 1620. STC 18508.

Niccholes, Alexander. *A Discourse of Marriage and Wiving.* London, 1615. STC 18514.

Parker Society, eds. *The Two Liturgies,* A.D. *1549 and* A.D. *1552.* Cambridge: The University Press, 1844.

Perkins, William. *Workes.* 3 vols. Cambridge, 1609. STC 19649.

Preston, John. *The New Covenant; or, The Saints' Portion.* London, 1629. STC 20241.

Pricke, Robert. *The Doctrine of Superioritie, and of Subjection.* London, 1609. STC 20337.

Rainolds, John. *A Defense of the Judgment of the Reformed Churches* (*Touching Adultery* & *Remarriage*). London, 1609. STC 20607.

Ramus, Petrus (Pierre de la Ramée). *The Art of Logic.* Ed. and trans. Anthony Wotton. Cambridge, 1626. STC 15248.

―――. *The Logicke of the Most Excellent Philosopher P. Ramus Martyr.* Trans. M. R. Makylmenaeus Scotus. London, 1574. STC 15246.

————. *Peter Ramus, His Dialectica in Two Bookes.* Trans. R. F. London, 1632. STC 15249.

The Reformation of the Ecclesiastical Laws (Reformatio Legum Ecclesiasticarum). Ed. Edward Cardwell. Oxford: The University Press, 1850.

Rogers, Daniel. *Matrimoniall Honour.* London, 1642. Wing STC 1797.

Sanderson, Robert. *Lectures on Conscience and Law.* Ed. and trans. Chr. Wordsworth. Oxford and Cambridge: Rivingtons, 1877.

Smith, Henry. *The Sermons of Maister Henry Smith.* London, 1597. STC 22722. *A Preparative to Mariage,* pp. 9-46.

Stockwood, John. *A Sermon Preached at Paules Crosse.* London, 1578. STC 23284.

Swetnam, J. *The Arraignment of Lewd, Idle, Froward, and Unconstant Women.* London, 1622. STC 23538.

Westminster Assembly of Divines. *The Directory for the Publick Worship of God.* Philadelphia: B. Franklin, 1745.

Whatley, William. *A Bride-Bush; or, A Wedding Sermon.* London, 1617. STC 25296.

————. *A Care-Cloth; or, A Treatise of the Cumbers and Troubles of Marriage.* London, 1624. STC 25299.

Wing, John. *The Crowne Conjugall; or, The Spouse Royall.* Middelburgh, 1620.

Secondary Sources

Books

Aiken, W. A., and Henning, Basil D., eds. *Conflict in Stuart England: Essays in Honor of Wallace Notestein.* New York: New York University Press, 1960.

Bailey, D. S. *Sexual Relation in Christian Thought.* New York: Harper & Brothers, 1959.

————. *Thomas Becon and the Reformation of the Church in England.* London: Oliver and Boyd, 1952

Barker, Arthur E. *Milton and the Puritan Dilemma.* Toronto: University of Toronto Press, 1942.

Blench, J. W. *Preaching in England.* New York: Barnes & Noble, 1964.

Burden, D. H. *The Logical Epic: A Study of the Argument of "Paradise Lost"* Cambridge: Harvard University Press, 1967.

Clebsch, William. *England's Earliest Protestants.* New Haven: Yale University Press, 1964.

Collinson, Patrick. *The Elizabethan Puritan Movement.* Berkeley: University of California Press, 1967.

Frere, Walter Howard. *A History of the English Church, Elizabeth—James I.* London: Macmillan & Co., 1911.

Frye, Roland M. *God, Man, and Satan.* Princeton: Princeton University Press, 1960.

Fuller, Thomas. *The Church History of Britain.* Vol. III. London: Thomas Tegg, 1842.

Gardiner, S. R. *The First Two Stuarts and the Puritan Revolution.* New York: Charles Scribner's Sons, 1893.

George, Charles H., and George, Katherine. *The Protestant Mind of the English Reformation.* Princeton: Princeton University Press, 1961.

Haller, William. *Elizabeth I and the Puritans.* Ithaca: Cornell University Press, 1964.

———. *Liberty and Reformation in the Puritan Revolution.* New York: Columbia University Press, 1955.

———. *The Rise of Puritanism.* New York: Columbia University Press, 1938.

———. *Tracts on Liberty in the Puritan Revolution.* 3 vols. New York: Columbia University Press, 1934.

Henson, H. Hensley. *English Religion in the Seventeenth Century.* London: John Murray, 1903.

———. *Puritanism in England.* London: Hodder & Stoughton, 1912.

Hill, Christopher. *The Century of Revolution, 1603-1714.* Camden, N.J.: Thomas Nelson & Sons, 1961.

———. *Economic Problems of the Church.* Oxford: Clarendon Press, 1966.

———. *Intellectual Origins of the English Revolution.* New York: Oxford University Press, 1965.

————. *Puritanism and Revolution.* New York: Schocken Books, 1964.

————. *Society and Puritanism in Pre-revolutionary England.* New York: Schocken Books, 1964.

Howell, Wilbur Samuel. *Logic and Rhetoric in England, 1500-1700.* Princeton: Princeton University Press, 1956.

Hutton, W. H. *A History of the English Church from the Accession of Charles I to the Death of Anne.* London: Macmillan & Co., 1903.

Kelley, Maurice W. *This Great Argument: A Study of Milton's "De Doctrina Christiana" as a Gloss upon "Paradise Lost."* Princeton: Princeton University Press, 1941.

Knappen, Marshall M. *Tudor Puritanism.* Chicago: University of Chicago Press, 1939.

Kurth, B. O. *Milton and Christian Heroism.* Berkeley: University of California Press, 1959.

Lacey, T. A. *Marriage in Church and State.* Rev. by R. C. Mortimer. London: S.P.C.K., 1947.

Little, David. *Religion, Order, and Law.* New York: Harper & Row, 1969.

Longueville, Thomas. *A Life of Archbishop Laud.* London: Kegan Paul, Trench, Trubner and Co., 1894.

McAdoo, Henry R. *The Spirit of Anglicanism.* New York: Charles Scribner's Sons, 1965.

————. *The Structure of Caroline Moral Theology.* London: Longmans, Green, & Co., 1949.

McNeill, John T. *The History and Character of Calvinism.* New York: Oxford University Press, 1954.

Masson, David. *The Life of John Milton in Connection with the History of His Time.* 3 vols. London: Macmillan & Co., 1859, 1871, 1896.

Miller, Perry. *The New England Mind: The Seventeenth Century.* Boston: Beacon Press, 1961.

Morgan, Edmund S. *The Puritan Family.* Rev. ed. New York: Harper & Row, 1966.

Morgan, Irvonwy. *Prince Charles' Puritan Chaplain.* London: Allen & Unwin, 1957.

New, John F. H. *Anglican and Puritan*. Stanford: Stanford University Press, 1964.

Notestein, Wallace. *The English People on the Eve of Colonization*. New York: Harper & Row, 1962.

Ong, Walter J. *Ramus, Method, and the Decay of Dialogue*. Cambridge: Harvard University Press, 1958.

Powell, Chilton L. *English Domestic Relations, 1487-1653*. New York: Columbia University Press, 1917.

Saurat, Denis. *Milton: Man and Thinker*. Rev. ed. London: J. M. Dent & Sons, 1944.

Tawney, R. H. *Religion and the Rise of Capitalism*. 13th ed. Mentor Books; New York: New American Library, 1954.

Weber, Max. *The Protestant Ethic and the Spirit of Capitalism*. Trans. Talcott Parsons. New York: Charles Scribner's Sons, 1958.

Willey, Basil. *The Seventeenth Century Background*. Garden City, N.Y.: Doubleday & Co., 1953.

Winnett, A. R. *Divorce and Remarriage in Anglicanism*. New York: St. Martin's Press, 1958.

Wolfe, Don M. *Milton in the Puritan Revolution*. New York: Humanities Press, 1963.

Wright, Louis B. *Middle-Class Culture in Elizabethan England*. Chapel Hill: University of North Carolina Press, 1935.

Articles

Barker, Arthur E. "Christian Liberty in Milton's Divorce Pamphlets," *Modern Language Review*, XXXV (1940), 153-61.

Duhamel, P. Albert. "Milton's Alleged Ramism," *PMLA*, LXVII (December 1952), 1035-53.

French, J. Milton. "Milton, Ramus, and Edward Phillips," *Modern Philology*, XLVII (1949), 82-87.

Frye, Roland M. "The Teachings of Classical Puritanism on Conjugal Love," *Studies in the Renaissance*, II (1955), 148-59.

Haller, William, and Haller, Maleville. "The Puritan Art of Love," *Huntington Library Quarterly*, V (1941-42), 235-72.

Howard, Leon. "The 'Invention' of Milton's 'Great Argument'; a Study of the Logic of 'God's Ways to Men,'" *Huntington Library Quarterly,* IX (1945-46), 149-74.

Owen, Evion. "Milton and Selden on Divorce," *Studies in Philology,* XLIII (1946), 233-57.

Powell, Chilton L. "Marriage in Early New England," *New England Quarterly,* I (1928), 323-44.

Scott-Craig, Thomas S. K. "The Craftsmanship and Theological Significance of Milton's Art of Logic," *Huntington Library Quarterly,* XVII (1953-54), 1-16.

Siegel, Paul N. "Milton and the Humanistic Attitude Toward Women," *Journal of the History of Ideas,* II (1950), 42-53.

Smith, G. C. Moore. "A Note on Milton's Art of Logic," *Review of English Studies,* XIII (1937), 335-40.

Unpublished Dissertations

Adams, A. C. "A Study of the Ethics of John Milton." Ph.D. dissertation, University of Missouri, 1961.

Clark, David L. "The Altar Controversy in Early Stuart England." Th.D. dissertation, Harvard University Divinty School, 1967.

Huguelet, T. L. "Milton's Hermeneutics: A Study of Scriptural Interpretation in the Divorce Tracts and in *De Doctrina Christiana.*" Ph.D. dissertation, University of North Carolina, 1959.

Irwin, H. Franklin. "Ramistic Logic in Milton's Prose Works." Ph.D. dissertation, Princeton University, 1941.

Kranidas, Thomas. "Milton's Concept of Decorum." Ph.D. dissertation, University of Washington, 1962.

Short-Title Catalogs

Pollard, A. W., and Redgrave, G. R., compilers. *A Short-Title Catalogue of Books Printed in England, Scotland, and Ireland, and of English Books Printed Abroad 1475-1640,* London: The Bibliographical Society, 1926.

Wing, Donald, compiler. *Short-Title Catalogue of Books Printed in England, Scotland, Ireland, Wales, and British America, and of English Books Printed in Other Countries, 1641-1700.* 3 vols. New York: Columbia University Press, 1951.

INDEX